For Neal and Jane Freeman

Threshold Editions
A Division of Simon & Schuster, Inc.
1230 Avenue of the Americas
New York, NY 10020

Copyright © 2012 by M. Stanton Evans and Herbert Romerstein

First Threshold Editions hardcover edition November 2012

THRESHOLD EDITIONS and colophon are trademarks of Simon & Schuster, Inc.

For information about special discounts for bulk purchases, please contact Simon & Schuster Special Sales at 1-866-506-1949 or business@simonandschuster.com.

The Simon & Schuster Speakers Bureau can bring authors to your live event. For more information or to book an event, contact the Simon & Schuster Speakers Bureau at 1-866-248-3049 or visit our website at www.simonspeakers.com.

Designed by Renata Di Biase

Manufactured in the United States of America

10   9   8   7   6   5   4   3   2   1

Library of Congress Cataloging-in-Publication Data

Evans, M. Stanton (Medford Stanton), 1934–
    Stalin's secret agents : the subversion of Roosevelt›s government / M. Stanton Evans and Herbert Rommerstein. — 1st Threshold Editions hardcover ed.
        p. cm.
    1. Espionage, Soviet—United States—History. 2. Subversive activities—United States—History—20th century. 3. Secret service—Soviet Union—History. 4. United States—Politics and government—1933–1945. 5. World War, 1939–1945—Secret service—Soviet Union. 6. Spies—Soviet Union—History. 7. Spies—United States—History—20th century. 8. Communists—United States—History—20th century. 9. Soviet Union—Foreign relations—United States. 10. United States—Foreign relations—Soviet Union. I. Rommerstein, Herbert. II. Title.
    UB271.R9E93 2012
    327.124707309′044—dc23
                                                                                    2012031055

ISBN 978-1-4391-4768-9
ISBN 978-1-4391-5554-7 (ebook)

STALIN'S

THE SUBVERSION OF

SECRET

ROOSEVELT'S GOVERNMENT

AGENTS

M. STANTON EVANS

AND

HERBERT ROMERSTEIN

THRESHOLD EDITIONS
New York   London   Toronto   Sydney   New Delhi

CONTENTS

Contents

STALIN'S SECRET AGENTS

THE GREATEST STORY NEVER TOLD

S ince the collapse of the Soviet empire in the early 1990s, we've learned a lot about Communist tactics used against the West in the long death struggle called the Cold War—much of it contrary to accepted wisdom in media/academic circles.

Some of this information is brand-new, some of it confirming things already known, some completely unexpected—but all of it important. The revelations are the more so as the story of what actually happened in the clash of global superpowers that dominated the second half of the twentieth century has yet to be told in adequate fashion. For numerous reasons—some legitimate, others not—significant facts about this conflict were the deepest-dyed of secrets, denied outright or held back from the public, and even today aren't common knowledge.

Of note in this respect, covert by nature and kept that way for decades, was the nonstop backstage warfare that was waged between the opposing forces even as peace in theory prevailed among the nations. Only by degrees have we come to understand the extent of this clandestine combat, and a great deal more is still waiting to be discovered. Even so, with the revelations of recent years we have enough data in hand to sketch the outlines of an astounding tale and fill in specifics about some matters long uncertain or contested.

Considering only its larger aspects, the Cold War story is of course well-known and doesn't need much elaboration. With the Bolshevik Revolution of 1917, conflict between the new Soviet rulers of Russia and the non-Communist nations was foreordained and, despite numerous tactical zigzags, would persist for generations. The hostility stemmed in part from conditions on the ground in Europe during World War I, but mainly from the belief of Soviet commissars Lenin and Trotsky that their victory would be the precursor to Red revolution elsewhere, and that the new Communist state would lead the way in making this happen. Soviet methods of secret warfare were developed to advance this revolutionary vision.

Generally speaking, what the new disclosures tell us about all this is that Communist covert actions against the United States and other target nations were relentless and effective, far more than most historians have imagined. The Kremlin used such tactics in systematic fashion, made them key elements of state policy, and devoted enormous resources to them. The data also show the manner in which the West fought back against this challenge, though in most cases we were on the defensive, playing catch-up, and far less practiced in secret warfare. We thus for many years experienced more defeats than triumphs, though with some victories to our credit.

As the record further shows, a main object of Moscow's subliminal onslaught was to plant secret agents in the United States and other Western nations, with emphasis on official agencies that dealt with military, intelligence, or foreign policy issues. From these positions, pro-Soviet operatives were able to engage in policy sabotage, spying, and other species of subversion that advanced the interests of the Kremlin. As shall be seen, activity of this type was involved in countless aspects of the Cold War story.

Among the information sources now available on such matters, those most often cited are the *Venona* decrypts compiled by the U.S. Army Signal Corps in the 1940s. *Venona* was the code name given to encrypted messages exchanged between the Red intelligence bosses in Moscow and their agents in this country. The Army code breakers intercepted thousands of these missives and by a painstaking process were able to decipher a substantial number. This information, reflecting the extent of the Soviets' activities in the United States and the identities of many of their contacts, was shared by the Army with the FBI to counter and eventually help break various of the pro-Red networks. These decrypts weren't made public until 1995, half a century after they were first recorded.[1]

Other revelations dating from the 1990s include material from the archives of the Soviet Union and other east bloc nations when for a brief period after the Communists were toppled from power such records were made available to researchers. The most recent such disclosures are the so-called Vassiliev papers, named for a former Soviet intelligence staffer who made voluminous copies of secret records and smuggled them out of Russia when he defected to the West. Similar revelations had been made by previous such defectors, including Oleg Gordievsky, Stanislav Levchenko, and Victor Kravchenko, along with native American defectors such as Whittaker Chambers and Elizabeth Bentley.

Of importance also—though an underrated resource—are the confidential archives of the FBI, which was tracking and recording the activities of Communists and Soviet agents in the United States before *Venona* came on line and before the advent of the Cold War. In some recent studies the efforts of the FBI in this regard have been disparaged, but, on close inspection, these negative comments aren't backed up by the record. In some cases of the New Deal years the Bureau may have missed clues it should have noted, but by the early 1940s it was far ahead of other U.S. agencies in spotting and combating the infiltration problem.

To all of which there should be added—though this too is much neglected—a sizable trove of information about Red activity in the United States collected by committees of the Congress, based on the testimony of ex-Communist witnesses, the findings of staff investigators, and information from intelligence agencies, security squads at the State Department, and other official bodies. Like the endeavors of the FBI, the work of the committees was often downgraded or ignored while the Cold War was in progress. As may be seen today in the light of the new disclosures, the hearings and reports of the House Committee on Un-American Activities, Senate Internal Security Subcommittee, and other panels of the Congress were (and are) a gold mine of useful information on Cold War issues.

Looking at this considerable body of data, and matching one set of materials with another, we can draw certain definite conclusions about the scope of Soviet-Communist activity in the United States and other target nations. First and foremost, it's evident from now-available records that Communist penetration of our government—and our society in general—was, over a span of decades, massive. Hundreds of Soviet agents, Communist Party members, and fellow travelers were ensconced on official payrolls, beginning in the New Deal era then increasing rapidly during World War II, when the Soviets were our allies against the Nazis.

As the record further shows, Communists and fellow travelers on official rosters in case after case were agents of the Soviet Union, plighting their troth to Moscow and striving to promote the cause of the dictator Stalin. This is of course contrary to the notion that American Reds were simply idealistic do-gooders, perhaps a bit misguided but devoted to peace and social justice, and thus shouldn't have been ousted from government jobs just because of their opinions. In countless instances, we know that domestic Communists in official posts were actively working on behalf of Russia, and thus were the minions of a hostile foreign power.

In due course many such pro-Soviet operatives rose to fairly high positions, which made their allegiance to Moscow even more problematic. The best known of these apparatchiks was Alger Hiss, who became a significant figure in the U.S. State Department in the war years and would play a critical role in planning for the postwar era. And while Hiss is the most remembered of Moscow's undercover agents, he was merely one of many. As the records prove, there were dozens of others like him at the State Department, White House, Treasury, Commerce, the wartime agencies, and other official venues.

In sum, as shown by a now substantial mass of data, a powerful and devious enemy had by the middle 1940s succeeded in planting myriad secret agents and sympathizers in offices of the U.S. government (and other posts of influence) where they were able to serve the cause of Moscow and betray America's national interests. The American people were blissfully ignorant of this danger, while a sizable number of high officials were either indifferent to the problem or in some cases complicit with it. A more alarming scenario for the safety and security of the nation would be hard to imagine.

Further confirmed by the recent revelations is something known before but in frequent need of stressing. Communist operatives in the United States were linked in multiple ways not only to their Moscow bosses but to Reds in other countries, all parts of a far-flung global apparatus. The most conspicuous of these ties were to the Cambridge University Communist cell of England, which produced such notorious Soviet agents as Anthony Blunt, Kim Philby, and Guy Burgess. There were, in addition, North American members of this ring who attended Cambridge in the 1930s and then returned to pursue official duties on this side of the ocean. Such pro-Red operatives as Philby, Burgess, and Donald Maclean would later be dispatched to Washington by Whitehall to liaise with U.S. officials. American and British security problems accordingly crisscrossed and interacted at many places.

Thus far our analysis and conclusions track closely with the views of others who have examined the relevant data and written about these matters. At this point, however, the story as we see it diverges sharply from that set forth in some other volumes—the main difference concerning the seemingly pervasive notion in Cold War studies that the major if not the only problem posed by

Communists on official payrolls was that of spying. In what seems to be the now standard version of the subject, it's assumed or said that the chief danger presented by Soviet agents in the United States was the theft of military or diplomatic secrets. Conversely, it's implied though seldom explicitly stated that if such spying didn't happen, the presence of Communists on official payrolls was not a huge security problem.

Our view is quite otherwise, in emphasis as well as in some respects in terms of substance. It's evident on the record before us that pro-Soviet spying did occur in the United States, sometimes in large doses, and was of great importance. This was most famously so concerning theft of our atomic secrets, but applied as well to confidential data such as the development of radar, jet propulsion, and other military systems. We not only acknowledge the significance of such spying, but stress it in most definite fashion. But that stipulation is different from the notion that spying was the *only* problem posed by Soviet agents. As important in some respects—and often more so—was the question of policy influence wielded by pro-Soviet apparatchiks on official payrolls (who were in fact dubbed "agents of influence" by their Moscow bosses).

Not, to be sure, that influence and espionage operations existed in separate, watertight compartments, nor could they in many cases have done so. The two aspects typically went together, as Communist or pro-Soviet moles in official positions might do one, the other, or both, as opportunity presented. The case of Alger Hiss provides a notable instance. Much has been made of the "pumpkin papers" (copies of diplomatic records) that his ex-Communist accuser Chambers produced in the course of their legal battles as proof that Hiss engaged in espionage when he was at the State Department. Attention has been focused pro and con on what these documents proved concerning his fealty to Moscow and (among his defenders) where else they might have come from. Less noticed is what the documents were *about*—namely, data from U.S. envoys abroad that would have disclosed to Moscow what American and other Western policy was going to be in the global turmoil occurring in the 1930s.

Guided by such inside information, the Soviets could plan their own strategies with assurance—like a card player who could read the hand of an opponent. Knowing what the United States or other Western nations would do with respect to Germany, Poland, Spain, Japan, or China, the commissars could make their moves with foreknowledge of the responses they would get from other powers. Thus the two facets of the Soviet project interacted—the spying handmaiden to the policy interest. And, of course, if *knowing* what the policies of the United States and other non-Communist nations would be was useful to the Kremlin, then being able to influence or guide those policies in some manner would have been still more so.

The degree to which such questions are glossed over in some recent studies is the more puzzling, as Cold War scholars generally are aware of the influence issue. No serious student of these matters, for example, can be ignorant of the Cold War role played by Chambers, who knew a lot about spying and was involved in it on a professional basis. Yet Chambers repeatedly stressed that spying as such was *not* the major issue. Rather, he said, with the likes of Hiss in federal office, policy influence was by far the leading problem. As Chambers expressed it:

> *In a situation with few parallels in history, the agents of an enemy power were in a position to do much more than purloin documents. They were in a position to influence the nation's foreign policy in the interest of the nation's chief enemy, and not only on exceptional occasions, like Yalta (where Hiss's role, while presumably important, is still ill-defined) or through the Morgenthau plan for the destruction of Germany (which is generally credited to [Soviet agent Harry Dexter] White) but in what must have been the staggering sum of day to day decisions.[2]*

As shall be seen, Chambers was correct about the roles of Hiss and White, though now accessible records that prove the point weren't open to inspection when he made this comment. As to the relative importance of policy influence compared to spying, Chambers further noted, "*That power to influence policy has always been the ultimate purpose of the Communist Party's infiltration. It was much more dangerous, and, as events have proved, much more difficult to detect, than espionage, which beside it is trivial, though the two go hand in hand.*"[3] (Emphasis added.) That sums up the matter about as well as it can be stated, and sets forth a major thesis of this volume.

In the face of this explicit testimony by one of the foremost experts on such subjects—whose expertise is well-known to researchers—it's remarkable that our histories continue to stress espionage in such one-sided manner. This focus has in turn been significant in limiting our Cold War knowledge, as journalists and scholars thus guided have been minutely examining a restricted, albeit important, set of issues. There is of course nothing wrong with espionage inquiries per se—quite the contrary—but they become misleading if they screen from view the issue of policy influence that was meanwhile being wielded by pro-Soviet agents in federal office.

Obscured by this approach, for instance, are numerous crucial questions about the establishment and growth of Communist global power and its threat to our survival. To what extent, if any, did pro-Soviet operatives in the West contribute to the success of the Bolshevik cause at the outset of the Soviet revolution? Or maneuver against the United States to Moscow's advantage in the run-up to Pearl Harbor? What role did concealed Communist agents of influence in the West play in the summit conferences of World War II among Franklin Roosevelt, Joseph Stalin, and Winston Churchill? In the standard treatments these and numerous other such questions aren't answered, or even raised, because they don't involve the issue of spying. The self-evident result of such omissions is an enormous gap in the historical record.

Apart from issues of this type, discovering the facts about the infiltration is no easy matter, as the pertinent data were so long kept secret. This stemmed initially from the subliminal aspects of the struggle, but was made worse by measures of official concealment used to prevent the public from seeing the scope and nature of the problem. The most explicit policies to this effect were presidential secrecy orders handed down by Washington administrations from the 1940s through the 1960s, denying FBI reports and other relevant information about the issue to Congress and the American people, with results that lingered on for decades.

Add to this a problem that in some respects was (and is) even more disturbing: the disappearance of many official records bearing on Cold War matters, either by way of "weeding" or transfer of important papers from one place to another, with no indication that this was done, or in some cases the outright destruction of security data. Several episodes of this nature will be examined in the pages that follow—some dating back to World War II, others as recent as the 1990s.

Further measures of concealment have included efforts by high-ranking U.S. officials to manipulate grand juries (at least two that we know of) to ensure that Communists and pro-Soviet henchmen in policy-making weren't brought to justice. The importance of such methods for purposes of the present survey is that not only did they corruptly influence the nation's legal system, they also warped the historical record available to researchers, so that treatments of the Cold War today often reflect a mistaken version of these cases and thus the true extent of the security problem.

From these considerations, the bottom line to be derived is in some ways the most distressing part of the story. In essence, the Communist conspirators of the 1930s and 1940s, assisted by some high-level U.S. officials, got away with their betrayal. A relative handful—Hiss, Carl Marzani, William Remington, the Rosenbergs—were indicted and convicted, but scores of others were repeatedly able to betray the United States and the non-Communist world to Moscow, then simply walk away from the policy damage they inflicted, with no accountability for their actions.

Even more to the point, most of these conspirators are getting away with it even now—in the pages of what purport to be histories of the Cold War. In numerous cases of the latter 1940s, as shall be seen, Communists and Soviet agents were pressured to leave the federal payroll (though in some instances even this didn't happen), but this too was done sub rosa, with no fanfare or public notice. Since there was thus in the overwhelming majority of cases no legal action or disclosure of the relevant background, the suspects would discreetly vanish from the historical record to savor in quiet retirement their clandestine exploits against U.S. and free-world interests.

A final element of obfuscation to be dealt with is that many official data that escaped destruction or removal have nonetheless been sanitized, so that even the documents we've been given are far from being full disclosure. A prime example involves the Yalta conference of February 1945, where President Roosevelt met with British prime minister Churchill and Soviet leader Stalin to make decisions that would dictate the postwar future and affect the lives of millions. Unfortunately, the official State Department compilation of the Yalta papers omitted or obscured many essential facts about the conference, what was done there, and how it happened. As this was the most crucial of the wartime summits, these omissions and obscurities have been of utmost importance in shaping—or misshaping—the long-accepted Cold War record.*

---

* A prime example of such omissions is that, when the compilation was put together, the State Department historians did not have full access to the papers of Edward Stettinius Jr., secretary of state at the time of Yalta. This resulted not only in an inadequate official record, but in reliance by historians on the sanitized posthumous Stettinius memoir about the conference, *Roosevelt and the Russians* (1949). As the now available Stettinius papers reveal, both the official Yalta compilation and the posthumous memoir are considerably less than the total story.

Our focus on Yalta in these comments is not coincidental, as this was the conference that more than any other determined the contours of the postwar landscape and led to some of the deadliest episodes of the Cold War. Yalta and the predecessor conference at Teheran were the culmination of a process that had been under way, in some respects, since the latter 1930s. In the pages that follow, we review some unreported aspects of the Yalta summit, before moving on to consideration of various historic issues and acts of state that resulted from the wartime meetings. As shall be seen, the now discernible facts of record are starkly different from the version of Cold War events set forth in many histories of the era.

1.

EVEN IF MY ALLY IS A FOOL

I t was, said Prime Minister Winston Churchill, "the greatest concentration of earthly power that had ever been seen in the history of mankind."[1]

Britain's inspirational wartime leader was referring to the Teheran conference of late November 1943, where he met with American president Franklin Roosevelt and Soviet dictator Joseph Stalin, his allies in the deadly struggle that was being waged against the Nazi Wehrmacht and (by the United States and Britain, though not by Russia) against Japan's Imperial legions. It was an accurate summary of conditions then prevailing. The allies at Teheran commanded land and naval forces more formidable than those deployed in any other conflict, before or after. Among them they controlled vast stretches of the earth and its major seaways, and were rapidly conquering others.

While Churchill's reference was to Teheran, it would be as valid, in fact a good deal more so, slightly over a year thereafter, when the three leaders met again near the Black Sea resort city of Yalta, in what was then the Soviet Union. By the time of Yalta, not only was the combined might of the Big Three even more prodigious; it was obvious that the Germans and Japanese were soon going to be defeated. At that point the victorious allies could together rule the world in toto, as there would be no other state or group of states remotely able to oppose them. Supremacy on such a scale was unprecedented in the annals of global warfare.

With such great power went huge responsibilities, opportunities, and problems. The superpowers held in their hands the fate of millions who had survived the ravages of war and would now dig out from beneath the rubble. These bewildered and battered peoples would be desperately seeking to put their lives back together in some semblance of peace and order. What the Big Three decided at the wartime summits would dictate their ability to do so, with impact that would last for decades.

Given all of the above, some understanding of what happened at these meetings would seem essential to an informed assessment of late-twentieth-century history and the further mortal combat that filled its pages. Yet, in standard treatments of the era, such understanding is hard to come by. Many of these are by-the-book accounts of campaigns and battles, Allied advances and reverses, steps taken to mobilize American forces, U.S.-British joint endeavors, and other facets of the military struggle. Others might be described as court histories, written on behalf of the people wielding power and meant to justify their actions. All, as noted, have been limited in that relevant data were long held back, ignored, or censored, and in some instances still aren't available for viewing. The net result of all these factors is that a complete and accurate record of what was done at these meetings in terms of geopolitical outcomes is still waiting to be written.

While making no pretensions to completeness, what follows is an attempt to fill in some historical blanks—to retrieve some of the missing data reflecting what happened at the wartime summits, and in the intervals between them, why it happened, and what resulted from the decisions taken. The principal focus is not on battles, generals, or naval forces, but on things occurring behind the scenes, as revealed by formerly secret records, memoirs of political and military figures, and confidential security archives now made public. In particular, we seek to trace the doings of certain shadowy figures in the background whose activities had significant influence on the decisions made and the Cold War policies that followed.

Briefly at Teheran, and more extensively at Yalta, discussions would be held among the Big Three powers about the shape of the postwar world, how its nations should be governed, and how to keep the peace among them. There was at Yalta specifically talk of a supranational body that would prevent outbreaks of future warfare and ensure the universal reign of justice.* This was a chief preoccupation of FDR, who in emulation of Woodrow Wilson before him thought the founding of such an agency would be his great legacy to the future.

These lofty notions were in keeping with the stated purposes of the war, as set forth in official speeches and manifestos. In the widely heralded Atlantic Charter of August 1941, issued in the names of Roosevelt and Churchill, the two leaders had vowed their commitment to self-government, national independence, and political freedom. The Anglo-American powers, said the charter, "desire no territorial changes that do not accord with the freely expressed wishes of the people." It underscored the point by stressing "the right of all peoples to choose the form of government under which they shall live." These thoughts would be reprised at Yalta, with a few verbal changes, in a "Declaration on Liberated Europe," agreed to by all of the Big Three allies.[2]

Of course, not all or even most discussions at Teheran and Yalta were conducted at this level. There were practical issues to be decided that were more immediate and pressing, and had to be settled while the war was still in progress. Among these was the destiny of the soon-to-be-conquered German nation, how its people should be dealt with, its assets distributed, and its lands divided. Also on the list of immediate topics were states of Eastern Europe that had initially been overrun by the Nazis and then captured by the Russians, whose prewar governments were in exile. How these

---

* The subject had earlier been raised, in tentative fashion, at meetings in Quebec and Teheran.

countries would be governed, inside what borders and by whom, would be major objects of discussion.

On the agenda also, somewhat obliquely at Teheran, explicitly at Yalta, was the future of China, though at both meetings this enormous subject would be handled in sub rosa fashion. Not quite so large, but large enough, was the issue of "reparations" that the Germans owed the Allies, which in practice mainly meant the Russians.* Added to these issues were questions involving refugees uprooted by the war, of whom there were several millions and whose plight affected all of Europe and much of Asia. All this compounded by the ravages of disease, hunger, and the mass destruction of industries, farms, and dwellings by saturation bombing and five-plus years of fighting.

In sum, just about everything imaginable was up for decision at these meetings, with Yalta in particular a veritable workshop for making over the world de novo, as so much of the preexisting global order had been demolished.

Of significance also, measured against the backdrop of the Atlantic Charter, was the way such matters would be handled. As things played out at Teheran and Yalta, the noble sentiments voiced in the charter amounted to little more than window dressing. In the vast majority of cases, the relevant choices would be made simply by the fiat of the Big Three powers: where borders would be drawn, what areas and assets belonged to whom, where populations would be moved because of such decisions. The three leaders would likewise decide, directly or indirectly, what political forces would prevail where and the forms of government to be installed in formerly captive nations, including those in alignment with the victors. No "freely expressed wishes of the people" about it.

---

* The Soviets were considered by the Allies to be the prime beneficiaries of "reparations" at the expense of Germany, as they were judged to have suffered the greatest losses at the hands of the Nazis.

Three prominent cases of this type were Yugoslavia, Poland, and China, all of which would be pulled into the vortex of Communist power when the war concluded. What the people of these countries thought about the decisions that shaped their destiny was immaterial, as they would have nothing effective to say about the subject. In these instances, governments would be imposed by top-down decree, intimidation, or outright violence. These results were both tragic and ironic, given the stated objects of the war, but especially so for Poland, as its independence had been the supposed casus belli of the conflict with the Nazis (as China was for the American war in Asia).

A similar fate would befall other nations of Eastern and Central Europe. Latvia, Estonia and Lithuania, Rumania, Bulgaria, Hungary, and Albania would be absorbed into the Soviet empire as the war proceeded. Czechoslovakia would hold out a few years longer but also be subject to Red conquest, as was self-evidently the part of Germany to be controlled by Moscow. All this was prelude to half a century of Cold War struggle, with numerous outbreaks along the way of hot-war fighting, in every quarter of the planet.

Nor was the absence of peace the only tragedy of this tragic era. As the forces of Communism advanced, the practices that prevailed in Russia would be extended also. With few exceptions, where the Soviet armies came to rest, they or their surrogates stayed, and would stay for years to come. Poland, Hungary, East Germany, et al. would—in another famous phrase of Churchill—be sealed up behind an Iron Curtain of repression. Behind that impenetrable barrier, concealed from view and their voices strangled, untold numbers of helpless victims would be killed, tortured, and imprisoned, with no hope of rescue or outside assistance, and no certain knowledge in the West of what had happened to them.

In the years to follow, similar results would occur in Asia. Millions would be slaughtered in China once the Communists got control there, and millions more would perish in Korea, Vietnam,

Cambodia, Laos. Red police states would in due course extend from the Baltic to the Pacific, and later to Africa and Latin America, denying freedoms, shutting down religious institutions, locking up dissenters. And even where Communist systems did not prevail, authoritarian governments of one sort or another were the rule instead of the exception. The supposedly progressive twentieth century thus became a saturnalia of tyranny and violence, surpassing in this respect also all previous records of such horrors.

These developments were obviously light-years from the visions of peace and justice proclaimed by the Western leaders in World War II and in jarring contrast to the objects of the war expressed in the Atlantic Charter. Viewed from any angle, nothing could have been further from the oft-stated aims of Roosevelt and Churchill, who had announced a series of high objectives but somehow accomplished the reverse of what they said they wanted. Though the law of unintended consequences often rules in the affairs of nations, history affords few examples of such totally counterproductive action and catastrophic failure on such a colossal basis. Yet there were many factors in the wartime equation that, to a discerning eye, could have foretold these dismal outcomes.

Fairly obvious at the time, and even more so later, were the geostrategic consequences of the war, given the opposing lineups that developed early in the fighting. The inevitable main effect was to enhance the strength of the Soviet Union, as the war would destroy the two major powers, Germany and Japan, that had contained it on its borders. With these states demolished, there was no country in Europe strong enough to resist the further advance of Communist power, while in Asia the only sizable obstacle facing Moscow was the shaky regime of Nationalist China, which by 1949 would itself succumb to Communist revolution.

The looming European imbalance had been visible early on to the veteran geostrategist Churchill. Though he held mistaken notions of his own that contributed to the postwar debacle, he became increasingly concerned about the growth of Soviet power as the war unfolded. He saw clearly that, while the conflict was being fought to free Europe from a genocidal tyrant, it would end by placing the continent at the mercy of another. The great tragedy of the struggle, he would write, was that "after all the exertions and sacrifices of millions of people, and of victories of the Righteous cause, we will not have found peace and security and that we lie in the grip of even worse perils than we have surmounted."[3]

Churchill's conclusion from these reflections was that the West urgently needed to shore up its defenses against the expansion of Soviet power, which was what eventually did happen in Europe toward the end of the 1940s. The same wartime phenomenon, meanwhile, would be apparent also to some high-level American observers, but was viewed by them in an entirely different light, leading to sharply different conclusions. In these official U.S. precincts, the impending dominance of Soviet power in Europe was not something to be combated, deplored, or counterbalanced, but rather an outcome to be accommodated and assisted.

The most explicit and seemingly authoritative statement of this startling view was a policy paper carried to one of the wartime meetings* by Roosevelt adviser Harry Hopkins. This document, among other things, asserted: "Russia's post-war position in Europe will be a dominant one. With Germany crushed, there is no power in Europe to oppose her tremendous military forces. The conclusions from the foregoing are obvious. *Since Russia is the decisive factor in the war, she must be given every assistance and every effort must be made to obtain her friendship.*"[4] (Emphasis added.)

Who drafted this astonishing statement is unknown, though Hopkins biographer Robert Sherwood tells us it came from a "very high level United States military strategic estimate." More certain is

---

* This was the Quebec conference between FDR and Churchill in August 1943. There would be a similar such meeting in Quebec a year thereafter.

that the thoughts expressed matched those of Hopkins himself and of his chieftain, FDR—presaging, as Sherwood notes, "the policy which guided the making of decisions at Teheran and, much later, at Yalta."

Seeking Soviet "friendship" and giving Moscow "every assistance" indeed summed up American policy at Teheran and Yalta, and for some while before those meetings. The most vivid expression of Roosevelt's ideas to this effect would be quoted by William Bullitt, a longtime confidant of the President, and his first envoy to Moscow. Bullitt recounted an episode early in the war in which he suggested to FDR that American Lend-Lease aid to Russia might provide some leverage with a balky Kremlin. To this, according to Bullitt, the President responded: "I have just a hunch that Stalin doesn't want anything but security for his country, and *I think that if I give him everything I possibly can and ask nothing from him in return, noblesse oblige, he won't try to annex anything and will work for world democracy and peace.*"[5] (Emphasis added.) Bullitt, who had learned about Stalin the hard way in Russia, tried to dissuade the President from this view but was not successful.*

This remarkable Roosevelt quote might seem implausible if there weren't other statements on the record a good deal like it. In October 1942, for instance, the President wrote to Churchill: "I think there is nothing more important than that Stalin feel that we mean to support him without qualification and at great sacrifice"— which was pretty close to the Bullitt version. As for the noblesse oblige, FDR at Yalta would be recorded by British Field Marshal

---

* Bullitt at the conclusion of World War I had been an enthusiast for the Soviet revolution, but when stationed in Moscow in the 1930s as U.S. ambassador he became disillusioned by the repression and mendacity that he witnessed. His views about the subject were expressed in his 1946 book, *The Great Globe Itself,* deploring among other things the Soviets' denial of religious freedom and continued efforts at worldwide subversion, contra pledges made to the United States as a basis for U.S. diplomatic recognition.

Alan Brooke as saying, "of one thing I am certain; Stalin is not an imperialist." And at a post-Yalta meeting, the President observed to his presumably nonplussed cabinet that as Stalin early on had studied for the priesthood, "something entered into his nature of the way in which a Christian gentleman should behave."[6]

When we recall that Stalin was one of the great mass murderers of all time, quite on a par with Hitler, these Roosevelt statements are most charitably described as surrealistic—less charitably, as irresponsible and dangerous nonsense. They were the more so as the President had at his beck experts on Soviet affairs including Bullitt, Loy Henderson, and George F. Kennan, all of whom had spent years in Moscow and knew much of the ghastly truth concerning Stalin. The President and his entourage, however, had no use for the counsel of such people, some of whom would in the 1930s and the war years be ousted from official posts because of their anti-Red opinions. (See chapter 19.)

Why Roosevelt believed the things he did concerning Stalin, or was willing to gamble the future of mankind on such "hunches," doesn't permit a definite answer. Undoubtedly a contributing factor was that he had close-in counselors who took a highly favorable view of Stalin and whose ideas trumped those of a Bullitt, Henderson, or Kennan. One such was Joseph Davies, who succeeded Bullitt as ambassador to Moscow and there became enamored of Stalin and the Soviet economic system. In a book about his experience in Russia, Davies would praise the Soviets in general, extenuate the bloody purge trials of the 1930s, and suggest that Stalin among his numerous virtues favored religious freedom and free elections (neither of which, despite some wartime gestures to placate U.S. opinion, ever existed in Stalin's Russia).

As to the up-close-and-personal Stalin, Davies would write in a memorable passage: "He gives the impression of a strong mind which is composed and wise. His brown eye is exceedingly kindly and gentle. A child would like to sit on his lap and a dog would sidle up to him."[7] No doubt a leader with these amiable qualities would have had a sense of noblesse oblige, and perhaps some aspect of a "Christian gentleman," so Davies may have been a source for these strange Rooseveltian notions. It appears in any event that the President's thoughts about such matters were generally influenced by Davies, who continued to advise the White House in the war years, though there were others on the scene who had a similar benighted view of Stalin.

Among these was Harry Hopkins, so close to the President he lived in the White House. Hopkins had at his own initiative been sent to Moscow by Roosevelt in July 1941—before America was in the war but a month after Hitler invaded Russia—to consult with Stalin about the kind of U.S. assistance the Soviets wanted. Hopkins thereafter wrote an admiring profile of Stalin, not quite so fawning as the Davies version but glowing with enthusiasm, then spent the war years zealously pushing through American aid to Russia.*

Hopkins's most famous statement about such matters—albeit one of many—was his pledge to a pro-Russian crowd at a June 1942 rally in New York promoting aid to Moscow. "We are determined," he said, "that nothing shall stop us from sharing with you all that we have."[8] In private comments, as discussed hereafter, he would make other even more emphatic statements of like nature. As events would show, these were faithful reflections of his—and Roosevelt's—attitude toward the Kremlin.

Also affecting Roosevelt's outlook toward Moscow were certain

---

* Not to be omitted in this context was the presence in the White House of Mrs. Roosevelt, who had around her a coterie of youthful leftists and was a point of contact for outside forces who took a favorable view of Moscow, the American Communist Party, and all manner of pro-Soviet causes. Add to these wartime influences the infinitely susceptible Henry Wallace, pro-Soviet staffers including Lauchlin Currie and David Niles, and numerous high-level officials in federal agencies who in fact were Soviet assets. Obviously, the forces around FDR pushing things in a pro-Soviet direction were many and effective.

personal traits and ideas he held about his own powers of persuasion. His confidence in Stalin was great, but his confidence in himself was greater. With some reason, based on his political successes at home, he saw himself as a charismatic figure who could persuade people to his way of thinking, if only they could be exposed to his irresistible person. He was convinced he could do this with Stalin, so that if they could just meet face-to-face FDR's charm and magnetism would set right the troublesome issues between them.

In pursuit of this conception, Roosevelt at Teheran and Yalta adopted a strategy of distancing himself from Churchill and making common cause with Stalin. This was rationalized as an effort to convince the dictator that the Anglo-Americans weren't "ganging up" on him, but degenerated into a series of unfunny Roosevelt jokes at Churchill's expense—plus side remarks to Stalin about the evils of British colonialism (no comments about Soviet colonialism)—that amounted to "ganging up" on Churchill.* This gambit was so tawdry even FDR interpreter Charles Bohlen, a supporter of Yalta, was offended, and, as backing for England was the main alleged reason for our involvement in the Atlantic conflict, it added yet another ironic reversal to America's wartime record.

Roosevelt's thoughts about such matters would be expressed early on to Churchill, when he wrote to the British leader: "I hope you will not mind my being totally frank when I tell you I think I can personally handle Stalin better than either your foreign office or my State Department. *Stalin hates the guts of all your people. He thinks he likes me better*, and I hope he will continue to do so."[9] (Emphasis added.) These comments were made before FDR had

---

* As Roosevelt explained to Labor Secretary Frances Perkins, he had allegedly broken the ice with Stalin at Teheran by saying, "Winston is cranky this morning, he got up on the wrong side of the bed." FDR added that "I began to tease Churchill over his Britishness, about John Bull. . . . Finally Stalin broke into a deep guffaw. . . . I kept it up until Stalin was laughing with me, and it was then that I called him 'Uncle Joe.'"

any direct contact with Stalin (they wouldn't meet until Teheran) and not much by way of indirect connection. They were rather clearly based on advice from Hopkins on his return from Moscow, and probably some input from Davies.

In fact, as with Stalin's alleged sense of noblesse oblige, or qualities as a Christian gentleman, there is no known evidence that he had any personal liking for FDR. As diplomat/historian Kennan would observe, for Roosevelt's notion that if only Stalin "could be exposed to the persuasive charms of someone like FDR himself" Soviet cooperation would be obtained, "there were no grounds whatever, and of a peculiarity unworthy of a statesman of FDR's stature."[10] It was also, unfortunately, the notion on which Roosevelt gambled the fate of the world at Teheran and Yalta.

Though the idea that Stalin liked Roosevelt in any personal sense may be questioned, he undoubtedly did like having, as leader of the powerful United States, someone prepared to give him unlimited favors, while America sought nothing in return from Russia. As Stalin was more than willing to receive and seldom hesitant in asking, this would have been an arrangement tailor-made for Moscow—the proverbial taking of candy from a baby. Concerning which, the dictator's true attitudes perhaps shone through a toast he made at Yalta, intriguingly linked to the issue of deception. On this occasion, Stalin held forth on the subject of deceit, saying, "Why should I not deceive my ally? I as a naive man think it best not to deceive my ally even if he is a fool."[11] To which he might have added that, if one's ally is indeed a fool, it doesn't take any great effort to deceive him, as he will do the deceiving for you.

2.

THE GHOST SHIP AT YALTA

With everything that was on the line at Yalta, one might suppose the U.S. government would have sent there a first-rate team of policy experts and negotiators to uphold American and free-world interests. Dealing with the tough and wily Soviets in such a context would have required the best that mid-century America had to offer. Such, however, was not to be the case at this world-changing summit.

Few people familiar with the American delegation at Yalta would have called it first-rate, or even adequate to the challenge. On the military side, there was an impressive show of brass and braid, but the diplomatic group was different. Among his entourage Roosevelt had two staffers knowledgeable of the Soviet Union—interpreter Bohlen and ambassador to Moscow W. Averell Harriman*—plus some support personnel to be discussed hereafter. But notably absent were ranking U.S. experts who knew a lot about the Soviets and diplomacy in general: top-line officials such as Undersecretary of State Joseph Grew, State's European chief James C. Dunn, Russia specialists Henderson and Kennan. None of these would make the trip to Yalta.

---

* Harriman was a millionaire businessman, heir to the Harriman railroad fortune, and an early promoter of U.S. investment in Russia. He was a personal friend of the Roosevelt family and close to Roosevelt's top assistant, Harry Hopkins. It was Hopkins who brought Harriman into the government in the war years to help administer the Roosevelt program of Lend-Lease aid to Britain and Russia. Harriman performed various other troubleshooting chores for FDR and Hopkins, which led to his 1943 appointment to the embassy in Moscow.

On hand instead to counsel FDR at the highest policy levels were his new secretary of state, Edward R. Stettinius Jr.—with all of two months' experience on the job*—and the President's chief confidant on domestic matters, Harry Hopkins. Stettinius by common consent was a foreign policy novice appointed simply because he was a protégé of Hopkins. Stettinius in essence got the job because he would have few independent notions (as occasionally happened with his predecessor, Cordell Hull). This was important to FDR, who prided himself on being his own foreign secretary, and typically functioned in that manner.

Hopkins had foreign experience of a sort, but this consisted mostly of shuttling back and forth as a special envoy to Stalin and Churchill before America was technically in the war, to see if they wanted our assistance (they did). This fit well with his earlier domestic role as dispenser of welfare dollars, and became official in the war years when he was made the overall head of Lend-Lease operations, providing aid to U.S. allies.

With Stettinius at his side and Hopkins hovering wraithlike in the background, Roosevelt at Yalta was indeed his own secretary of state, and we have briefly seen what this would have meant for dealings with the Soviet Union. He was intent on making Stalin like him via personal magnetism and unrequited favors, while distancing American interests from those of England. His main object was to get Stalin to agree with the Rooseveltian vision of a peaceable kingdom to come via the United Nations, establishing a U.S.-Soviet condominium to manage the postwar world between them.

All that, however, was just a beginning. In addition to his

---

* Like Harriman, Stettinius was a big businessman (U.S. Steel) recruited by Hopkins for wartime duty in the Lend-Lease program. In 1943 Stettinius was made undersecretary of state and less than a year later was appointed secretary when Cordell Hull retired from the department. Stettinius's lack of qualification for the assignment was proverbial at the time and acknowledged even in pro-FDR and pro-Hopkins histories of the era.

peculiar view of Stalin and the negotiating process, there were definite signs at Yalta that the President was failing badly in his powers. As known to some people at the time, and widely acknowledged now, Roosevelt was a dying man at Yalta, and indications were many that his illness had affected his performance for some while before then. Exactly how to measure its impact is uncertain, but that it was a significant factor can't very well be doubted.

Roosevelt's health had been an issue—for him and others—from the day in 1921 when he was struck down by polio, as a result of which he would never walk again unaided. His battle to overcome his disability, and refusal to let it blight his prospects, were of epic nature—something again known at the time to a handful of people but now a matter of general knowledge. Even his bitterest critics must marvel at his two decades of struggle with his affliction, and the heroic spirit in which he waged it.

Not so heroic, but perhaps commendable in its way, was the role of the Washington press corps in concealing his infirmity from the public. Photographs or newsreels of FDR being carried, pushed in a wheelchair, or otherwise appearing physically helpless were discouraged by the White House. The media of the time usually complied with these restrictions. And so long as projecting a presidential image of physical vigor was the only point of the charade, there was arguably no major damage being done to the nation's interests.

As we now know, however, Roosevelt had other health problems of a more daunting nature in terms of his official performance. These concerned not the paralysis of his lower body or even his physical health in general, but involved instead his mental balance, judgment, and powers of comprehension. A good deal of information about such matters has become available in recent decades, all of it disturbing. Two informative essays are *The Dying President* (1998) by presidential historian Robert Ferrell and *FDR's Deadly Secret* (2009) by Dr. Steven Lomazow and journalist Eric Fettmann. These studies differ in suggesting the causes of Roosevelt's illness but are alike in describing its effects on his ability to carry out his duties. And for policy purposes, of course, the effects are the important features.*

Eyewitness accounts of Roosevelt's declining state began at the Teheran conference with Churchill and Stalin (November 1943) and would become more frequent in the days that followed. There had been signs of weakness before, recorded by a doting cousin who was with him on a regular basis, but it was at Teheran that these first seemed to affect his official conduct. On November 28, at a dinner meeting with Churchill and Stalin, FDR collapsed and had to be taken to his quarters. According to Charles Bohlen, the President "turned green and great drops of sweat began to bead off his face." [1] The episode was put down to "indigestion," but events that followed would suggest a different diagnosis.

By early 1944, Roosevelt's decline was so apparent that observers who saw him at close range knew he was gravely ill. One such was journalist Turner Catledge, then a reporter for the *New York Times*, later executive editor of the paper. On returning from Europe in March 1944, Catledge would write, he talked with the President at the White House and was profoundly shaken by the experience.

"When I first entered the President's office," said Catledge, "I had my first glimpse of him in several months. I was shocked and horrified—so much so that my impulse was to turn around and leave. I felt I was seeing something I wasn't supposed to see. . . . He was sitting there with a vague, glassy eyed expression and his mouth hanging open. . . . Reluctantly, I sat down and we started to talk. . . . He would start talking about something, then in mid-sentence he would stop and his mouth would drop open . . . and he sat staring at me in silence. I knew I was looking at a terribly sick man." [2]

This was eleven months before the Big Three would convene at

---

* Ferrell discusses in some detail the evidence that Roosevelt had long suffered from chronic heart disease. Lomazow and Fettmann advance the thesis that he was suffering also from a metastasizing cancer.

Yalta. In the weeks ensuing, there was considerable other testimony of like nature. Among those who remarked on FDR's declining powers was former Democratic national chairman Jim Farley, a main architect of Roosevelt's early political triumphs. In his memoirs, Farley would recount the comments of many observers of this era about the President's illness.

"From the time of his return from Teheran in December," said Farley, "there were disturbing reports about Roosevelt's health. Hundreds of persons, high and low, reported to me that he looked bad, his mind wandered, his hands shook, his jaw sagged and he tired easily. Almost everyone who came in had some story about the President's health—directly or indirectly—from any one of various doctors who examined him. . . . Members of the Cabinet, senators, congressmen, members of the White House staff, various Federal officials and newspapermen carried a variety of reports on the President's failing health."

All this, again, in early 1944. By midsummer, at the time of the Chicago Democratic convention, which nominated Roosevelt for a fourth term in office, Farley recalled: "Everywhere the President's health was a major topic, though it was discussed largely in whispers. . . ." The political implications weren't lost on the experienced pols of the Democratic Party.* "Anyone with a grain of common sense," wrote Farley, "would surely realize from the appearance of the President that he is not a well man and there is not a chance in the world for him to carry on for four years more . . . he just can't survive another presidential term. . . ."[3] On which evidence, the Democratic leaders at Chicago nominated a dying man—the man who seven months later would go to Yalta.

Roosevelt himself didn't attend the Chicago convention, instead wending his way by train across the country to San Diego, where

---

* One product of this concern was the replacement as vice presidential nominee of the mistrusted Henry Wallace with the more reliable Harry Truman.

he would embark on a leisurely ocean voyage. At San Diego he delivered his nomination acceptance speech by radio, being snapped by a *Life* magazine photographer in an unflattering picture that made the President look old and ailing. He then left on a five-week Pacific cruise, the main stated purpose of which was a Pearl Harbor meeting with General Douglas MacArthur and Admiral Chester Nimitz to discuss the war in Asia.

At this meeting, MacArthur explained to FDR his plan to return to the Philippines and his tactic of bypassing enemy strongpoints in the Pacific. The general later recorded his impressions of FDR, which matched those of Catledge and Farley. "I was shocked," said MacArthur, "at the personal appearance of President Roosevelt. I had not seen him in a number of years and he had failed immeasurably. I predict that he will be dead within the year."[4] That grim forecast would be distressingly on-target.

Similar comments would be made by others who saw Roosevelt soon thereafter. Canadian prime minister William Lyon Mackenzie King, who would host a September Roosevelt-Churchill summit at Quebec, remarked that the President "had failed very much since I last saw him." In the run-up to Quebec, War Secretary Henry Stimson made like observations. "I have been much troubled," said Stimson, "by the President's physical condition. . . . I rather fear for the effects of this hard conference upon him. . . . I am particularly troubled that he is going up there without any real preparation for the solution of the underlying problem of how to treat Germany." (Stimson added that FDR seemed to have made "absolutely no study" of the German problem—a premonition borne out by what happened at the conference.[5] See chapter 15.)

After the fall election, during which FDR briefly seemed to rally, Labor Secretary Frances Perkins was likewise alarmed by his condition. As she would recall it, "the change in appearance had to do with the oncoming of a kind of glassy eye, and an extremely drawn look around the jaw and cheeks, and even a sort of dropping of the muscles of control of the jaw and mouth . . . if you saw him close, you could see that his hands were weak. . . . When he fainted, as he did occasionally, that was all accentuated. It would be very brief, and he'd be back again."[6]

On the eve of Yalta, similar thoughts would occur to interpreter Bohlen. Though saying that FDR's condition didn't then affect his speech or mental powers, Bohlen too would be disturbed by the President's illness. "I was shocked," said Bohlen, "by Roosevelt's physical appearance. His condition had deteriorated markedly in the less than two weeks since I had seen him. He was not only frail and desperately tired, he looked ill. . . . Everyone noticed the president's condition, and we in the American delegation began to talk among ourselves about the basic state of his health."[7]

All of this, however, was kept secret from the public. Principal blame for this has been laid at the door of Dr. Ross McIntire, the Navy admiral who was Roosevelt's physician. McIntire insisted at the time of the President's death, and later, that the stroke that ended his life came out of the blue, that there had been no previous signals of disaster. McIntire has been attacked for taking this position, going along with the White House line that the President was in fine fettle. Again, however, the main point from a policy angle isn't the issue of medical scandal or malpractice, but FDR's ability to carry out his duties.

At the time of Yalta, reports about Roosevelt's mental state were varied, which may reflect the fact that he had good days and bad, but also that different people had different motives in describing his condition. Tellingly, those who said he was on top of his game included close-in confidants and advisers—Bohlen, Stettinius, Harriman, and Admiral William Leahy.* All had rea-

---

* Leahy was a career naval officer who first met Roosevelt in 1913, when FDR was assistant secretary of the Navy. Over the next two decades Leahy ascended to ever-higher naval office and in 1937 was appointed Chief of Naval Operations. In the war years he was named by FDR as chief of staff to the President, making him the top-ranking military officer in the nation (and the most conservative of Roosevelt's top advisers). He later served in the same capacity with President Truman.

son to defend FDR at Yalta, but also to defend Yalta itself, as all were to some degree responsible for its outcomes. Others on the scene would have different notions. James Byrnes, present as an observer but without responsibility for things decided, expressed grave concern about the President's failing health and obvious lack of preparation.* Even the admiring Harry Hopkins, who did have policy input at Yalta, would later say he "doubted that Roosevelt had heard half of what had been said at the Yalta sessions."[8]

Still more severe were the comments of the British, who had no great interest in making Roosevelt look good, and probably had an opposite view because of his attitude toward Churchill. The prime minister's version was that when Roosevelt arrived at Yalta, "he looked frail and ill," and Churchill's thoughts at the end of the conference were even more apprehensive. When the leaders parted, he said, "the President seemed placid and frail. I felt that he had a slender contact with life."[9]

The most critical of British observers was Lord Moran, Churchill's own physician. "To a doctor's eye," wrote Moran, "the President appears a sick man. . . . The President looked old and thin and drawn . . . he sat looking straight ahead with his mouth open, as if he were not taking things in. . . ." Similar comment would be made by Sir Alexander Cadogan of the British Foreign Office: "Whenever [FDR] was called on to preside over any meeting, he failed to make any attempt to grip it or guide it, and sat generally speechless, or, if he made any intervention, it was generally completely irrelevant."[10]

---

* In his autobiography, *Speaking Frankly,* Byrnes said of FDR at Yalta, "I was disturbed by his appearance. I feared his illness was not due entirely to a cold. . . . The President had made little preparation for the Yalta conference. . . . I am sure (this) was due to the President's illness."

FDR's Condition at Yalta

A visibly failing President Roosevelt confers with British prime minister Winston Churchill at the Yalta conference of February 1945. At the conference and in the weeks preceding, numerous observers said that they were shocked by the President's appearance. (Source: *AP Photo*)

Suggesting that the British were more accurate than FDR's admirers were episodes at Yalta—and other summits before then—that indicated an alarming lack of mental balance in his performance. There had been at least one suggestive incident at Teheran, reported by both Elliott Roosevelt and Bohlen, when Stalin urged the shooting of fifty thousand Germans as soon as they could be captured. This outraged Churchill as being contrary to the rules of warfare. FDR then interjected, saying perhaps they could compromise by shooting only 49,500. (This related by Elliott Roosevelt as an example of the President's humor.)*[11]

---

* This episode was also recounted by FDR himself to Turner Catledge at their March 1944 meeting. Catledge didn't think it funny. Churchill's version appears in his book *Closing the Ring*, volume 3 of his history of the war.

At Yalta, FDR would make even more peculiar statements, in terms highly embarrassing to his supporters. One of his strangest comments concerned an upcoming visit with Saudi Arabia's King Ibn Saud, scheduled immediately after the Yalta summit. When Stalin asked what concessions Roosevelt might make to Saud in dealing with Middle Eastern issues, the President replied that there was only one concession that he might make and that "was to give him [Ibn Saud] the six million Jews in the United States."[12]

Though this astounding comment was edited out of the official record, it survives in the minutes preserved at the Roosevelt Library in Hyde Park, New York, and in the Stettinius papers. Such a remark of course did nothing to burnish the President's reputation as a crusading liberal—which is doubtless why it got excised—and might be construed as evidence of anti-Semitism, of a type not unknown among the patrician classes from which he was descended. An alternative explanation is that this response suggested a kind of aphasia—the lack of the sort of mental filter that keeps people from blurting out impulsive statements.

Slightly less strange, but strange nonetheless, was the President's reference to Wendell Willkie. A moderate Republican who had run against Roosevelt in 1940, Willkie in the war years became a kind of roving U.S. ambassador, visiting heads of state in Europe and Asia. He died of a heart attack at the relatively young age of fifty-two in the autumn of 1944, some weeks before the Yalta summit. Churchill at Yalta recalled that he had given Willkie a copy of a speech the prime minister made about colonialism and the British Empire. In response, according to the Bohlen minutes, "the President inquired if that was what had killed Mr. Willkie."[13]

FDR Comment on Jews Omitted

TOP SECRET   February 10, 1945

who he felt had merely been waiting during the war for the worst catastrophes to happen.

MARSHAL STALIN then said he thought more time was needed to consider and finish the business of the conference.

THE PRESIDENT answered that he had three Kings waiting for him in the Near East, including Ibn Saud.

MARSHAL STALIN asked whether the President intended to make any concessions to Ibn Saud.

THE PRESIDENT replied that there was only one concession he thought he might offer and that was to give him the six million Jews in the United States.

MARSHAL STALIN said the Jewish problem was a very difficult one--that they had tried to establish a national home for the Jews in Virovidzhan but that they had only stayed there two or three years and then scattered to the cities. He said the Jews were natural traders but much had been accomplished by putting small groups in some agricultural areas.

THE PRESIDENT said he was a Zionist and asked if Marshal Stalin was one.

MARSHAL STALIN said he was one in principle but he recognized the difficulty.

During the course of the conversation, MARSHAL STALIN remarked that the Soviet Government would never have signed a treaty with the Germans in 1939 had it not been for Munich and the Polish-German treaty of 1934.

MARSHAL STALIN came over and spoke to the President and said he did not think they could complete the work of the conference by three o'clock tomorrow.

THE PRESIDENT replied that if necessary he would wait over until Monday, to which Marshal Stalin expressed gratification.

It was tentatively agreed that there would be a plenary session tomorrow at twelve noon, after which the Prime Minister and Marshal Stalin would lunch with the President.

TOP SECRET

President Roosevelt's statement at Yalta that he might make a concession to the king of Saudi Arabia by giving him "the six million Jews in the United States." This FDR comment was edited out of the State Department record on Yalta but appears in minutes of the meeting preserved in other official archives. (*Source: Stettinius/Yalta records, University of Virginia*)

What Roosevelt could possibly have meant by this we can only surmise, as there is in the record no follow-up by Churchill.* It seems likely FDR's listeners were not only puzzled by what he said, but embarrassed for him, and moved on quickly to other topics. Again, the extreme oddness of the comment suggests a lack of judgment, mental balance, or just plain common sense. Like the plight of the Jews, or killing fifty thousand Germans, the death of Willkie would not strike most people as a matter of amusement.

These episodes, though troubling, were not the most disturbing aspects of Roosevelt's conduct at the summits. More worrisome in policy terms were cases in which he signed or agreed to things of which he later said he had no knowledge. One significant instance occurred in September 1944, at his second Quebec conclave with Churchill. At this meeting, Roosevelt approved a summary of the so-called Morgenthau Plan for Germany but later said he couldn't recall having done so. (At this period, he would also sign an important letter about the U.S.-German occupation drafted verbatim by a Soviet secret agent. See chapter 15.)

There were other incidents of like nature. Bohlen would recount an episode in which FDR was given a paper on U.S. Latin American policy, observing that "Roosevelt signed the document without understanding its contents." In some cases, the President's staffers simply took things into their own hands, making decisions in his name without his knowledge. Robert Sherwood reports that, shortly after Quebec, FDR approved a cable saying Churchill spoke for him on a certain matter. As Hopkins disagreed with this, he had the cable halted, without bothering to consult the President. (Sherwood cites this as an example of "Hopkins' willingness to act first and ask for authority later.") In an instance concerning Poland, Hopkins ordered cables withheld

---

* It's possible that this was another of Roosevelt's alleged jokes at Churchill's expense.

from FDR that had been sent by Churchill and the U.S. ambassador in London.*[14]

Students of our politics know, of course, that documents signed and sent out in the name of the president are often or even usually drafted by others, subject to the president's approval. But if the president is unable to give his approval, or know what he has approved, the implications of such practice are alarming, to put the matter no more strongly. In the case of FDR, it's known that cables and memos issued in his name during the last year of his life were routinely the work of others—what the President knew about them being problematic. As Churchill would remember:

> . . . *at this time Roosevelt's health and strength had faded. In my long telegrams I thought I was talking to my trusted friend and colleague . . . [but] I was no longer being heard by him. . . . The President's devoted aides were anxious to keep their knowledge of his condition in the narrowest possible circles, and various hands drafted in combination the answers that were sent in his name. To these, as his life ebbed, Roosevelt could only give general guidance and approval.*[15]

Because of his declining health, Roosevelt spent long periods away from Washington, going as often as possible to his home in Hyde Park or his retreat at Warm Springs, Georgia, taking a month's vacation in the spring of 1944 at Bernard Baruch's estate in South Carolina, and embarking on his lengthy voyage to Hawaii. Even when at the White House, he was under doctor's orders to sleep as much as possible (ten hours a night, plus daily naps) and was limited to four hours of work per day, if that. All this at the height of

---

* The cables withheld concerned efforts by the British to coordinate assistance for Polish freedom fighters in Warsaw who were battling against the Nazis. For reasons to be discussed, such assistance was opposed by Moscow—and by Hopkins. See chapter 10.

World War II, with the President supposedly governing a mighty nation, running for a fourth term of office, and commanding a global coalition in the greatest war that was ever conducted. And all of it prelude to Yalta, where he would contest the fate of the world with Stalin.

In effect, Roosevelt's tenure during his final months in office was a kind of regency, not unlike that existing in the incapacitated last days of Woodrow Wilson, when Mrs. Wilson was in some sense the ruler of the nation. There is no evidence that Mrs. Roosevelt wanted or had similar power, as she exerted her considerable influence through other channels. But there were those who did aspire to wield such power, as indeed somebody had to if the President was still holding office but unable to carry out its duties.

Commenting on all this, historian Ferrell observes that, because of Roosevelt's illness and absenteeism, the administration was, in its last months, a kind of ghost ship, running on inertia. To the outside observer, says Ferrell, "the appearance of things was of incessant activity. In actual fact, things were not so active. Behind the façade of movement, of decision, of control from the executive offices to the rear of the White House, there often was little but emptiness, with the government virtually running itself." [16]

But of course, at the highest levels, the government couldn't "run itself," especially not in the midst of a massive global struggle affecting the lives of millions, with a further deadly struggle looming up at Yalta. Bureaucrats down in the ranks could carry on with administrative tasks as prescribed by law or regulation, but at the topmost levels somebody had to read the cables, draft the responses, issue the orders, and make the decisions that would affect the fate of the world for years thereafter. This would have been all the more true at Yalta, where there was no routine to fall back on and the President and his party were called upon to make decisions on the fly, settling issues of colossal import on the spur of the moment.

Though Hiss is now well-known to history, in January 1945 he was merely one State Department staffer among many, and of fairly junior status—a mid-level employee who wasn't even head of a division (third ranking in the branch where he was working). It thus seems odd that Roosevelt would single him out as someone who should go to Yalta— the more curious as it's reasonably clear that FDR had never dealt with Hiss directly (a point confirmed by Hiss in his own memoirs).

At all events, Hiss did go to Yalta, one of a small group of State Department staffers there, and would play a major role in the proceedings. Such a role would have been in keeping with the President's expressed desire to have him at the conference. It's not, however, in keeping with numerous books and essays that deal with Yalta or Cold War studies discussing Hiss and his duel with Chambers.

In standard treatments of the era, the role of Hiss at Yalta tends to get downplayed, if not ignored entirely. Usually, when his presence is mentioned, he's depicted as a modest clerk/technician working in the background, whose only substantive interest was in the founding of the United Nations (which occurred some three months later). Otherwise, his activity at the summit is glossed over as being of no great importance.

A prime example of such comment occurred ten years after Yalta, when papers from the conference were belatedly published. When these were leaked to the *New York Times*, correspondent Peter Kihss began his story this way: "Alger Hiss, whose role at the Yalta conference long has been a subject of hostile speculation, *spent his time there exclusively on planning for the United Nations*."[2] (Emphasis added.)

Similar statements denying any linkage of Hiss at Yalta to non-U.N.-related issues were made by other news outlets. The *Washington Post*, for one, described him as a mere "note-taker," "a technician working among other technicians." The *Washington Sunday Star* commented that Hiss at Yalta "was one notch above a glorified office boy."[3] As these statements were made after Hiss was sent to prison for lying about his Red connections, their obvious main effect was to shield Yalta itself, and its vast concessions to Moscow, from any hint of Communist influence in the American delegation.

Though not describing himself in such disparaging terms, Hiss would testify in similar fashion, saying his interests at the time of Yalta were focused strictly on the United Nations. In 1948, he was asked by Representative Karl Mundt (R-SD) if he had any involvement with China policy (a hot topic in 1948) at the era of Yalta or in the months thereafter. On this the colloquy went as follows:

> HISS: No, I did not. I had been connected with far eastern affairs before, but about February 1944 I was assigned to United Nations work and *specialized entirely in that field thereafter.*

> MUNDT: Referring especially to that portion of the Secretary's [George C. Marshall's] proclamation [in December 1945] which said that we must have peace and unity with the Communists in China.

> HISS: I was not consulted on that. *It was not in my area at all.*[4] Emphasis added.

These and other statements suggesting that Hiss dealt only with U.N. affairs at Yalta would be recycled many times in Cold War histories and become accepted wisdom on the topic. But based on now available data, we know these comments were mistaken—were, indeed, an almost exact inversion of the record. Noteworthy in this respect are the Stettinius diaries and other of his confidential papers, significant portions of which in the authors' possession have not previously been published.

The Stettinius papers are most revealing on the role of Hiss at Yalta, as the two worked together closely there and Stettinius leaned heavily on Hiss for expertise on many issues. The documents indicate that Hiss was an outspoken participant in the Yalta sessions, addressing a wide array of topics and at times dealing virtually as an equal with British foreign secretary Anthony Eden and other high officials. As Hiss was the American on the scene most conversant with U.N. affairs, he of course had a lot to say about that subject, but his role was by no means limited to such matters.

Among the topics on which Hiss held forth, often in authoritative manner, were the conduct of China policy by the Allies, establishment of a high commission to govern peacetime Europe, the role of France in the postwar era, and occupation zones in Germany once the Nazis had surrendered. The Stettinius diaries likewise depict Hiss as a knowledgeable source on one of the most contentious issues raised at Yalta—the use of German compulsory labor as a form of human "reparations." (See chapter 16.) Along with other data on such matters, the Stettinius papers show there were few subjects at the meeting on which Hiss wasn't a significant player.

Unfortunately for students of Cold War history, numerous items relating to all this have been omitted from official records. Of note in this regard is the case of China, concerning which Hiss under oath denied involvement at Yalta and for some while before then. The Stettinius papers show the reverse: that on February 1, 1945, at a meeting with Anthony Eden on the eve of the conference, Hiss explicitly raised the China issue, in terms indicating that he spoke for the U.S. government on the matter. This entry from the Stettinius diaries tells us:

> *At this point* Mr. Hiss brought up *the question of China and stressed the* importance which the United States attaches *to U.S., British-Soviet encouragement and support for an agreement between the Commintern* [sic] *and the Chinese Congress* [sic] *in order to further the war effort and prevent possible civil strife.*[5] Emphasis added.

In the State Department Yalta compilation, there is a version of this exchange, but the role of Hiss is conspicuously not mentioned. This entry says the issue of Chinese unity "was raised,"[6] but doesn't say Hiss was the person who raised it. The omission is the more noteworthy as this was precisely the point brought up by Mundt, concerning which Hiss disclaimed interest or knowledge after February 1944—a full year before these Yalta-eve discussions. So Hiss testified falsely on this, as he did on other matters.

Hiss Raises Issue of China

Prime Minister that we should put everything on the table at the forthcoming conference. He said that the British have so little to give that it should be pointed out in connection with all the other matters to be discussed. He thought the Russians might bring up the Far East. He thought we should try to settle the Polish question and the question of voting in the Council.

China

At this point, Mr. Hiss brought up the question of China and stressed the importance which the United States attaches to U.S.-British-Soviet encouragement and support for an agreement between the Comintern and the Chinese Congress in order to further the war effort and prevent possible civil strife. Mr. Eden said that Mr. Hopkins had said that the President has it in his mind that the President has it in his mind that the British want to keep the Comintern and Congress from reaching agreement. Mr. Eden said he couldn't imagine where that idea could come from. He said we all desire Chinese unity and wish to get the Russians to take the same position.

Emergency European High Commission

Mr. Hiss was asked to describe the main purpose behind this suggestion. He pointed out the desirability of unity in fact and in appearance among the great powers

TOP SECRET

The official State Department compilation of papers relating to the Yalta conference says the issue of unity between the anti-Communist Chiang Kai-shek and the Communists of China "was raised" in discussions between U.S. and British officials, but doesn't say who raised it. The papers of Secretary of State Edward R. Stettinius Jr. show that the person who raised it was Alger Hiss—contrary to his later sworn statement that he had no involvement with or interest in China policy at the time of Yalta. (*Source: Stettinius/Yalta records, University of Virginia.*)

Of note also is the way Hiss stressed the "importance which the United States" attached to Chinese unity, as if he were a person of authority speaking officially on the subject. Likewise significant is that he made these statements in the presence of Stettinius, who would have been the logical person at a meeting with Eden to set forth the U.S. position. However, Stettinius as noted at the time had been secretary of state for just two months, was inexperienced in many such matters, and was uncertain about the details of numerous topics. He would in such cases defer to Hiss, letting him state the American view of things and later citing him as an expert on events at Yalta.

This reliance was evident in the drafting of Stettinius's 1949 memoir, *Roosevelt and the Russians*, when he repeatedly told historian Walter Johnson, who helped out with the drafting, to check with Hiss about decisions made at Yalta—the role of France, reparations, occupation zones—along with U.N. issues. The Stettinius archive contains copious notes about the handling of such topics at Yalta, all starkly different from the notion of Hiss as low-level technician focused strictly on the United Nations.

On the subject of assigning a German occupation zone to France, for instance, Stettinius told Johnson: "Alger Hiss can fill in the background." In further comment about the role of France, the former secretary said: "See Alger Hiss about this." On the issue of forced German labor as a form of reparations: "See Alger and we'll discuss this again." In later discussions of the German occupation: "Hiss would remember. Consult him." On the question of who drafted the Yalta Declaration on Liberated Europe: "[See] Alger Hiss again." On voting arrangements for the United Nations: "See Alger Hiss about this." And again: "Alger Hiss can fill in important background on that."[7]

These references were the more telling as Stettinius in other comments showed himself extremely shaky, in some cases totally misinformed, about what went on at Yalta. (See chapter 16.) He relied on Hiss because the latter was knowledgeable and assured, as Stettinius himself frequently wasn't. There are still other Stettinius entries that emphasize the role of Hiss at Yalta. These show Hiss holding forth on a considerable range of topics, again in seemingly authoritative manner:

> Hiss talked further *with Sir Alexander Cadogan [Britain's perma-*
> *nent undersecretary for foreign affairs] . . . on trusteeships. . . . Sir*
> *Alexander* agreed with Hiss' statement of the United States posi-
> tion. . . . Mr. Hiss was asked to explain the main purpose *behind*
> *this suggestion [for a European High Commission] . . .* He pointed
> out *the desirability of unity in fact and in appearance among the*
> *great powers. . . .* Mr. Hiss pointed out *that [quarterly meetings of*
> *the foreign ministers] might lessen the dignity of the Commission. . . .*
> He said it was the Department's view *that the French should be*
> *recognized as the fifth sponsoring power. . . .* He said that the State
> Department did not propose *to give any Dumbarton Oaks [con-*
> *ference] documents to the French. . . .*[8] (*Emphasis added.*)

Once more, the tone of assured authority comes through, as does the scope of the issues on which Hiss expressed the "United States" or "State Department" position. Still further insight into his role would be provided when *Roosevelt and the Russians* was published. Among other things, Stettinius in this volume recounted his Yalta schedule, in which he conferred on a twice-daily basis with advisers Hiss, Freeman Matthews, Wilder Foote, and interpreter Bohlen. The author was complimentary toward all, but particularly so toward Hiss, who, per Stettinius, "performed brilliantly" at Yalta.

Among further such Stettinius notations were comments on meetings where Hiss, along with others, met directly with FDR. On February 4, at the outset of the conference, said Stettinius, "Harriman, Matthews, Hiss, Bohlen and I met with the President to review our proposals for the conference agenda." On February 7, the secretary recorded, "the President asked me to get a lawyer to consult with him over the wording of the Polish boundary statement [regarding a dispute between Moscow and the Polish exile government in London]." The lawyer Stettinius got was Hiss. ("I called Alger Hiss and as the two of us were trying to work out a solution for the President, Roosevelt looked up at us and said, 'I've got it.'")[9]

As for his access to diplomatic data, including Far Eastern matters, Hiss in private comments was more forthcoming than in his answer to Mundt and in other public statements. In documents prepared during his legal battles with Chambers (unearthed by Allen Weinstein in writing his book about the case), Hiss recalled the assignments he had been given in preparing for the summit, as follows:

"Stettinius put me in charge of assembling all the background papers and documentation of the State Department group before we left Washington. . . . I was in charge of receiving and dispatching reports from and to the State Department. . . . *I was also responsible for any general matters that might come up relating to the Far East or Near East.* Before leaving Washington I was also given by Mr. Hackworth* papers relating to a possible agreement on the trial of war criminals. . . ."[10] (Emphasis added.) Once more, all sharply different from the notion of Hiss as mere clerk-technician dealing only with U.N. issues.

In fact, the Yalta compilation published by the State Department, though incomplete, contains numerous items showing the role of Hiss in handling all manner of important data at the summit. The wide-ranging authority given him by Stettinius appears in one official entry as follows: "At the Secretary's staff committee meeting of January 10, the Secretary asked that all memoranda for the President on topics to be discussed at the meeting of the Big Three should be in the hands of Alger Hiss not later than Monday, January 15."[11]

---

* State Department legal adviser Green Hackworth.

Stettinius and Hiss at Yalta

Secretary of State Edward R. Stettinius Jr., Alger Hiss, and unidentified companion at the Yalta conference. In their respective memoirs, for different reasons, Stettinius and Hiss would each express satisfaction with the outcome of the meeting. (*Source: Franklin D. Roosevelt Library, Hyde Park, N.Y.*)

This was just nine days after FDR and Stettinius discussed having Hiss go to Yalta, in which span he had somehow risen from obscurity to become the custodian of "all memoranda for the President" on topics to be considered at the summit—not bad positioning for a Soviet agent whose nominal chieftain, FDR, would soon be meeting with his real one, Stalin. Nor was this the only indication in the records of the role played by Hiss and his skill at collecting information.

The point would be made by State Department historian Bryton Barron, who was charged with compiling the Yalta papers but got into a wrangle with department higher-ups as to what should be made public. In writing about this internal conflict, Barron stressed the unusual nature of the documents Hiss had in his possession, which the department collected from his files in assembling its Yalta record.

Among these documents was a copy of a Soviet proposal on German reparations—concerning which, as seen, Hiss was referenced by Stettinius as an authority to be consulted. A related item was the original Soviet proposal concerning an Allied commission to be established on such matters; another was the draft of a U.S. position paper on the status of Poland. The acquisition of these papers by Hiss would of course have been facilitated by his role as coordinator of documents relating to the summit.

The ability of Hiss to position himself at the crossroads of information was displayed often in his tenure at State. Even as a junior staffer in 1936, he had impressed his fellow Communists as a shrewd operator in such matters. As recorded by Alexander Vassiliev, one KGB report quoted State Department official Laurence Duggan, himself an oft-identified pro-Soviet agent, as saying Hiss was "the one who had everything important from every division on his desk, and must be one of the best informed people" in the department. The KGB lamented that Hiss was already spoken for by the rival Soviet agency GRU (military intelligence), saying that if the KGB had such a source at State "no one else would really be needed."*[12]

---

* The accomplishments of Hiss in this respect would be on display also in the matter of the "pumpkin papers" (actually microfilm) and other official documents

Against that backdrop, the manner in which Hiss wound up receiving data at Yalta looks like more of the same from an accomplished master. Indeed, his task there would have been far simpler than in other assignments, as he was operating not from a second- or third-tier position, but at the apex of the system, cheek by jowl with Stettinius and one remove from FDR, to whom all important information whatever would have been directed. Add to this the complete trust Stettinius placed in Hiss, which meant no relevant papers would have been denied this Soviet agent.

As to whether Hiss used his position to advance the Red agenda, the conventional wisdom says he didn't—or at least that there is no plausible evidence that he did. One theory holds that since he was an agent of military intelligence, and since the bulk of discussion at Yalta was political or diplomatic, he would have had nothing of interest to share with his Soviet bosses. This, however, assumes a degree of compartmentalization that seldom obtains anywhere and certainly didn't at Yalta, where military questions (most notably the Pacific war) were inextricably mixed with diplomatic issues.

In one account it's said Hiss met secretly with a Soviet official at Yalta, perhaps to share information or agree on tactics. This story is of anecdotal nature and thus hard to verify, and it seems doubtful

---

Chambers said he received from Hiss (and Harry Dexter White) in the latter part of 1937 and early months of 1938. These papers were of wide-ranging nature, many stemming from high-level sources, including U.S. embassies in Tokyo, Paris, London, and Vienna. They discussed Japanese, German, and British military, political, and economic developments, all of consuming interest to Moscow as the world moved relentlessly toward war and the Soviets sought to play off the potential combatants against each other, while themselves staying on the sidelines. A similar mix of data obtained by Hiss was discovered in 1946 by State Department security forces investigating the leak of a secret policy memo concerning Greece to newspaper columnist Drew Pearson. The document had been held in Hiss's Office of Special Political Affairs (SPA), among other places, and security screeners believed Hiss was the culprit. The investigators also found other records in his office, including material concerning the atomic bomb and data concerning American policy toward China (a subject as seen allegedly of no concern to Hiss after 1944).

someone as careful as Hiss would have taken such a risk in such confined surroundings. Nor is it evident that he would have had to do so. He had had ample opportunity in the weeks preceding to meet in secure conditions with Soviet operatives in Washington, as he would have known from early January that he was going to Yalta, and by January 10 had been named as point man for assembling all pertinent U.S. data for the summit.

Hiss would thus have known going in what Moscow's interests were, if he wasn't well aware beforehand, and what American policy was on the relevant issues. This would have been especially so concerning the German occupation, forced labor as reparations, or turning anti-Soviet fugitives over to the Russians. On these and other topics pro-Moscow agents in the United States had been developing plans for months preceding Yalta, dating back to earlier meetings at Quebec and elsewhere (see chapter 15). Hiss as a top-level Soviet functionary wouldn't need to be briefed about such matters *after* he arrived at Yalta.

In this respect, also, we need only recall the peculiar episode with which our discussion started—when Roosevelt, out of the blue, told Stettinius he didn't much care which staffers would be at Yalta, but thought Hiss and Isaiah Bowman should be there. As FDR at that time had no particular reason to know, or even know of, Hiss, the obvious implication is that someone with access to the President made this suggestion to him—and, as seen, Roosevelt in his final days was all too susceptible to suggestion. That the person who made this one was concerned to advance the Soviet cause at Yalta seems about as plain as such an inference can be.

4.

MOSCOW'S BODYGUARD OF LIES

The long-secret backstage role of Alger Hiss at Yalta casts retrospective light on aspects of the Communist operation that were seen but dimly, if at all, when the Cold War was in progress.

Most obviously, his skill in positioning himself at the vectors of diplomatic information indicates the degree to which Soviet undercover agents were able to penetrate the U.S. government in crucial places, up to the highest policy-making levels. The importance of Hiss in this respect appears more clearly still when we recall that he wasn't an isolated instance, but only one such agent out of many.

Others involved in similar pro-Communist machinations will be considered in the following pages. For now enough to note two other ranking U.S. officials who were in their way as significant as Hiss—Harry D. White at the Treasury and Lauchlin Currie at the White House—both of whom would show up in *Venona*, FBI reports, and other security records as spies and agents of influence for the Kremlin. Because of their top-line positions, the ability of these twin apparatchiks to serve Moscow was great, enhanced still further when they worked together behind the scenes on pro-Soviet projects.*

---

* Harry Dexter White was a monetary economist of some stature. He was chiefly responsible for the Bretton Woods conference of 1944, which created the International Monetary Fund; had taught at Harvard; and like many others moved from academia to federal service when the New Deal was hiring. Treasury Secretary Henry Morgenthau Jr. relied heavily on White for advice and counsel and gave him

A further thought suggested by the activity of Hiss at Yalta is the previously noted point that the frontier between espionage and policy influence was often murky, so that exclusive emphasis on the former mistakes the nature of the problem. The data that the spies obtained were in numerous instances valuable to Moscow because they supplied advance knowledge of what American or other Western policy would be or, even better, permitted operatives such as Hiss, White, and Currie to push that policy in pro-Red directions.

Otherwise the role of Hiss at Yalta, and his career in general, suggest the great importance in the Moscow scheme of things of secrecy and deception. This was true not only of the part that he and others played as clandestine Soviet agents, but also of the decades-long dispute that would ensue when Whittaker Chambers went public with his charges of subversion involving Hiss and others. In this colossal struggle, Red deceptions and obfuscations would repeatedly confuse the issues and distort the record—and continue to do so even now. Through it all, over a span of decades, Hiss himself maintained a pose of injured innocence, despite the ever-thickening mass of evidence against him. His was a lifelong study in deception, in service to the cause of Moscow.

Deception and concealment have of course been used by many nations for many ages, most famously in times of warfare. Some well-known examples from the modern era occurred during World War II, when each side made extensive efforts to dupe the other and conversely penetrate the smoke screens of the foe to figure out what he was up to. Of particular note were Anglo-American

---

wide-ranging powers. These were especially far-reaching in foreign dealings, where White was in essence Mayor of the Palace. A friend and political ally of White, the Canadian-born Currie was another academic economist who served at the Treasury, later moving to the White House on the executive staff of FDR. In the latter role, Currie's portfolio included policy toward China, which would become a hugely significant issue in the war years and the postwar era.

schemes to mislead the Germans as to the site of the D-Day landings of 1944, and British success in co-opting German agents in England, who then radioed back false intel to their Nazi bosses.

While such practices have long existed, seldom have they been used more aggressively or to greater effect than by the Soviet Union. In the Soviet world, deception was an everyday occurrence, used in peace as well as war, aimed at both foes and allies and fine-tuned to the level of a science. Such methods were for the Communists a matter of doctrine, propounded early on by Lenin and pursued with zeal by his successors. Stalin was a great exponent of the art, using it against internal enemies as well as in his global dealings. All this was consonant with Soviet theory, wherein the goals of the Communist Party justified any ruse that got the job done.

In turn, nowhere was the Red commitment to deception more comprehensive than in the Soviet intelligence units—in the modern era known as the KGB (state security service) and GRU (military intelligence), assisted in their efforts by the Comintern (Communist International), the worldwide web of Communist parties and controlled front groups that flourished in the 1930s. The intelligence units, as the term implies, were chiefly devoted to gathering information useful to the Kremlin, with focus on obtaining data needed for political-military planning. But these agencies also had purposes that were the reverse of information gathering—disseminating alleged facts about the Soviet Union, or some individual, group, or nation, on issues of concern to Moscow, that were anything but factual.

Of course, the concept of infiltrating secret agents into other countries to serve the purposes of the Kremlin was deceptive by its very nature. It was made the more so by the Communist system of dual concealments: the creation of "illegal" networks in the United States and elsewhere, consisting of operatives using false identities and bogus cover assignments; and official representatives at Soviet embassies, consulates, and trade missions who were legally in the host countries, but whose real business was to carry out secret in-telligence tasks for Moscow.

In the propaganda sector, meanwhile, deception was the stock-in-trade of the pro-Soviet false flag operations called fronts, which broadcast Communist themes and messages under auspices that were nominally of non-Communist nature. Such operations proliferated in the 1930s, when innumerable committees, rallies, manifestos, books, articles, and plays were brought forth in this misleading format.

As all of the above suggests, the Kremlin's deception tactics usu-ally weren't ad hoc—though in the nature of the case that of course did happen—but were carefully developed stratagems set forth systematically in the training of its agents. These practices were referred to by the Soviets as "active measures," a concept embracing a whole gamut of activities meant to mislead and guide into pro-Soviet channels the thoughts and actions of target nations. An om-nibus definition of the term as used by Moscow would be provided by the U.S. Central Intelligence Agency as follows:

> *The Soviets use the term active measures . . . to refer to activities by virtually every element of the Soviet party and state structure. . . . [Such activities and elements include] foreign Communist parties and international and national front organizations; written and oral disinformation, particularly forgeries, manipulation of foreign media through controlled assets and press placements; agents of influence; . . . ad hoc political influence operations, often involving elements of deception, blackmail, or intimidation.*[1]

In some cases the "agents of influence" referred to might be govern-ment officials in the West or members of parliamentary bodies, denizens of the press corps, academics, or spokesmen for certain captive labor unions. In others, they might be leaders in some agitational project, as with the front groups of the 1930s. Degrees of commitment might vary from hard-core devotion to fellow traveling to delusion—though people in the last-named category couldn't be used as full-fledged agents. The common feature was that all such activity was geared to promoting alleged data, ideas, or themes that were counterfactual in ways that served the Moscow interest.

To define their goals and instruct their agents, the Soviets developed a body of expertise about such matters and a vocabulary to explain it. Central to their lexicon was the concept of "disinformation," which wasn't a slur devised by their opponents but rather a term used by the Soviets themselves to describe what they were doing. A KGB document called the Directorate RT Handbook informs us, for instance, that "active measures" included "disinformation, denunciation, compromise" and other species of deception. "Disinformation" was in turn defined as *the overt presentation to the enemy of false information* or specially prepared materials and documents in order to mislead him and to induce him to make decisions and take actions which correspond to the interests of the Soviet Union...."[2] (Emphasis added.)

That summed up the matter well, again highlighting the routine nature of the resort to falsehood and the importance of influence operations in the doings of the Kremlin's henchmen. In some cases, disinformation schemes might be relatively simple projects, such as planting a false news story, spreading a rumor, or making a false accusation against an opponent. On other occasions they would be more elaborate and require extensive planning. One favored technique was the use of forgeries—another art in which the Reds were practiced. Such methods extended from fake passports and identity papers to currency counterfeiting to documents allegedly stemming from the U.S. government showing warlike or other evil purpose. (The fake IDs and passports were integral parts of the global revolutionary mission, allowing operatives to move in secret fashion from one target country to another.)

In certain cases the deceptions were so complex as to constitute a kind of alternate reality—of the type later made famous by the *Mission: Impossible* television series. Soviet talents along these lines would be on display in the earliest going, after the October 1917 Bolshevik coup against the provisional Russian government of Alexander Kerensky. As a small minority in the country, the Communists faced numerous internal foes who opposed their seizure of power, plus outside forces hostile to their program. The French, English, and Americans engaged in World War I were in particular alarmed by the announced intention of Lenin and Trotsky to pull Russia out of the wartime coalition against the Central Powers, headed by Germany's kaiser Wilhelm II.

To neutralize their internal foes and befuddle the outside forces, the Communists came up with a scheme that outdid the *Mission: Impossible* series. This was an ersatz resistance group nicknamed "the Trust," used to disorient their enemies abroad and on the home front. Involved in this amazing venture were a whole variety of ruses—make-believe resistance leaders, imaginary armies, intelligence chicken feed* to establish bona fides, staged events to convince the doubtful. By such devices, authentic resistance leaders were drawn into the net, and, after the deception had run its course, arrested and imprisoned.[3]

This Potemkin village scenario would be repeated, with variations, at later stages of the Cold War. Similar ruses were employed in Czechoslovakia, Albania, Ukraine, and other regions under Communist domination. The most obvious direct parallel was the so-called WIN project, developed in Poland in the 1940s when the Communists imposed their tyranny in that country via a group of Soviet-sponsored puppets. WIN was another ersatz group that compromised the anti-Communist forces and, as a kind of bonus

---

* This was true but inconsequential information that could be checked for authenticity by the recipients but would do no harm to Moscow. See note on page 58.

siphoned off resources from the West intended for the opposition. Like the Trust, WIN pulled into its orbit a host of legitimate resistance leaders, meanwhile feeding false data to the Western powers that misled them as to the strategic moves they should make in Poland.*[4]

Other Red deception schemes weren't so complex but were in their way effective. A choice example would be recalled by the British Communist Claud Cockburn, describing a disinformation project that occurred during the Spanish Civil War of the 1930s. Cockburn said he had been told by Communist higher-ups to write an "eyewitness account" of a pro-Red uprising against the Falangist opposition in Spanish Morocco. The purpose of this gambit was to convince the government of France that the Communists were making headway in the fighting, and that a shipment of arms being held by the French should be approved for transit.

As Cockburn told it, he would write the "eyewitness account" requested, though he had never been in the town where the combat happened (if in fact it did), supplying fictitious details about street fighting and the people who allegedly led it. This story duly appeared in the press and per Cockburn convinced the authorities the Reds were for real and should be assisted. Whatever the other merits of this tale, its most striking aspect was the prosaic manner in which Cockburn described the process of deception, again suggesting the routine nature of Communist falsehood in promoting favored causes.[5]

Similar fables about Communist valor would be common

---

* "WIN" was an acronym for the Polish phrase meaning "freedom and independence." The success of the scheme provided a text for self-congratulation by the Communists in Poland, who boasted after the fact about the way they had tricked their opponents, and provided some further insight into pro-Red disinformation methods: "The information we sent out was often weighted with authentic data. . . . Disinforming the enemy involved giving him authentic information [to establish credibility] as long as it was devoid of official or state secrets . . . basically this was the best disinformation."

during World War II, when it was claimed that Red guerrillas were bravely carrying the battle to the foe, while their anti-Red competitors among the Allies were collaborationists or traitors. Exhibit A in this respect was China (though the same occurred in Yugoslavia, Rumania, and Poland), where it was said the Communists under Mao Tse-tung were single-handedly fighting against Japan, while the anti-Communist Nationalists of Chiang Kai-shek did nothing or colluded with the invaders. Propaganda to this effect, repeated by U.S. officials in China and influential in shaping U.S. policy toward Asia, was as spurious as Cockburn's mythical Spanish battle.

As we now know from mainland Chinese Communist sources, the Red cadres under Mao in fact did little to fight the Japanese and were more likely to be in collusion with them—in essence doing what they accused the Nationalists of doing. The reason for this, as explained by former Red Guard Jung Chang in her definitive biography of Mao, was that the Communists were waiting to seize the ground Chiang surrendered when he and the Japanese moved on to other battles. As she phrased it, "Mao did not want the Red Army to fight the invaders at all. . . . He said years later that his attitude had been, the more land Japan took the better."[6]

As this suggests, a propaganda tactic in which the Reds specialized was to accuse their foes of what they themselves were doing—a method all the more effective since, as practitioners of the act complained of, the Communists knew a lot about it. Another important instance occurred during World War II, when they incessantly criticized the United States and Britain for not opening a "second front" in Europe to relieve Nazi pressure on the Russian armies. Seldom mentioned by the Soviets was that for four years running they not only failed to open a "second front" in Asia but in fact had a neutrality treaty with Japan that lasted until the war was nearly over, meanwhile assisting the Japanese against the Allies.

As discovered by the U.S. Office of Strategic Services (OSS), the Soviets were diverting American Lend-Lease supplies shipped to Russia via the Pacific to the control of the Japanese, in exchange for materials Moscow was receiving from Japan. This Soviet double cross also revealed another facet of the problem—this of an internal nature. According to OSS Major Donald Downes, when U.S. officials learned of the Soviet betrayal, they were "ordered by highest authority: drop the subject; make no mention of it." Defending or concealing Moscow's actions thus had a higher priority in some U.S. circles than protecting American lives and interests.*[7]

Yet another aspect of Soviet "disinformation" tactics is helpful in understanding the way the Cold War unfolded. Of note in the KGB Handbook was use of the terms "compromise" and "denunciation" as methods for discrediting Moscow's opponents. The handbook entry on this says that "compromise is used for . . . subverting the authority and weakening the position of state institutions, political organizations, individuals, government, political, public, religious and other figures of capitalist nations, and anti-Soviet emigrant organizations, bringing to the attention of interested parties especially selected materials and information *which either conform to reality or are fabricated. . . .*" [8] (Emphasis added.)

The meaning of this technique would be sharpened by the term "denunciation," which suggested going beyond the idea of weakening someone's influence to the notion of outright destruction—or character assassination, as we have come to call it. This was yet another practice in which the Reds excelled, repeatedly used against anti-Communist forces in the countless power struggles that occurred throughout the Cold War. The method was so widely used it might be considered the most distinctive feature of pro-Red polemics, employed constantly in policy battles overseas and on the home front (and still evident in radical left discourse today).

---

* According to Major Downes, "The [OSS] Seattle listening post for Russian ships [monitoring radio transmissions] . . . reported that American machine tools, loaded as supposedly lend-lease for Russia, were being delivered to Jap ports. . . . The Japs were exchanging rubber . . . in return."

The prototype of this tactic was the fusillade of accusations leveled at Leon Trotsky and other early leaders of the Bolshevik Revolution in the Moscow purge trials of the 1930s, in which a host of formerly lauded Soviet heroes were accused by Stalin as agents of the Nazis. Similar charges would elsewhere be directed at anti-Communist forces, including Chiang Kai-shek of China, Draza Mihailovich of Yugoslavia, the exile government of Poland, and other foreign leaders who stood between the Reds and their objectives. Like treatment would be meted out in the security battles of the United States, as anti-Communist diplomats, members of Congress, military figures, investigative bodies, and many others would have their character and conduct assailed by pro-Red agents.

Conspicuous among the targets of such attacks were defectors from the Soviet operation who knew the truth of what was going on and tried to warn the West about it. Vituperation directed at these people probably exceeded all other forms of Communist denunciation. Foremost among such defectors in the United States was Whittaker Chambers, the former Soviet courier who broke with Moscow in the 1930s and whose testimony against Alger Hiss would become a cause célèbre. What Chambers had to say was dangerous not only to Hiss but to Hiss's Soviet sponsors and their worldwide subversion project. Hence no effort would be spared to destroy Chambers, a campaign that came within a hair's breadth of succeeding.

Revelations about all this would come from the archives of the KGB, as disclosed in the 1990s by onetime Soviet operative Alexander Vassiliev. As noted, this former Moscow agent copied down voluminous reports about the goals and tactics of Soviet intelligence, including disinformation schemes concerning Chambers. One entry on Chambers, using the code name "Karl," discussed the feasibility of forging records to destroy his reputation, as follows:

Find a file on "Karl" in the German archives revealing that he is a German agent, that he worked as a spy for the Gestapo [the Nazi secret police] in the U.S. and on a mission from them infiltrated the American Comparty [Communist Party]. If we print this in our newspaper and publish a few "documents" that can be prepared at home, it would have a major effect.[9]

This proposal was rejected by KGB higher-ups on the grounds that it would create problems for party members who had worked with Chambers, suggesting that they were Gestapo agents also. The planned destruction would have to proceed by other channels (and did). However, what comes through again is the matter-of-factness of the proposal. Noteworthy also was the Communist penchant for branding opponents as fascists or Nazis—charges routinely made against their foes in the USSR, defectors from the Soviet operation, anti-Communists in target countries, and government officials everywhere who opposed the Soviet program.

All of the above had serious consequences for the conduct of the Cold War, especially for the people targeted by such methods, many of whom in fact had their reputations and lives destroyed. More broadly, the policy impact of such deceptions in numerous cases was to turn Western influence and support against the anti-Communist forces and in favor of their Red opponents, as U.S. and other Allied leaders based decisions on false intelligence from pro-Soviet agents. The effects were calamitous for the cause of freedom, as numerous countries were thus delivered into the hands of Stalin and his minions.

Analogous to these developments were battles on the home front, as Communist and pro-Red forces were proclaimed as heroes or martyrs, while the people who opposed them were denounced as villains. Thus ex-Communist witnesses Chambers, Elizabeth Bentley, Louis Budenz, and others were derided as "paid informers," liars, drunks, and psychopaths. Similar allegations would be made against members of Congress, investigative committees, the FBI, media figures, and others who opposed the Communist program. "Witch hunting" and "character assassination" were among the milder epithets hurled at the anti-Communist forces—providing yet another instance of pro-Red spokesmen accusing others of what they themselves were doing.

Nor were these the only victims of Red disinformation. A further casualty would be the cause of historical truth, eroded by an ongoing process of falsification, corruption, and inversion. Over the course of decades, Communist falsehoods about nations, people, and issues were repeated with such frequency and volume and from such seemingly divergent sources that many in non-Communist circles accepted them at face value. The pages that follow examine several Red deception schemes that unfolded in this manner, the geopolitical consequences that followed, and some of the mistaken history that has been written on such topics. Given the vastness of the subject and the still developing condition of the data, we recognize that our treatment will merely scratch the surface. Even so, we think the extent to which the Cold War record has been distorted will be apparent.

5.

THREE WHO SAVED A REVOLUTION

In consolidating their control of Russia, deceiving their internal foes was for the Bolsheviks only half the battle. There remained the task of neutralizing the Allied powers still fighting in Western Europe, who opposed the Soviets' plans for pulling Russia out of the conflict with the Kaiser.

To gain their objective and fend off the Allies, the Communists would use disinformation tactics similar to those deployed against their homegrown opponents. These schemes were generally successful, and not merely because the West was taken in by the Trust, its ersatz armies, and bogus leaders. As it happened, the United States, France, and Britain all had their own indigenous sources of confusion who would serve the cause of Lenin, Trotsky, and—eventually—Stalin. These would be the original "agents of influence" in the West, the vanguard of a numerous host that would flourish over the next six decades.*

Though there were others in the field who helped the Soviets in this fashion, three in particular sent to Russia by American organizations were especially useful to the comrades. The first of this trio on the scene was a U.S. citizen named Raymond Robins,

---

* The most publicized Western fan of Russia's new political system was the American Communist John Reed, a romantic figure who wrote a famous book about the revolution and would long be considered a hero by leftward forces. However, because of his open Communist sympathies it's doubtful he had much impact on U.S. opinion in the immediate aftermath of the coup.

a mysterious figure who traveled to Petrograd* in the summer of 1917 on an alleged mission of mercy. Robins held the assimilated rank of colonel in the U.S. Army but was actually a civilian, part of a Red Cross team sent to Russia ostensibly for humanitarian reasons. He had an unusual background for this duty, as he was by profession a mining engineer/promoter. The Red Cross group to which he was attached was unusual also, consisting mainly of businessmen and lawyers, with only a handful of (soon departed) medical staffers included.

If Robins's background and the purpose of his mission were puzzling, his activities in Russia would be even more so. From the beginning, these were more political than humanitarian, of ambitious scope and conducted at the highest levels. In the wake of the Bolshevik October uprising, he quickly became a major player in America's dealings with the Soviet leaders, wielding influence in ways that had little connection to Red Cross issues. At times, indeed, he seemed to be the most important American in Russia, more so than others with official duties.

Robins was able to wield this remarkable influence—often in opposition to U.S. ambassador David Francis, who had hung on in Russia despite the coup and U.S. nonrecognition of the Red regime—because he enjoyed unprecedented access to Lenin and Trotsky. The colonel by his own account saw one or the other of the Soviet bosses on a regular basis, enjoying walk-in privileges at their makeshift quarters. His prestige was so great that the Bolsheviks assigned a railway car for his use, arrested people at his instigation, and in general treated him as a VIP of the highest standing. These privileges gave him enormous leverage over the flow of data to U.S. officials as to the thoughts and purposes of the Soviet leaders.[†w1]

---

* Formerly—and again today—called St. Petersburg. Also, during the Communist era renamed Leningrad.

† By interposing himself between the Bolshevik leaders and U.S. officials, Robins

Robins achieved this unusual status in large measure through the good offices of one Alexander Gumberg, a Russian-born naturalized U.S. citizen who was even more mysterious than Robins. Gumberg's brother, who went by the nom de guerre of GZorin, was a leading Bolshevik; and though Gumberg himself professed a stance of nonattachment, he was a Soviet agent also, as the Communist leaders gave him the task of interpreting for, and otherwise guiding, non-Russian-speaking tourists such as Robins. In short order, Gumberg-Robins became an inseparable duo, which meant the American was in effect co-opted by the Soviet rulers. Hence his extraordinary access to Lenin and Trotsky, and the influence that he wielded.[2]

It thus developed that Robins was uniquely positioned to promote to U.S. officials views of the Soviet revolution that were in essence Communist propaganda. He preached that Lenin and Trotsky were reasonable people who could be dealt with by the West, that their regime should not only receive American recognition but could be induced to take a cooperative stance by economic aid and credits, and that no help whatever should be given to the anti–Red Russian resistance forces (of which there were many), since Bolshevism was firmly in the saddle and nothing could be done to overturn it.

These comments ran contrary in many respects to the views of

---

became the main conduit by which information—or, more accurately, misinformation—about the Soviet revolution was conveyed to Washington policy makers. The twin results of his activity, both beneficial to Lenin and Trotsky, were to darken counsel in Washington, thus muddling prospects for action, and to divide American policies concerning Russia from those of France and Britain. Eager to keep Russia in the war against the Kaiser, Paris and London tried to concert measures with the Wilson administration to support anti-Bolshevik resistance. Buffeted by conflicting reports from Russia, Wilson delayed action for six months, and when the United States finally intervened, it did so in minimal, hesitant fashion. With the lack of any consistent Allied policy during the latter months of 1918—and the virtual dissolution of the Western Alliance when the war concluded—the Bolsheviks were able to recover from a position of weakness to deal with the widely scattered and ill-equipped opposing forces one by one, until resistance was extinguished.

other U.S. observers, including Ambassador Francis and Edgar Sisson of the Committee on Public Information (a precursor to the Office of War Information in World War II). Robins and Sisson had begun their Russian tenure together on friendly terms and with similar views about the revolution but parted company on the subject of trusting the new rulers. Robins guided by Gumberg seemed mesmerized by Lenin, whom Sisson came to consider dangerous and untrustworthy.[3] The two Americans specifically differed as to whether the Bolsheviks were acting as agents of the Germans, who obviously stood to gain if Russia were subtracted from the fighting. Their dissonant voices were part of a cacophony of diverse reports from amateur U.S. observers in the country.

Given conflicting streams of information coming out of Russia, Washington policy makers were unsure what course to follow. Accordingly, when U.S. intervention to help the anti-Bolsheviks in some manner was at last approved, it was minor, belated, and halfhearted—a classic case of too little, too late, and predictably ineffective. The Robins counsel of aid and accommodation and resulting muddle and delay thus helped achieve a prime objective of Lenin and Trotsky: to buy time and forestall outside involvement as long as possible while they mopped up their internal opposition.

Exactly why Robins did these things would be a topic of dispute. In the view of diplomat/historian George F. Kennan, the colonel was a naïve idealist who got taken in by Lenin and Trotsky, was misled about the nature of the revolution, and accordingly was a victim not a villain.[4] But it appears that in so arguing, Kennan was unaware of an extensive record compiled by Robins, well after the revolution was over, in which he expressed no misgivings about the homicidal regime whose power he helped consolidate. On the contrary, his statements over a span of decades show him to have been a lifelong admirer of the Soviet system.

In the 1940s, for instance, Robins would write to Communist

author Albert Kahn that, in the event of global revolutionary war, armed legions would fight "under the leadership of the Red Army" for the "freedom which was ended by British and American capitalist exploitation." In another letter to Kahn and coauthor Michael Sayers, Robins said "capitalism, imperialism and British colonial tyranny" were plotting "with the Jesuit machine" to "destroy the Soviet Union." He wrote likewise to Jessica Smith, of *Soviet Russia Today*, that "monopoly capitalism and the Roman Catholic hierarchy" were out to "destroy the fruits of the Soviet revolution."*[5]

From all this it would appear Raymond Robins was a figure of historical importance, who might be accounted the most significant American player promoting the cause of Moscow in the early going. And he would indeed seem deserving of that title—except that there was waiting in the wings an even more remarkable agent of influence who would even more zealously carry on the mission.

This was a youthful Russian-American with the improbable name of Armand Hammer, who in the 1920s and '30s built diligently on the pro-Red foundations Gumberg and Robins had established. Hammer arrived in Russia in August 1921, there by launching one of the most astounding careers of global intrigue that have ever been recorded. Like Robins, he would develop personal ties with Lenin and use these to advantage in dealings with Soviet commissars and U.S. officials. In which respect he invariably

---

* Later, British Communist Cedric Belfrage would pen a eulogy of Robins, saying the colonel had been an early advocate of recognizing the Red regime and in 1933 had conveyed his thoughts about the matter to Stalin directly. Thereafter, said Belfrage, Robins returned to the United States and met with President Roosevelt, conferring with him for upwards of an hour. If this account is to be believed, Robins was a go-between linking Stalin with FDR, a potential catalyst in the process by which American recognition was granted Moscow. Given his previous record of high-level Russian dealings, it seems possible Robins did play some such part in the recognition drama. And whatever the facts in that regard, his pro-Soviet advocacy over a span of decades suggests no remorse for his role in helping out the revolution.

had two closely linked objectives—to act as an advocate for Moscow in the West, and to create a personal business empire based on his Red connections.

Virtually everything about Armand Hammer was bizarre, beginning with his unusual name. He was the son of Dr. Julius Hammer, a Russian-born naturalized U.S. citizen, physician, and cosmetics entrepreneur in New York City and leading member of the Socialist Labor Party—a section of which would morph into the Communist Party USA.* Because of his professional activities, Dr. Hammer was fairly affluent and a financial supporter of the American Communist apparatus. In this role he helped set up a Soviet pseudo-embassy and trade mission in New York, a 1920s forerunner of the official Washington embassy that was still years in the future. This pseudo-embassy, as later information would reveal, was a conduit for funds moving between New York and Moscow to underwrite pro-Red subversion.[6]

Armand Hammer thus came by his pro-Soviet leanings naturally, and would follow closely in his father's footsteps. In 1921, when Hammer senior was sent to Sing Sing Prison for three years after performing a bungled abortion, Armand would take his place on a trip to Russia, in pursuit of financial deals that would advance the Communist interest. It was on this journey that he met Lenin, and though Hammer always embellished accounts of such occasions, the available data indicate that he made a strong impression on the Soviet leader.

Following this meeting, Lenin would inform the comrades that Armand was in the country, had brought gifts to show his backing for the cause, and could be useful to the Soviets in their quest for U.S. assistance. "If Hammer is earnest in his desire to help," said

---

* The symbol of the Socialist Labor Party was the arm and hammer, which it is believed by some was the source of the younger Hammer's curious name.

Lenin, "he could be used to develop a business enterprise in Russia that would encourage other U.S. businesses to follow his example. ... This is a small path leading to the American business world, and this path should be made use of in every way."[7]

To shore up Armand's credibility in this role, he would be given a series of Russian business deals that could be touted as money-makers. This meant his success had to be guaranteed by Moscow, as he could hardly play his part as shill if he were seen to be a failure. The deals included an asbestos mine, a pencil-manufacturing concern, and, most famously, a franchise selling Russian art (both real and fake) to Western buyers. He would later parlay these ventures into others, including the well-known Hammer galleries and control of Occidental Petroleum Corporation, which would one day be a significant player in global energy markets.

Like Robins, Hammer was afforded many signs of Soviet favor. For years he was the only foreigner whose private plane could be flown into Russian airspace, and the commissars made available to him sumptuous quarters when he was in Moscow. On the U.S. end of things, he would establish contacts with businessmen, officials, and notables of all descriptions. These included two sons of FDR; Tennessee Democratic senator Albert Gore (father of the vice president to be), who went on to work for Hammer after he left the Senate; Senator Edward Kennedy; and, on the Republican side, Senator Styles Bridges of New Hampshire and (somewhat fatefully) President Richard Nixon. In his latter days, Hammer even wangled a photo op with President Ronald Reagan, making him the only person known to history directly acquainted with Lenin, founder of the Soviet empire, and (however briefly) Reagan, who worked to bring that empire down in ruins.[8]

Hammer did all this and a good deal more with considerable gusto because he enjoyed having high-level contacts and the trappings of celebrity, but also because the influence thus obtained or suggested could be used to advance his invariable main agenda:

promoting détente between the United States and Russia, leading to the U.S. investment that Lenin had envisioned.*

The importance of Hammer's U.S.-Soviet business dealings can't be overstated, as the Communists would be chronically reliant on Western funding, credits, and technology to help them through their economic troubles. (Conversely, it was when the credits and technical assistance were cut back under Reagan that the creaking Soviet machinery collapsed and Mikhail Gorbachev had to adjourn the Cold War.) U.S. capitalists who followed the trail blazed by Hammer included W. Averell Harriman, Henry Ford, the Morgan interests, Cyrus Eaton, Mack Truck, Chase Manhattan, Control Data, and several other U.S. corporations. Such dealings were of utmost importance in keeping the Soviets economically afloat for a span of nearly seven decades.

Meanwhile, the Hammer-channeled flow of funds between East and West supported still other Soviet projects of sinister nature. The doings of both Hammers in this respect were of interest to FBI Director J. Edgar Hoover, who had been on the trail since the 1920s when British security sleuths raided a Hammer-connected London outfit that was laundering funds from Moscow. Information to this effect would be circulated by the FBI (and later the CIA), noting that Russian money had been disbursed to Soviet agents through the British cutout, and that New York police had found documents "revealing the activities of a clandestine Soviet network in the United States."[9]

An FBI/CIA report about all this further stated that pro-Soviet operatives in the West "were receiving considerable amounts of

---

* A pursuit that included portraying the Soviet leaders as admirable human beings. In this respect he was something of a virtuoso, along the lines of Joe Davies. (Hammer found in Leonid Brezhnev, for example, "a man of great humanism and vast warmth. . . . His eyes quickly filled with tears when his sentiments were stirred." The Hammer view of Lenin was even better: "Like One before him, he forbade not little children to come to him, and rejoiced that they should be happy.")

money from Dr. Julius Hammer in Moscow," and that in London "Dr. Julius Hammer's name and cryptonyms were seized before the Soviet code clerk could destroy them." To which the report added, "a source of known reliability [a common reference to intercepted communications] has stated that Armand Hammer had the job of paying Soviet agents in France under the cover of commercial trans-actions from 1929 until his departure for New York in 1934."*[10]

Having done all the above, the remarkable Armand Hammer passed away in 1990, at the ripe age of ninety-two. Before he did so he added yet another odd distinction to a flamboyant record. Despite seventy years of serving as a Moscow front man, promot-ing the interests of the Kremlin and carrying water for Russian leaders from Lenin to Brezhnev, he was never arrested or indicted as a Soviet agent. He did, however, get into trouble for his political wheeling and dealing, having made an anonymous contribution to the 1972 presidential campaign of Nixon, in violation of newly adopted campaign limits, for which offense Hammer would be in-dicted and convicted.† Thus in the United States as of the 1970s, being an agent of Moscow was not a matter causing legal problems, but an illicit contribution to Richard Nixon could lead to prison.

Hammer and Raymond Robins performed for Russia's new rulers two essential services: helping stay the hand of the Western allies early on, when the Red regime was extremely weak and might have

---

* This and similar information was known decades later to Reagan's national security adviser Richard V. Allen, who was cognizant of the role that credits and technology transfer played in keeping the Soviets afloat. Allen blocked efforts by Hammer to gain access to the Reagan government as long as the security adviser was in the White House. It was only after Allen departed that Hammer worked his way into the fringes of the Reagan circle, using as a device to gain entry a professed interest in a philanthropic cause supported by Mrs. Reagan.

† Hammer was later pardoned by President George H. W. Bush.

been toppled, and helping the Soviets secure the capital, credits, and technology they needed to keep the revolution going. In terms of public opinion, however, it's probable that the third member of our troika was the most influential of the lot. This was the noted journalist Walter Duranty, Moscow correspondent for the *New York Times*. Though British born and Cambridge educated, Duranty became a U.S. newsman in Europe during World War I, moving on when the war ended to an assignment in Latvia, before being posted farther east to Moscow.

Duranty arrived in Russia in August 1921, at the same time as Hammer, and over the next decade would establish himself as the dean of Western journalists in the country. After a brief early period of hostility, he would experience a complete conversion and become an avid promoter of the Soviet system. Why he did so is uncertain. It doesn't appear he was an ideological Communist, as he reportedly had no ideology at all beyond a kind of Nietzschean will-to-power view that didn't mind dictators and apparently hardened him to scenes of suffering. This would have been useful emotional armor in the Soviet Union of the 1930s, when the suffering was intense and would get more so.

Duranty was but one of a considerable number of Western journalists, tourists, and academics who showed up in Moscow in the 1920s and '30s and emerged with glowing reports about the wondrous future unfolding in Russia. But he was among the most influential, as he was not a mere visiting amateur or parachute correspondent but a longtime resident and reputed expert for a major American paper. This standing made it the more significant that as with Colonel Robins so much of Duranty's reportage was pro-Soviet propaganda.

Duranty's most important contributions in this respect occurred in the period 1932–33, when Stalin's policy of forced collectivization was being inflicted on Russia's downtrodden peasants, and they tried to resist the seizure of their crops and livestock. This led to a brutal crackdown as recalcitrants were denied food and the ability to produce it—in essence, a policy of forced starvation. These harsh measures resulted in the deaths of countless victims—numbering by most estimates between five and ten million—many of whom perished in the streets of Russian towns and cities.

The famine and death toll were reported by a few correspondents, notably William Henry Chamberlin of the United States and Britain's Malcolm Muggeridge. But most of the Western press corps in Moscow ignored or downplayed the horrendous story. Leading the way in this respect was Duranty, whose reportage touched on the subject in ways suggesting he knew the facts, but so couched as to obscure their meaning. His best-known offering in this vein was his denial/nondenial of the famine, as follows: "Any report of famine in Russia today is an exaggeration or malicious propaganda. The food shortage which has affected almost the whole population . . . has, however, caused heavy loss of life."[11] The distinction between a "famine" and a "food shortage" causing "heavy loss of life" was not explained to Duranty's readers.

This tortured prose, which would become notorious in the annals of obfuscation, followed another Duranty quote suggesting his pro-Soviet stance, acceptance of dictatorial rule, and indifference to its victims. This was his extenuation of Stalin's despotic methods as steps on the road to progress, which the backward peasants were allegedly blocking. As Duranty famously put it: "You can't make an omelet without breaking eggs." That the omelet was a ghastly system of repression, and the eggs the lives of helpless human beings, evidently did not concern him.*

---

* Double-talk and outright denials of the famine would be supplied by other journalists following Duranty's example—so much so that Eugene Lyons, himself a Moscow correspondent of this era, would title an essay on the subject "The Press Corps Conceals a Famine." Lyons was a former sympathizer with the regime who became a staunch anti-Communist because of what he saw in Russia, admitting that he had taken part in the cover-up and expressing shame for having done so.

What made all this strategically crucial was that the period 1932–33, when famine was raging and Russians were dying in massive numbers, was a turning point in U.S.-Soviet relations. It was at this time that American recognition of the Moscow regime was being seriously weighed and, once Roosevelt gained power, granted. Had the truth been reported about the atrocities inflicted on Russia's peasants, the death and misery that resulted, and the cruelty of a government that could crush its people in such fashion, it could have badly damaged Moscow's prospects for recognition. Duranty and company by their denials and obfuscations prevented this embarrassment for the Soviet tyrants.

Subsequently, when recognition was conferred, Duranty, like Robins and Hammer, would achieve a place of honor with the Kremlin. When Soviet ambassador Maxim Litvinov traveled to Washington to seal the deal, Duranty accompanied him on the journey, a well-publicized fact that further enhanced the journalist's reputation as the consummate Russian expert with high-level contacts. It's noteworthy also that Duranty would receive a Pulitzer Prize for his reporting at this era. As this is considered American journalism's highest honor, he thus was rewarded in both Russia and the U.S. for his blatant Soviet propaganda. Like the curious tale of Armand Hammer, who suffered in legal terms for illicitly supporting Nixon but not for being a Soviet agent, Duranty's Pulitzer says a lot about some American priorities in the struggle of East and West, as well as those that prevailed in Russia.

6.

THE FIRST RED DECADE

The first major Communist penetration of the American government occurred in the 1930s. The Communist Party USA had been founded more than a decade before, encouraged by Moscow and financed through such helpful go-betweens as Julius and Armand Hammer. But the party of that era was small, ineffective, and far outside the national mainstream, mostly headed by leaders who were foreign born, with a membership tilted to émigrés, many of whom could not speak English. Its chances of infiltrating federal agencies, or other important institutions, were meager.

All this began changing in the 1930s, chiefly though not entirely as a result of the Great Depression. Thanks to the political/economic crisis of the age, a lot of people would become disillusioned with capitalism and the American system in general and begin casting about for something different. A number of these would be attracted by the pat and seemingly cogent "class struggle" slogans of the Marxists and the claimed successes of the Soviet Union, and decide that Communism was the answer they were seeking. This would in particular be true with certain members of the intellectual classes, and at some prestigious centers of higher learning.

Meanwhile, the Communist Party USA was undergoing a makeover of its own at the behest of Moscow and American party chief Earl Browder, downplaying its more violent aspects and presenting itself as a peaceful, democratic group of patriotic nature. Given cover by the 1930s proliferation of party-sponsored front groups that seemingly blended Red revolutionary concepts with less threatening leftward causes, the Communists appeared to many unfamiliar with such tactics as simply promoting a more rigorous version of widely held progressive notions.

The net result of all these changes was the emergence in the United States of a new class of party members, many of them on the college campus, in some cases from Anglo families of long standing—the ranks from which government workers of the middle and upper echelons typically got recruited. In many cases they, their families, or their faculty mentors personally knew the people who did the hiring, and so had easy access to federal payrolls. And when one of the young radicals got hired, he could help to bring in others.

Greatly aiding the infiltration process was the advent of FDR's New Deal, this also, of course, in response to the Depression. As is well-known, President Roosevelt throughout the 1930s launched a host of federal agencies, programs, and regulations to deal with the nation's myriad economic problems. This activity required the hiring of a lot of new employees and attracted numerous would-be planners and reformers eager to get in on the action. Among these were scores of converts to Marxist doctrine, many of whom would later emerge in confidential security records as Communists or Soviet agents.

Further aiding the penetration effort was FDR's decision in the fall of 1933 to recognize the Red regime in Moscow, which had been a prime objective of such as Robins, Hammer, and Duranty. Once this had been achieved, not only was an aura of legitimacy conferred on the Soviet Union, but, as earlier seen, Stalin was able to send to Washington ostensible diplomats and embassy staffers who were in fact intelligence agents. Working with Soviet "illegals" already in the country, these newcomers would create a formidable network of apparatchiks on American soil liaising with Communists on official payrolls.

A good deal of what we know about all this would be disclosed toward the end of the decade by Whittaker Chambers, one of the earliest native-born recruits, who worked in the mid-1930s as a courier linking Soviet intelligence with Communists in the federal workforce. In 1939, shocked by the Hitler-Stalin pact* and otherwise disenchanted, Chambers decided to break openly with Moscow and tell the authorities what he knew about the infiltration. In September 1939, accompanied by anti-Communist writer-editor Isaac Don Levine, he had a lengthy talk with Assistant Secretary of State Adolf Berle, then doubling as a specialist on security matters for the White House.

Chambers would later repeat his story to the FBI, at legislative hearings, and in federal courtrooms, as well as in a bestselling memoir, becoming in the process the most famous and in some ways most important witness in American Cold War history. However, it's evident from the record that much of what he had to say was revealed in this initial talk with Berle. And what he would reveal, both then and later, was an astonishing picture of subversion, reaching into numerous government agencies and rising to significant levels.

Specifically, Chambers would name a sizable group of suspects then holding federal jobs, most notably Alger Hiss, and provide examples of activity by official U.S. staffers working on behalf of Moscow. Judging by Berle's notes—and a parallel set recorded by Levine—it was a shocking tale that should have set alarm bells ringing and led quickly to corrective action.[1] But so far as anyone was ever able to tell, no bells were rung or action taken. It appears, indeed, that virtually nothing would be done about the Chambers data for years thereafter.

Berle himself would later downplay the Chambers information, saying the people named were merely members of a "study group"

---

* The pact between the two dictators was signed in August 1939 and lasted until June 1941, when Hitler invaded Russia.

and thus not a security danger.[2] But this version was belied by Berle's own notes about his talk with Chambers. The heading he gave these wasn't "Marxist study group," but "Underground Espionage Agent." As Chambers would comment in his memoir, he was obviously describing "not a Marxist study group, but a Communist conspiracy." And the people named would fully live up to that description. They, and the offices they held, in the order that the Berle memo gave them, were as follows:

Lee Pressman—Agricultural Adjustment Administration (later with the CIO)
Nathan Witt—National Labor Relations Board
Harold Ware—Agricultural Administration
John Abt—Department of Justice
Charles Kramer—La Follette Committee (Senate)
Vincent Reno—Aberdeen Proving Grounds
Philip Reno—Social Security
Elinor Nelson—Federal Employees Union
Richard Post—State Department
Laurence Duggan—State Department
Julian Wadleigh—State Department
Leander Lovell—State Department
Noel Field—State Department
Lauchlin Currie—White House
Solomon Adler—Treasury Department
Frank Coe—Treasury Department
Donald Hiss—Labor Department
Alger Hiss—State Department

To these identifications Chambers would eventually add others: Harry Dexter White at the Treasury, George Silverman of the Railway Retirement Board, Henry Collins of Agriculture (subsequently at the State Department), and several more of like persuasion. Harold Ware, according to Chambers, had been the original head of this secret Communist unit but was now deceased, replaced first by Nathan Witt, and thereafter by John Abt. Chambers further noted that the group, while under his own immediate supervision, was ultimately responsible to Soviet foreign commissar J. Peters, who worked with Communist leader Alexander Trachtenberg of the U.S. party.

Based on what was eventually learned about these people, this was a formidable crew of Soviet agents, Reds, and fellow travelers, many of whom would appear in later chapters of the story. Chambers referred to the core members as the "Ware cell" and in this context expanded on the "study group" description. While "political instruction and discussion" did occur within the cell, he said, it wasn't simply a "study group," nor was it chiefly an espionage operation. Since this, as has been noted, remains a point of confusion in such matters, his further explanation is worth recalling:

> *The real power of the group lay at much higher levels. It was a power to influence, from the most strategic positions, the policies of the United States government, especially in the labor and welfare fields. Moreover, since one member of the group [Witt] was secretary of the National Labor Relations Board, and another member of the group [Pressman] was in the top council of the CIO, the Communist Party was in a position to exert a millstone effect, both in favor of policies and persons it supported, and against policies and persons it disliked.*[3]

The Chambers information would subsequently be confirmed by other witnesses in legal proceedings and the disclosures of *Venona*. Foremost among the witnesses reinforcing his assertions was ex-Communist Elizabeth Bentley, also a former courier linking Red intelligence operatives with comrades on the federal payroll. In 1945, she too would break with Moscow and tell her story to the FBI, triggering a massive investigation that in substance confirmed the Chambers data, leading in time to dramatic hearings by congressional committees and some historic grand jury sessions. (See chapter 20.)

Elizabeth Bentley was a highly intelligent, well-educated member of the 1930s generation, typical in many ways of recruits into the Communist Party at that era. A graduate of Vassar, she was attracted by the rhetoric of the Communist-front American League for Peace and Democracy, migrated from there to the Communist Party, then moved into her role as espionage courier for the Soviet underground apparatus. Her career in Communist/Soviet circles lasted for roughly a decade, until 1945, when she broke with the Soviets and went to the FBI.

Before the Bentley inquest was over, she would name more than one hundred people who allegedly were or had been Communists or Soviet assets, about half of whom had been in federal office and two dozen of whom were still holding official jobs when she approached the Bureau. In addition, the FBI would track scores of other people connected to her suspects, seemingly of similar outlook. Surveillance data, wiretap logs, and reports to government agencies about these cases fill tens of thousands of pages in Bureau records, indicating that FBI warnings about the penetration were supplied to top officials early, in detail, and often.[4] In some cases these reports resulted in backstage efforts to force resignations, but until the latter 1940s, when Congress got actively on the case, little else by way of action. The indifference that met the Chambers revelations thus persisted for almost a decade.

While the Bentley suspects would be found in numerous U.S. agencies, the largest single group that she identified was at the Treasury, which on her evidence had been well infiltrated by the middle 1930s, with a steady influx of new recruits thereafter. Her main Treasury contact was Nathan G. Silvermaster, who earlier served at other federal agencies and had drawn the notice of security forces, again without effective action. The most important

Treasury suspect otherwise was Assistant Secretary Harry White (named as well by Chambers), who by common consent exerted enormous influence with Treasury Secretary Henry Morgenthau Jr. Other Morgenthau staffers on Bentley's list included Harold Glasser, V. Frank Coe, Solomon Adler, and Victor Perlo (all also named by Chambers), plus half a dozen additional suspects. And this was the pro-Moscow lineup at just one agency out of many.

The Treasury group in turn was linked to suspects at numerous other federal venues. The most important of such connections was to high-ranking White House assistant Lauchlin Currie, himself a former Treasury staffer and pro-Soviet asset well-known to the Silvermaster circle. Similar contacts could be traced down many official byways—Pressman and Witt linked with Alger Hiss at State, Solomon Adler rooming and working with a key diplomatic figure, Bentley suspect William Remington at Commerce allied with a staffer in Foggy Bottom, and so on. All of which would seem to have justified the boast of Soviet commissar Peters, as relayed by Chambers: "Even in Germany, under the Weimar Republic, the party did not have what we have here."[5]

While it's apparent that these backstage doings were something other than "study group" deliberations, it should be noted that, as with the Ware cell, there were in fact certain New Deal units called "study groups," so that Berle in using this term was describing something that actually existed. However, as observed by Chambers, a "study group" might have several different functions, ranging from discussion of philosophical issues to pro-Red propaganda to covert subversive action. So membership in such a unit could mean much or little or something in between, depending on what the group was up to and the member's level of involvement with it.

One thing that seems to have been generally true about these groups was that they provided mutual protection and support to their members serving on official payrolls. In a bureaucratic system where networking was—and is—of prime importance, this made them a considerable force, wielding leverage on job placement, approval for promotions, clearance on security grounds, and so on. The members routinely hired and promoted one another, gave each other recommendations, and vouched for one another when trouble threatened.

One of the more significant of these groups was, like the Ware cell, based mainly at Agriculture, an agency then considered of key importance because of problems afflicting the nation's farming system. Connected with this unit (though not an Agriculture employee) was Harry Hopkins, later the most powerful figure in the government next to FDR himself, playing a pivotal role in World War II and the beginning phases of the Cold War. Other members included Chambers suspect Pressman, FDR "brain truster" Rexford Tugwell, Agriculture official Paul Appleby, his departmental ally Gardner Jackson, and youth activist Aubrey Williams.[6]

All these would eventually have key parts to play in the New Deal drama. As noted, Pressman was identified as a Communist by Chambers, an identification Pressman would one day admit, after first taking the Fifth Amendment about it. He had left Agriculture in 1935 to work for the National Research Project (subsequently going to the CIO), an offshoot of the Works Progress Administration (WPA). The Research Project was a prime example of networking in action, described by Chambers as a "trap door" into federal service for Communist Party members.* Its operational chiefs were David Weintraub and Irving Kaplan—both identified under oath and in now available security records as pro-Moscow assets. The overall head of the project, and the person who hired Lee Pressman, was fellow study group alumnus Hopkins.†[7]

---

* Chambers himself obtained a job there, with Communist assistance, when he sought to establish a public identity after years in the Soviet underground.

† The ostensible purpose of the National Research Project was to gather statistics and economic data to be used as a basis for projects pursued by the WPA under

Pressman had a continuing relationship with yet another study group alum, Agriculture staffer Gardner Jackson. A longtime activist for radical causes, Jackson would be listed in a 1940s House Committee on Un-American Activities roster of "veteran fellow travelers." He would justify that billing through agitational efforts on behalf of the International Labor Defense, Veterans of the Abraham Lincoln Brigade, and the Washington Committee for Democratic Action, all later officially cited front groups. Behind the scenes, he would take up the cudgels for the Soviet agent Louis Gibarti, when that notorious apparatchik was seeking entry into the country (an effort opposed by security-minded staffers at the State Department of that era).[8]

Jackson's extracurricular projects brought him to the notice not only of the House Committee but of executive branch officials concerned about security matters. A security squad inquiry in 1942 prompted an angry outburst from the undersecretary of Agriculture (the number-two official at the department), denouncing the investigation of Jackson as a waste of time, vouching for Jackson, and rebuking the agency's security people for even daring to look into the matter. The official coming thus to Jackson's aid was his study group colleague Paul Appleby. The Appleby protest was successful, and soon after it was lodged the investigation of Jackson ended abruptly in his favor.[9] Many other cases of the era would be handled in like fashion.

Among the most impressive of the New Deal networking efforts was that at the Treasury, led by the powerful Harry White, whose impact on Cold War policy matters for many years would be extensive. Because of his great influence with Secretary Morgenthau, White was able to bring into the agency a host of ideological allies, including the earlier noted Adler, Coe, Glasser, Silvermaster, and

---

Hopkins. Chambers's assignment there during his brief tenure was to compile information concerning America's railroads—the object of which was not apparent from his discussion of the matter.

others. Beyond which, White's networking also extended outside the Treasury to other bureaus and departments, with suggestive implications for policy matters.

Among the more ambitious of White's networking ventures was a series of meetings that applied the "study group" concept across the organizational spectrum. While we don't know what was discussed at these sessions, we do have the names of some of the people who attended. These formed an intriguing mix of agencies, groups, and individuals. Among the people called together by White, and their affiliations, according to official records:

Paul Appleby, Budget	Murray Latimer, Railway
C. B. Baldwin, CIO-PAC	Retirement Board
Oscar Chapman, Interior	Isador Lubin, Labor
Benjamin Cohen, White House	Robert Nathan, WPB
Oscar Cox, FEA	David Niles, White House
Wayne Coy, Budget	Randolph Paul, Treasury
Lauchlin Currie, White House	Milo Perkins, BEW
Jonathan Daniels, White House	Paul Porter, OES
Mordecai Ezekiel, Agriculture	Edward Prichard, OES
Abe Fortas, Interior	James Rowe, Justice
Robert Hannegan, DNC	Michael Straus, Interior
Leon Henderson, RIA	Aubrey Williams, NYA*[10]
Major Charles Kades, Army	

On even a cursory survey, this was an impressive sampling of U.S. agencies and outside groups, especially so in view of the prominent posts held by the attendees. Among the entities represented were the

---

* Glossary of acronyms: CIO-PAC—Congress of Industrial Organization– Political Action Committee; FEA—Foreign Economic Administration; DNC— Democratic National Committee; RIA—Research Institute of America; WPB—War Production Board; BEW—Board of Economic Warfare; OES— Office of Economic Stabilization; NYA—National Youth Administration.

White House, five cabinet departments, and several special bureaus, plus political auxiliaries and think tanks that wielded leverage on policy issues. Their aggregate impact would have been the greater had they worked to achieve some object or the other in typical networking fashion. Since the group was assembled by White, and since we know from other data that numerous attendees shared his outlook, the potential for coordinated action would have been substantial.

Of particular interest in this lineup were attendees who had contact with Soviet intelligence agents or members of the Communist Party. These attenndees included White himself, his ally Lauchlin Currie, and executive staffer David Niles (concerning whom more later), all of whom would make appearances in *Venona*. Joining this trio was C. B. "Beanie" Baldwin, identified in other confidential records as a secret member of the party. Baldwin was another former Agriculture employee, who like his colleague Lee Pressman would move on to the CIO. (Baldwin would subsequently be the majordomo of the 1948 Progressive Party presidential bid of Henry Wallace.)

Also of interest in this group were four attendees then working at the White House: Currie, Niles, Benjamin Cohen, and Jonathan Daniels. Add to this quartet two staffers at the Bureau of the Budget, which was then a White House adjunct with access to the Oval Office. So Appleby, in his new role at the bureau, and his colleague Wayne Coy could be included in this number also. Here was great potential influence at high levels.

The official on this roster by all accounts closest to White was Currie. The two had been students and instructors together at Harvard, had common academic interests, and, according to Chambers-Bentley and *Venona*, shared an even more significant link as fellow travelers and agents of influence. As Bentley would testify, they were among the most important Soviet contacts in federal office, as they were both high-ranking and well-known and their word would be accepted. Singly, either would have been a formidable asset. Together, they were a powerful combination.

A significant example of how these several players came to the aid of endangered fellow staffers was the case of Nathan Silvermaster, Elizabeth Bentley's main contact in official circles when she performed her role as Soviet courier. As seen, Silvermaster had early on attracted the notice of security forces, but when he did so members of the various backstage networks sprang quickly, and effectively, to his defense.

Silvermaster had touched a host of relevant bases on his long federal journey. In the 1930s, he had worked at Agriculture for the secret Communist Baldwin, in the war years moving to the Board of Economic Warfare to serve with Currie, then transferring at the instigation of White to the Treasury payroll. When security forces objected to Silvermaster, the White-Currie axis came vigorously to his rescue. As Paul Appleby explained it, Silvermaster was "very close both to Harry White and Lauchlin Currie. There is no reason to question his loyalty and good citizenship." The backing of those two pro-Soviet assets would thus help keep their friend Silvermaster on the federal payroll.[11]

Though the emphasis of such networking in the 1930s was perforce on domestic matters, it's notable that the list Chambers gave Berle also included a group of suspects—six of the people named—who were or had been at the State Department (Richard Post, Laurence Duggan, Julian Wadleigh, Leander Lovell, Noel Field, Alger Hiss). In this connection, a final instance of networking would be instructive. This was a research/advocacy group called the Institute of Pacific Relations, which as the name suggests was focused on Far Eastern issues. Though a private organization, it was quasi-official, working in close conjunction with State, featuring diplomats among its members and trustees, and furnishing Asia policy expertise to the department.

Among U.S. officials who at various times served on the board of the IPR were such prestigious mainstream figures as General George C. Marshall and Undersecretary of State Sumner Welles, plus others who were of lesser stature but in their way important. Government staffers who served as IPR trustees included Soviet agents of influence Hiss and Currie and State Department official John Carter Vincent. Meanwhile, Owen Lattimore and Joseph Barnes, both on the IPR payroll in the 1930s, would become government information specialists in the war years. Others connected to the IPR included State Department Far East experts Michael Greenberg and Haldore Hanson and Soviet intelligence asset T. A. Bisson, who like others mentioned shows up in the pages of *Venona*.

Further enhancing its networking efforts, the IPR had affiliates in numerous countries, including England, Germany, China, Japan, and—as of the middle 1930s—the Soviet Union. As this last suggests, there were enrolled in the group a substantial number of Communists and Soviet agents from other nations, who were thus able to liaise at IPR conventicles with American colleagues, many of whom had no idea they were dealing with Soviet agents (though there were others who in fact knew the connection). The nature of the operation would be summed up by a U.S. Senate committee as follows:

> *The IPR . . . was like a specialized flypaper in its attractive power for Communists. . . . British Communists like Michael Greenberg, Elsie Fairfax Cholmeley, and Anthony Jenkinson; Chinese Communists like Chi Chao ting, Chen Han seng, Chu Tong, or Y.Y. Hsu; German Communists like Hans Moeller . . . or Guenther Stein; Japanese Communists (and espionage agents) like Saionji and Ozaki; United States communists like James S. Allen, Frederick Field, William Mandel, Lawrence Rosinger, and Alger Hiss.*[12]

Here was networking potential on a global scale, which by the end of the 1930s would become a powerful force in shaping events in Asia. Its considerable influence in this respect would in the next few years grow even more so.

7.

REMEMBER PEARL HARBOR

Among important features of the Communist apparatus glossed over in the usual histories—arguably one of the most important—was its interactive, global nature: the degree to which it collaborated with its sponsors/paymasters in the Kremlin and pro-Red forces in other countries.

This angle tends to get ignored or downplayed not only in leftward comment that portrays the CPUSA as a well-meaning indigenous outfit, but also by anti-Communist spokesmen who have viewed the party chiefly as a domestic menace (as with the prosecution of its leaders for violation of the Smith Act*). Debate conducted at this level frames the issue as the threat of coup d'état or revolution in the streets, as happened in Russia, and whether there was any realistic chance of similar dire events occurring in a U.S. context. Fixation on this kind of danger ignores the CP's far more important Cold War role as fifth-columnist agent of a hostile foreign power.

Even when the international angle is noted, the image of the party provided in standard treatments is frequently misleading. In numerous cases, as has been seen, discussion of the Communist link to Moscow centers on the issue of spying—the theft of military or diplomatic secrets—but this too misses the crucial aspect.

---

* The Smith Act, named for Representative Howard Smith (D-VA), adopted and amended at the era of the Hitler-Stalin pact, made it a federal crime to "teach and advocate the overthrow of the government of the United States by force and violence," of which offense the Communist leaders were convicted.

Such spying as noted did occur, but generally speaking was subordinate to the overarching Communist goal of influencing U.S. policy in favor of the Soviet interest.

For reasons that are apparent, such policy influence was most extensive during World War II, when the Soviets were our allies and anti-Communist safeguards were virtually nonexistent. In a macabre way this was apropos, as pro-Soviet machinations had a pivotal role to play in America's involvement in that conflict. Of note in this respect was the complex maneuvering of Communist and pro-Moscow elements during the run-up to Pearl Harbor, the surprise attack by Japanese forces on December 7, 1941, in which more than two thousand Americans perished, and which launched the nation into catastrophic conflict.

Though the Pearl Harbor raid was a surprise as to location, war somewhere in the Pacific had been in prospect for some years before then. In the latter 1930s and early '40s, storm clouds had gathered over Asia as over Europe, mainly as a result of Japan's attack on China. In 1931, Japan had annexed the northeastern Chinese province of Manchuria, and in 1937 embarked on a more extensive campaign against the rest of China, battling the Nationalist government of Chiang Kai-shek, then based at the inland city of Chungking. In this long-running struggle, American sympathies were overwhelmingly on the side of China, and U.S. officials had imposed a series of economic sanctions to punish Tokyo for its transgressions.

Though Japan at this time was the most powerful state in Asia, it had vulnerabilities the United States was able to exploit because of our own great economic power. In contrast to conditions existing later, America in the prewar years was the foremost petroleum-producing country in the world, while Japan as a resource-poor island nation had to import oil to fuel its economy and military system. The United States was also then, as today, a world financial power, serving as a banking center for many nations, Japan included. Our dominant role in both respects gave us enormous economic leverage and made our sanctions doubly effective when in the summer of 1941 we shut off oil exports to Japan and froze its financial holdings in U.S. banking channels.

An X factor in this volatile equation was the Soviet Union, whose Asian regions adjoined Manchuria, had long been a foe of the Japanese, and had had border clashes with them where the two empires came together. Fear of Japan was chronic in Soviet strategic thinking and would become still more intense with the Manchurian invasion. The Soviets at this period were thus like the United States on the side of China, and extended aid to Chiang to help keep him in the battle. The logic of which from a Soviet standpoint was fairly simple, as Chiang by his resistance was draining Tokyo's resources and pinning down a million-plus Japanese who might otherwise have invaded Russia.

To deal with this complex of issues and protect their flank in Asia, the Soviets had on the ground in China a formidable group of undercover agents. Foremost among these was the German Communist Richard Sorge, perhaps the most effective secret agent in Soviet history (enshrined in the Moscow pantheon of intelligence heroes).[1] As of the latter 1930s, Sorge was a ten-year veteran of the GRU (military intelligence) and head of an extensive pro-Red network based in Shanghai.* His group was a veritable microcosm of the Soviet global project, including as it did the Red Chinese apparatchik Chen Han Seng, the American pro-Soviet writer Agnes Smedley, the German-born naturalized Briton Guenther Stein, and influential Japanese Communists Hotsumi Ozaki and Kinkazu Saionji.[2]

---

* Sorge was a battle-wounded German veteran of World War I, disillusioned by the carnage inflicted by that struggle and accompanying economic chaos, who became convinced that capitalism was the source of these social evils. In 1929 he joined the German Communist Party and would later be sent to Moscow for training as an agent of the Comintern, dealing in "political intelligence." He was subsequently transferred to Soviet military intelligence, specializing in Far Eastern matters.

As the Soviets became increasingly worried about Japan's expansionist ambitions, Sorge moved his operations to Tokyo to follow events there more closely. Here he worked as a correspondent for a German newspaper, posing as a devoted Nazi. In this guise, he had access to the German embassy and, since the Reich was allied with Japan, entrée to Tokyo policy-making circles. This access was enhanced by the presence of Ozaki and Saionji, both respected figures in Japan with contacts in the Imperial cabinet.

Sorge's associates used their contacts to keep him apprised of happenings in Japanese inner circles, a subject that for Moscow became even more urgent in the summer of 1941, when Hitler invaded Russia. The Nazi onslaught sent the Soviet armies reeling backward and raised in Stalin's mind the grim specter of a two-front war should Japan attack him from the east while he was embroiled in Europe. Whether this was going to happen, if so when, and what to do about it would now become the main preoccupations of Sorge and his agents.

Luckily for Moscow—less so for others—Tokyo's leaders had for some time before this been divided on the subject of how to handle Russia. The army for the most part favored striking north against Siberia, which would have capitalized on Stalin's conflict with the Nazis and forced him into the two-front war he dreaded. But the navy wanted to go south against U.S. or European Pacific outposts to get the resources—petroleum above all else—that the empire sorely needed. In the latter months of 1941, these questions were being thrashed out daily in the Tokyo cabinet.

As this dispute unfolded, Sorge and company exerted their influence behind the scenes to affect the outcome in favor of the Soviet interest. As he would divulge later in a memoir, Sorge and his colleagues sought to convince Japan's officials that there was no percentage in attacking Russia, but that a move against British, Dutch, or American targets in the Pacific would be to their advantage. The argument Ozaki used in official councils Sorge would sum up as follows:

The Soviet Union has no intention whatsoever of fighting Japan [which was true both in 1941 and in the Pacific war that followed]. . . . It would be a shortsighted and mistaken view for Japan to attack Russia, since she cannot expect to gain anything in Eastern Siberia. . . . should Japan aspire to further expansions elsewhere than in China, the Southern area alone would be worth going into, for there Japan would find the critical resources so essential to her war-time economy, and there would confront the true enemy blocking her from her place in the sun.[*3]

While all this was happening, a mirror-image debate was occurring in the United States, where there was also a sharp division of views on what to do in Asia. The tightening of sanctions against Japan, as American strategists knew, would affect not only the military power of the empire but its economy in general, a threat that for Japan might be considered a casus belli. (Ironically, the point was made by FDR himself on the day before the freezing order was issued. As he told a group of business leaders, "if we cut the oil off, they [the Japanese] probably would have gone down to the Netherland East Indies a year ago and we would have had war.")[4]

This prospect was a matter of concern to many in the United States who wanted to avoid a head-on conflict and talked about a possible truce to prevent or postpone a military showdown. Especially interested in reaching such a truce were U.S. Army Chief of Staff General George C. Marshall and Chief of Naval Operations Admiral Harold Stark, who advised the White House that

---

* Ozaki pursued this line even though the Soviets had issued no instructions to do so, but didn't forbid such conduct outright. Sorge and Ozaki construed this omission as license to influence the course of Japanese thinking in behalf of Moscow. As observed by U.S. Far East intelligence chief Major General Charles Willoughby, Sorge's "right hand man (Ozaki), who had exceptional facilities and an exceptional position within the highest quarters of the Japanese government," exercised "his influence toward keeping Japan from attacking Russia and . . . to encourage them to move south toward a collision with England and the United States."

America's depleted peacetime forces weren't ready for all-out warfare. Among other advocates of a modus vivendi was U.S. ambassador to Tokyo Joseph Grew, who conferred with Japanese premier Fumimaro Konoye about a possible Konoye-Roosevelt meeting—which Konoye, according to Grew, emphatically wanted—to reach a compromise arrangement.[5]

However, when it seemed that the truce idea was gaining favor, other U.S. officials with different notions would spring quickly into action. One such was White House assistant/Soviet asset Lauchlin Currie, whose portfolio included China and who would vehemently deplore the concept of a truce with Tokyo as a betrayal of our Chinese allies. Any agreement with the Japanese, Currie said in a memo to FDR, "would do irreparable damage to the good will we have built up in China." U.S. fealty to Chiang Kai-shek, in Currie's view, precluded any compromise with Japan, so the modus vivendi idea had to be abandoned.[6]

Also opposed to the truce concept, and voicing grave concern about the well-being of our China allies, was the Treasury's Harry White, who had been a major player in imposing economic sanctions to punish Japan for its aggressions. As talk of a modus vivendi spread, White bitterly denounced the concept as "a Far Eastern Munich," saying that "persons in our country's government" were hoping to "betray the cause of the heroic Chinese people" and undermine the chance of a "world-wide democratic victory." To "sell out China to her enemies," he said, would "dim the bright luster of American world leadership in her democratic fight against fascism."[7]

In which martial spirit, White issued a call for U.S. officials and activists to stand fast for Chiang Kai-shek and China. As later testified by Edward C. Carter of the Institute of Pacific Relations, White contacted him in November 1941 to warn against the truce proposal and convene an emergency meeting in the nation's capital to prevent a "sellout of China" (Carter added that by the time he got to Washington for the meeting, the modus vivendi danger had subsided).[8]

Also weighing in at this juncture was Professor Owen Lattimore of Johns Hopkins University (and the IPR), a close associate of Carter and Currie and a contact, as he would one day reveal, of the Soviet agent White. Lattimore at this time was serving in Chungking as U.S. adviser to Chiang Kai-shek, a post to which he had been assigned by FDR at the behest of Currie. In this job, the professor became a frequent go-between in U.S. dealings with Chiang (who spoke no English). On November 25, at the height of the modus vivendi wrangle, Lattimore dispatched a cable to Currie saying the idea was repugnant to Chiang and should be rejected. In setting forth Chiang's views, Lattimore told Currie:

> *I feel you should urgently advise the president of the generalissimo's very strong reaction. I have never seen him really agitated before. Loosening of economic pressures or unfreezing [of Japanese financial assets] would dangerously increase Japan's military advantage in China. . . . Any modus vivendi now arrived at would be disastrous for Chinese belief in America . . . [Chiang] questions his ability to hold the situation together [should Japan succeed in] escaping military defeat through diplomatic victory.*[9]

Given the events that immediately followed, it's noteworthy that this cable was Lattimore's version of what Chiang Kai-shek believed or knew and that Chiang's knowledge of what was transpiring would have been influenced to some unknown extent by what Lattimore had told him. Such thoughts, however, did not occur to Washington officials, who took the Lattimore cable at face value and referred to it as a cable not from Lattimore, but from Chiang.

This Lattimore cable turned out to be hugely important, as it coincided with and helped trigger a decision by Secretary of State

Cordell Hull to abandon the modus vivendi concept and pave the way for warfare. Reflecting later on Pearl Harbor, War Secretary Henry Stimson recalled Hull as saying he had renounced the truce idea "because the Chinese had objected. . . . Chiang Kai-shek had sent a special message to the effect that that would make a terrifically bad impression in China." Chief of Naval Operations Stark likewise remembered that prominent in Hull's thinking was "the message from Chiang Kai-shek." Accordingly, Hull had announced, he was ready to "kick the whole thing over." [10]

Which was what did then happen. On November 26, Hull met with Japan's Washington envoys to give them the final U.S. offer, which they, as foreseen, would view as an ultimatum their government could not agree to. This Hull proposal included some further input from the Treasury's White, who drafted yet another memo on the subject, forwarded to the State Department for its guidance. Foremost among the demands set forth in this memo was that the Japanese pull out of China entirely, or else pay the price for their refusal.

In all of this we can now also see the hidden hand of the KGB, which for reasons noted was concerned that there be no easing of Washington-Tokyo tensions. As disclosed later by KGB officer Vitaliy Pavlov, he had traveled to Washington some months before this to brief White on points to stress in preventing a U.S.-Japanese rapprochement. White, who didn't need much prompting, followed through by drafting and redrafting his tough-talking memo. As comparison would show, his demands concerning China and Indochina were in substance identical to Hull's proposal.

The parallels between the Pavlov-White talking points and the document presented by Hull, indeed, are striking. As revealed by Pavlov, he had emphasized to White that Japan must "halt its aggression in China and nearby areas" and "recall all of its armed forces from the mainland." [11] The Hull proposals were the same: "The government of Japan will withdraw military, naval, air and police forces from China and Indochina." That these stipulations were known by Hull to be unacceptable in Tokyo was indicated by his later statement that he had thus left matters "in the hands of [War Secretary] Stimson and [Navy Secretary Frank] Knox—the Army and the Navy."*[12]

Thus did policies promoted in official U.S. circles by White, Currie, and Lattimore dovetail with those advanced by the Sorge-Ozaki network in Japan—all converging toward the result that there would be no American-Japanese rapprochement and, even more to the point, no Japanese attack on Russia. The meaning of it all from the Soviet angle would be summed up by Pavlov, who said his goal in dealing with White had been to "prevent or at least complicate any decision by Japanese militarists to attack our Far Eastern border and stop Tokyo's Northward expansion." As for White himself, Pavlov added, he "well understood that in shielding us from Japanese aggression in the Far East, he would help strengthen the Soviet Union in the face of the threat in Europe."† (Despite this, Pavlov contended that White wasn't acting as a Soviet agent.)[13]

There is no way of telling whether Pearl Harbor would have happened anyway absent these machinations, as there were other forces at work pushing toward Japanese-American confrontation, a clash implicit in much that had preceded (particularly the oil embargo). Nor is there any indication in this history that the Soviets knew Pearl Harbor would be Japan's intended target. From

---

* The Army Pearl Harbor board that eventually reviewed this sequence concluded that the Hull proposals amounted to "touching the button" that had triggered the Pacific warfare. As the board expressed it, "the action of the Secretary of State in delivering the counterproposals of November 26, 1941, was used by the Japanese as the signal to begin the war by the attack on Pearl Harbor."

† Pavlov in this discussion further stated that White in so acting had performed as an American patriot—neglecting to note that the blow evaded by Russia would be launched instead against the United States.

a Moscow perspective, the important thing was that Japan strike south rather than north against the Russians. Where the southern blow was struck would have been, comparatively speaking, a matter of indifference.

Of interest on the American side of things was the emphasis placed throughout by leftward spokesmen on the well-being of China and the urgent need for the United States to stand firm for the gallant Chiang Kai-shek. According to such as White, Lattimore, Currie, and Edward Carter, there could be no truce with Tokyo because this would have been disloyal to our ally Chiang, who was leading a "heroic" resistance against Japan's aggression. But a few years later, when Chiang was no longer of any value to Moscow and was fending off a Red rebellion, these onetime admirers would become his most virulent critics.

Significant also was the degree of collaboration exhibited by this heterogeneous cast of players. Sorge, Ozaki, and company in Tokyo, White and Currie in Washington, and Lattimore in Chungking among them had most of the bases covered. This harmonization becomes the more comprehensible when we note that all these people were part of a global apparatus that agitated Far Eastern issues—the most visible manifestation of which was the IPR. Thus numerous members of the Sorge ring—Agnes Smedley, Guenther Stein, Chen Han Seng, Ozaki, and Saionji—were linked to the IPR in one fashion or another, while similar interactions would be apparent among the U.S. contingent. Lattimore, Currie, and White all had IPR connections, were well-known to one another, and were of pro-Soviet outlook. It was obviously a far-flung operation, well positioned to influence events in Asia. Its successes in struggles yet to come would be many and important.

8.

THE ENEMY WITHIN

Though extensive, Communist penetration of the federal government in the 1930s was but prologue to the vast infiltration that would occur during World War II, when the Soviets were our allies against the Nazis and pro-Moscow views were pervasive in official U.S. circles.

Among other effects, such Soviet-friendly wartime attitudes trumped earlier legal safeguards against hiring Reds for federal office, and in some cases dictated efforts to recruit them. Most notably, high-level military orders would be issued that "mere membership" in the Communist Party wasn't a bar to commissions in the military or access to restricted official data. The rationale for these decrees was that we couldn't ban CP members from holding federal jobs while the number-one Communist power in the world was fighting as our "noble ally." (See chapter 10.)

Given that background, it should hardly be surprising that a sizable crew of Communists, pro-Reds, and Soviet agents would wind up on official wartime payrolls. It would have been far more surprising if they hadn't. Based on what we know today, it appears that hundreds of such people—possibly thousands—got hired by the government in the early to mid 1940s, reinforcing the already numerous corps of agents named by Chambers in the prewar era. As seen, the first revelations of this further penetration were supplied in November 1945 by defecting Soviet courier Bentley. Her disclosures picked up where those of Chambers ended, though there were multiple overlaps between the rosters that the two provided.

In other respects as well, Bentley's allegations weren't totally new to the FBI, which had been keeping watch on pro-Red suspects in other investigations, especially of Communist efforts to infiltrate the atomic energy project in the early 1940s and the *Amerasia* case, which would develop in the spring of 1945 (see chapter 18). In the wake of Bentley's revelations, the Bureau laid on a dragnet investigation of her people, combining the leads that she provided with findings from these earlier inquests. The net result was a startling picture of the Communist penetration that had developed in the war years. This was summed up in a spring 1946 memo from FBI special agent Guy Hottel to FBI Director Hoover, as follows:

> *It has become increasingly clear in the investigation of this case that there are a tremendous number of persons employed in the United States government who are Communists and who strive daily to advance the cause of Communism and destroy the foundations of this government. . . . Today nearly every department or agency of this government is infiltrated with them in varying degree. To aggravate the situation, they appear to have concentrated most heavily in those departments which make policy, particularly in the international field, or carry it into effect . . . [including] such organizations as the State and Treasury departments, FEA, OSS, WPB, etc. . . .*[1]

This grim assessment would be confirmed two years later by the so-called Gorsky memo, named for Anatoly Gorsky, the KGB rezident operating out of the Soviet Washington embassy in the 1940s. As recorded by KGB defector Alexander Vassiliev, Gorsky in December 1948 advised Moscow of a series of Red intelligence

---

* FEA—Foreign Economic Administration; OSS—Office of Strategic Services; WPB—War Production Board.

failures caused by the Chambers-Bentley defections, plus revelations from two other former Communists, Louis Budenz and Hede Massing. These renegades, said the memo, had blown the cover of numerous agents with whom the Soviets were working. All told, Gorsky named upwards of sixty people who had been compromised, of whom more than forty had been holding federal office. The names he provided, with affiliations, included the following:

Alger Hiss, State Department
Donald Hiss, Interior Department
Henry A. Wadleigh [Julian], State Department
F. V. Reno, Aberdeen Proving Grounds
Henry Collins, Department of Agriculture
William W. Pigman, Bureau of Standards
Lee Pressman, CIO [formerly Agriculture Department]
Noel Field, State Department
V. V. Sveshnikov, War Department
Harry White, Treasury Department
G. Silverman, Air Force
Harold Glasser, Treasury Department
Laurence Duggan, State Department
Franz Neumann, OSS/State Department
Harry Magdoff, Commerce Department
Edward Fitzgerald, Commerce Department
Charles Kramer, Senate Staff
Donald Wheeler, OSS/State Department
Allan Rosenberg, FEA [Foreign Economic Administration]
Stanley Graze, OSS/State Department
Gerald Graze, War Department
Charles Flato, FSA [Farm Security Administration]
Gregory Silvermaster, Treasury Department
Lauchlin Currie, White House
Frank Coe, Treasury Department

Bela Gold, Commerce Department
Sonia Gold, Treasury Department
Irving Kaplan, Treasury Department
Solomon Adler, Treasury Department
Ludwig Ullman, War Department
David Weintraub, UNRRA [United Nations Relief and
    Rehabilitation Administration]
Maurice Halperin, OSS/State Department
Duncan Lee, OSS
Helen Tenney, OSS
Ruth Rivkin, UNRRA
Bernard Redmont, State Department
Robert Miller, State Department
Joseph Gregg, State Department
William Remington, Commerce Department
Julius Joseph, OSS
Willard Park, State Department[2]*

As may be seen from analysis of this roster, most of the Gorsky cases had indeed been named by Chambers-Bentley, who between them had thus exposed several dozen Soviet agents in official positions. Of the Chambers group made known to Berle (supplemented in other Chambers statements) we find, for example, the Hiss brothers, Currie, Adler, Pressman, Duggan, and Frank Coe, to name an influential handful. From the list of Bentley suspects the Gorsky memo supplied confirming data on White, Silvermaster, Glasser, Maurice Halperin, Robert Miller, Harry Magdoff, Donald Wheeler, and numerous others. The memo thus indicates, as do further available data, that the disclosures of the defecting Communists were very much on target.

---

* Nongovernmental operatives named in the Gorsky memo are excluded from this listing.

Of interest also is that certain of the Soviet contacts thus named were still holding down official jobs as late as 1948, the year that Gorsky penned his memo, three years after Bentley made her disclosures to the FBI, and almost a decade after Chambers talked to Berle. These included Adler at the Treasury, Franz Neumann at the State Department, William Remington at Commerce, and Coe at the International Monetary Fund, making up a significant foursome. So, despite the fact that Gorsky considered them to have been compromised by the defections, this didn't seem to be enough, measured by security standards of the day, to get them off official payrolls.

(A further point worth noting is that the people Gorsky named weren't Moscow's only secret U.S. contacts. As suggested by Gorsky's statement that he had "avoided renewing ties with agents who hadn't been exposed," the Chambers-Bentley people weren't the total story. This matched their own assertions that there were other Soviet rings in existence with which they weren't personally connected.)

Also a conspicuous feature of Gorsky's list was the appearance of numerous suspects from temporary wartime units thrown together at the outset of the fighting. These agencies were assembled in a hurry, with little or no attention to anti-Red security vetting, and so were easy targets for penetration. This was most obviously true of the Office of Strategic Services (OSS) and Office of War Information (OWI), which were by all accounts the most heavily infiltrated of the wartime bureaus, though the Board of Economic Warfare (later called the Foreign Economic Administration) ran a close third in this unusual competition.

The importance of OSS and OWI in Cold War context was that, along with the military intelligence units, they were relied on by U.S. officials for supposedly impartial, accurate data about what was happening in the war zones, who was doing what against the Axis, and who thus should receive support from the United

States and other of the Allies. The activities of OSS were especially crucial in this respect, as this service, among its several functions, worked with guerrillas and other elements overseas to promote resistance to enemy forces.

Little was known about OSS at the time, because like its successor, the Central Intelligence Agency, it was by its nature ultrasecret, engaging in clandestine actions of all types around the globe, presumably unknown to the enemy but also unknown to Congress and the American public. However, we now have a fair amount of information about the service, the people in it, and what some of them were up to. What this tells us, in a nutshell, is that there was indeed a substantial Communist penetration of OSS, and that this had considerable impact on the course of policy in the war years and the Cold War struggle that would follow.

The scope of this infiltration is suggested again by the Gorsky memo, as no fewer than seven of the people named in it (Franz Neumann, Donald Wheeler, Stanley Graze, Maurice Halperin, Duncan Lee, Helen Tenney, and Julius Joseph) had been OSS employees. Four of these in turn (Neumann, Wheeler, Halperin, Graze) would migrate to the State Department when the war concluded. Among the others, based on the evidence supplied by Bentley, the most influential seems to have been Duncan Lee, a ranking OSS official, who turns up often in the chronicles of the FBI and the annals of *Venona*.

As described by Bentley, Lee was important in his own right, but even more so because he was a top assistant to General William "Wild Bill" Donovan, commanding officer of OSS, and thus privy to confidential data that came to Donovan's office. A prime example of this access was a secret list that, per *Venona*, Lee had given the Soviets in September 1944, indicating what U.S. security forces knew about Red penetration of the service, making it possible for the KGB to take preventive action to protect its agents.

Alleged Communists at OSS

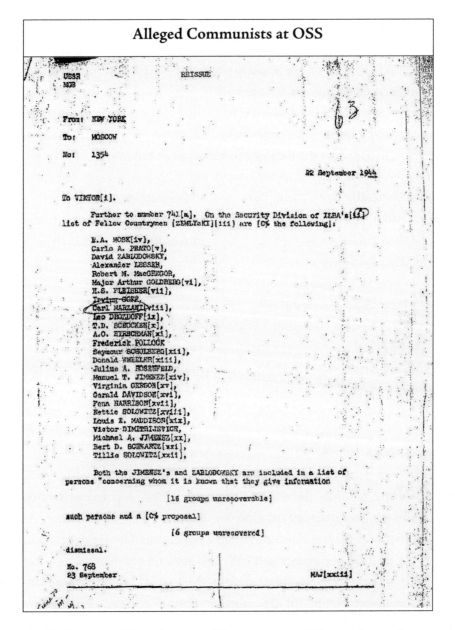

From: NEW YORK

To: MOSCOW

No: 1354

22 September 1944

To VIKTOR[i].

Further to number 741.[a]. On the Security Division of ILBA's[ii] list of Fellow Countrymen [ZEMLYaKI][iii] are [C% the following]:

E.A. MOSK[iv],
Carlo A. PRATO[v],
David ZABLODOWSKY,
Alexander LESSER,
Robert M. MacGREGOR,
Major Arthur GOLDBERG[vi],
H.S. PLEISHER[vii],
Irving GORE,
Carl MARZANI[viii],
Leo DROZDOFF[ix],
T.D. SCHOCKEN[x],
A.O. HIRSCHMAN[xi],
Frederick POLLOCK
Seymour SCHULBERG[xii],
Donald WHEELER[xiii],
Julius A. ROSENFELD,
Manuel T. JIMENEZ[xiv],
Virginia GERSON[xv],
Gerald DAVIDSON[xvi],
Fena HARRISON[xvii],
Nettie SOLOWITZ[xviii],
Louis E. MADDISON[xix],
Victor DIMITRIJEVICH,
Michael A. JIMENEZ[xx],
Bert D. SCHWARTZ[xxi],
Tillie SOLOWITZ[xxii],

Both the JIMENEZ's and ZABLODOWSKY are included in a list of persons "concerning whom it is known that they give information

[16 groups unrecoverable]

such persons and a [C% proposal]

[6 groups unrecovered]

dismissal.

No. 768
23 September

MAJ[xxiii]

The "unredacted" list of suspected Soviet agents and Communists in the U.S. Office of Strategic Services during World War II, compiled by OSS security staffers, provided to the Soviets by an inside contact. In the version of this message published in the *Venona* papers, all the names but one were blacked out by official censors. (*Source: OSS records, National Archives*)

This list of OSS suspects would be featured in the *Venona* decrypts, but as often happens in such cases all the names but one (Donald Wheeler) were blacked out by official censors. However, an unredacted copy of the list appears in OSS records at the National Archives, and various of the names provided there are suggestive. As recorded by Duncan Lee, the "fellow countrymen" (Communists) at OSS identified by the security forces were as follows:

E. A. Mosk	Seymour Schulberg
Carlo A. Prato*	Donald Wheeler
David Zablodowsky	Julius A. H. Rosenfeld
Alexander Lesser	Manuel T. Jimenez
Robert M. MacGregor	Virginia Gerson
Major Arthur Goldberg	Gerald Davidson
H. S. Fleisher	Fena Harrison
Irving Goff	Nettie Solowitz
Carl Marzani	Louis E. Maddison
Leo Drozdoff	Victor Dimitjevich
T. D. Schocken	Michael A. Jimenez
A. O. Hirschman	Bert D. Schwartz
Frederick Pollock	Tillie Solowitz[3]

Why the security sleuths named these people and not others on currently available information we have no way of knowing. As shown by collateral data, there were numerous Communists, pro-Reds, and Soviet agents at OSS who weren't on this roster—Lee himself being an obvious example, Maurice Halperin being another, Franz Neumann yet another. This of course simply meant the security forces couldn't know everything they would have liked to. Conversely, there were people on the list—for instance, future Supreme Court justice Arthur Goldberg—concerning whom there

---

* So given in the memo. The name was actually "Carlo á Prato."

is no known evidence for such suspicion. But there were others on the roster about whom a good deal would be learned through independent sources.

Thus Carlo á Prato would show up in discussion of security issues at OWI, sister agency of OSS, as brought out in the inquests of Congress. David Zablodowsky, Alexander Lesser, and Carl Marzani, like others noted, would move from OSS to State when the war was over. (Marzani would one day become famous as a Cold War figure, convicted in federal court for falsely denying his Red connections.) Zablodowsky, Marzani's sidekick at both OSS and State, later moved on to the United Nations. As his case suggests, the suspects were tenacious, well connected, and skilled at maneuver, and thus survived many changes and vicissitudes to stay on official payrolls.

Security problems at the Office of War Information were similar to those at OSS, arguably as bad in terms of numbers and more visible during the war because of OWI's more public mission. The similarities stemmed from the common hectic conditions in which the units were founded and the fact that both were initially part of a single agency under Donovan, called the Coordinator of Information. However, as OSS-style clandestine functions and OWI's public propaganda didn't fit together very well, the units would be subdivided, OWI being spun off as an independent outfit in 1942.

Because of its relatively high profile, OWI drew the sort of notice in the war years that OSS generally speaking didn't. Members of Congress and some outside observers would lodge complaints about allegedly pro-Communist staffers at OWI and asserted pro-Red slanting of its propaganda efforts. Representative Martin Dies (D-TX), of the Committee on Un-American Activities, Representative John Lesinski (D-MI), and Representative Fred Busbey (R-IL) took to the House floor to list OWI staffers with radical leftist backgrounds. In 1943 spokesmen for the AFL and CIO said the OWI official in charge of labor matters was of radical outlook and that he slanted coverage of workplace issues in favor of the Communist interest. Likewise, representatives of European exile governments charged that OWI broadcasts about their homelands were laced with pro-Red propaganda.[4]

While we don't have rosters for OWI like those provided for OSS by Lee and Gorsky, we do have a fair amount of information about some of the OWI divisions. Prominent in this respect was the Pacific office, headquartered in San Francisco. Based on a combination of tips and surveillance, the FBI in 1942–44 was, as noted, monitoring Communist efforts to infiltrate the atomic energy project, originally based at the University of California at Berkeley. The Soviet ring trying to penetrate the project was run by the KGB agent Gregori Kheifetz of the Russian consulate in San Francisco and the wealthy American Communist Louise Bransten, a resident of that city.

In this early 1940s probe, the FBI found the Kheifetz-Bransten group had frequent contacts with OWI personnel, including West Coast staffers Robin Kinkead and Philip Lilienthal and filmmaker Charles A. Page. Also drawing notice from security forces were OWI ethnic Chinese employees Chew Hong and Chi Kung Chuan, protégés of Owen Lattimore of the San Francisco unit, though attached to the office of Lattimore's OWI colleague Joseph Barnes in New York City. Lattimore himself would eventually be the target of an FBI investigation, as would Barnes, who was found by the Bureau to be in contact with the Kheifetz-Bransten combine. Once more, a wide-ranging operation with multiple interactions among the players.[5]

Still other OWI inquiries by Congress and executive security forces would reveal numerous such connections. Manning the Italian desk was Carlo á Prato, who, as seen, would show up on the roster of OSS "fellow countrymen" provided to the Soviets by Duncan Lee. The principal influence on the Polish desk was said by the FBI to be the naturalized Polish-American Oscar Lange, who after the fall of Poland would go on the payroll of the Red regime there. A comparable role was played in Yugoslav affairs by Louis Adamic, an indefatigable champion of the Communist leader who went by the nom de guerre of Tito. The main influence on the German desk was reportedly émigré Paul Hagen (né Karl Frank), a sometime member of the German Communist Party—with which, however, he said he had broken (see below).[6]

OWI would be of further interest as its history revealed some of the unusual methods by which the infiltration happened. Because of its global mission, the agency needed staffers who could speak and write the languages of foreign nations, read their literature, and know something of their cultures. This often meant utilizing émigrés, which presented a problem under then-existing law that barred hiring aliens as federal employees. The answer to this dilemma was supplied by a private group called Short Wave Research Inc., which had employed Bentley suspect Helen Tenney in OSS-related work before that agency and OWI divided.

The value of Short Wave Research from the standpoint of OWI was that, as a private entity, it could hire foreign nationals as the agency at that time could not. These employees would be put to work at scriptwriting, translating, editing, and broadcasting as Short Wave staffers, though on the premises of OWI. Short Wave would then bill OWI for services rendered, taking a 10 percent commission. As shown in testimony to Congress, roughly 60 percent of the foreign nationals performing tasks for OWI were brought in by this method. (Later, when the law was changed, many would go to work for OWI directly.)[7]

By this convoluted process, Short Wave would become a kind of trapdoor for entry into the federal workforce, not unlike the National Research Project of the 1930s as described by Chambers. Another factor in the equation was a related private outfit called the International Coordination Council, closely linked to Short Wave by common officers and sponsors. This group would bring into the country foreign nationals who were then hired for Short Wave projects on behalf of OWI. The Coordination Council, Short Wave, and OWI together thus formed a kind of pipeline by which alien workers could be recruited, imported into the United States, and in effect placed on the federal payroll.

This remarkable series of cutouts would draw the notice of the FBI when it began looking into Bentley's allegations about former OSS employee Tenney. Among other things, the Bureau found, Tenney's supervisor in OSS-related tasks had been one Marya Blow, née Mannes, who worked with Short Wave in its original OSS incarnation and again in conjunction with OWI. Delving back into its security records, the Bureau further discovered that, "according to a New York file, 100 59703, it was ascertained that one Maria Mannes was a member of the Greenwich Village Club, First and Second districts, of the Communist Political Association of Manhattan."[8]

A Bureau investigation revealed as well that Mannes-Blow was linked to the German émigré Hagen (Karl Frank), who, in the interlocking fashion common in these circles, was also among her associates at the Coordination Council. Like Mannes-Blow, Hagen was a mysterious figure. By his own account he had been a member of the German Communist Party for a decade (1919–29) and was a friend of the Soviet agent Gerhart Eisler. Questioned about these linkages, Hagen said he had broken with the Communists in Germany and set up his own competitive group there, though when and how this occurred were unclear. (He also said he had steered away from Communists when he came to the United States, but according to FBI surveillance of his activities this was untruthful.)[9]

The Bureau also discovered that Hagen had been assisted in obtaining his entry visa into the United States by White House staffer Lauchlin Currie, who appeared as a witness in Hagen's behalf and vouched for him as someone not inimical to security interests. As we know that Currie himself was a Soviet asset, this endorsement of the émigré seems less than reassuring. The same might be said of Franz Neumann, who according to Hagen could likewise vouch for his bona fides. Since Neumann too appears in *Venona* and the Gorsky memo as a Soviet asset, his vouching for Hagen would seem to be about as persuasive as that of Currie.

An additional player in these maneuvers, already introduced herein, was Edward Carter, like Marya Mannes and Hagen a director of the tightly interlocking Coordination Council, and the person who had introduced the émigré to Currie. The ubiquitous Carter was also head of the Russian War Relief and, more famously, the Institute of Pacific Relations. This leads us to a final (for now) serendipitous angle of the story, as OWI's Joseph Barnes had worked with Carter at IPR before going on to a career in journalism and federal service. And it was Barnes—identified as yet another strategically placed Communist agent by both Louis Budenz and Whittaker Chambers—who would negotiate OWI's contract with Short Wave Research and Mannes.[10] By such ingenious methods did things get done behind closed doors at certain U.S. agencies of the war years.

9.

FRIENDS IN HIGH PLACES

While pro-Moscow elements were infiltrating the government at ground level, related influences were working in the upper regions, exerting pressure downward on the lower echelons of power. Between them, these converging forces made for wartime policy that was pro-Soviet in the extreme and would stay that way for a considerable time after the fighting had concluded.

The most obvious and most powerful influence of this nature was the President himself, whose curious notions about Soviet dictator Stalin, the Soviet system, and the proper way of dealing with the Russians have been noted. Roosevelt stated his views about these matters often, practiced them at Teheran and Yalta, and promoted them in other ways, including his choice of White House staffers and the people he took with him to the wartime summits.

Also to be included among pro-Red policy influences at the top were the President's wife and the unusual but effective role she played in pushing forward radical causes. Her leverage was wielded mostly at the retail level, involving random lesser appointments and minor favor seekers, rather than larger geopolitical questions. But the net impact of her advocacy—prompted and aided by a numerous crew of activists with whom she consorted—was in the same direction.*

---

* Mrs. Roosevelt, as her admirers often noted, was herself a "progressive" of some standing, apart from her marriage to FDR, and by most accounts was a constant advocate with him for leftward causes. She was in particular interested in domestic welfare projects and partial to young radical activists whose purposes were less well-meaning than her own.

And, of course, no such compilation could possibly omit Vice President Henry Wallace, arguably the most prominent pro-Soviet political figure of the time, as shown by his later emergence as White House candidate of the Communist-dominated Progressive Party. Though considered an oddball even in left-wing circles and seemingly not a policy influence on major issues, Wallace by his position nonetheless was able to give aid and comfort to other U.S. officials who worked in favor of pro-Red causes.

In terms of White House staffing, by far the most important member of the Roosevelt team, in this respect and others, was the President's longtime aide and crony, Harry Hopkins. For much of his tenure in Washington, Hopkins held no cabinet post, but for the better part of a decade was Roosevelt's most powerful adviser. So close was he to the President, indeed, that for three-plus years he actually resided at the White House. That's as good as high-level access gets, and during most of the wartime era no cabinet member could compete with him for influence.*

Hopkins's unique position, literally at the President's elbow, made it the more consequential that he held pro-Soviet views of the most fervent nature. We had a glimpse of these in an earlier chapter, when he declared to a pro-Russian rally that "nothing shall stop us from sharing with you all that we have. . . ." As overall director of the Lend-Lease program extending aid to America's wartime allies, and in other foreign dealings, he would back those words with action. Throughout the war years, Moscow had no better official U.S. friend than Hopkins.

Hopkins had an unusual background for involvement in world affairs, since his prewar experience was in the field of domestic

---

* The cabinet member who came the closest was Treasury Secretary Morgenthau, a New York neighbor and personal friend of FDR. However, as Morgenthau and Hopkins were allies on issues involving the Soviet Union and wartime diplomacy, this linkage would in all likelihood have enforced the Hopkins influence, rather than providing competition.

welfare. A native of Iowa, and a 1912 graduate of Grinnell College, he would thereafter register as a member of the Socialist Party and support its candidates for office. In the latter 1920s and early '30s, he would become a social worker/executive in New York, where his path first crossed with that of New York governor FDR. One of those with whom Hopkins was connected at this era was his mentor and longtime friend Joseph Kingsbury, a social worker/ executive also, one with a considerable history of Communist front involvement (defending, for example, the Communist Party USA and its Soviet sponsors). It was the kind of association Hopkins would continue in 1933 when the New Deal brought him to Washington to pursue relief efforts at the federal level.*[1]

The new appointee's background in welfare work made him a natural for disbursing dollars in the New Deal setup, and he soon became famous for the speed with which he moved money out the door and the volume at which he moved it. It was his talent in this respect that first commended him to FDR, and made his later transition to the global stage seem fairly natural also when Lend-Lease became a major wartime program. In this new endeavor, Hopkins showed he could dispense American aid even more lavishly overseas than on the home front.

Though first conceived as a way of helping England against the Nazis, Lend-Lease under Hopkins would increasingly be conducted for the benefit of Moscow, with British (and American) interests tagging after. An instructive tale to this effect would be told

---

* Among those with whom Hopkins dealt in Washington were some of the "study group" personnel considered in chapter 6. Specifically, he would connect up with such U.S. officials as then-secret Communist Lee Pressman, inveterate Red front activist Gardner Jackson, and Agriculture official Paul Appleby (a Grinnell classmate), who like Pressman was also an ally—per the State Department's security chief—of the Soviet agent Alger Hiss. As we have seen, members of this group were proficient at networking, hiring each other, furnishing each other with recommendations, and backstopping one another when questions were raised about security matters.

by Army Air Corps Major George Racey Jordan, in charge of war-time shipments to Russia via an air base in Montana. Jordan described the manner in which Soviet operatives in the United States demanded priority treatment and other privilege, and when U.S. officials weren't quick to comply, invoked the name of Hopkins. When this happened, Jordan testified, they got their way posthaste, no further questions asked about it.

Especially memorable in Jordan's account were massive shipments to Russia of official U.S. documents, running to many thousands of pages, concerning technical and scientific matters far in excess of Lend-Lease requirements. Among these, said Jordan, were papers containing such expressions as "uranium" and "heavy water," phrases that had no meaning for him in 1944 but would mean a great deal the following year when nuclear weapons were used against the Japanese. (Jordan further testified—backed by official bills of lading—to physical shipments of uranium-235 to Russia.)

The most shocking Jordan testimony concerned specifications he had seen involving an installation at Oak Ridge, Tennessee, a supersecret wartime site for work on atomic weapons. The specs were accompanied by a note reading, "_____ had a hell of a time getting these away from Groves." The blank space was for the name of the individual who obtained the documents (too smudged, according to Jordan, to be legible), and "Groves," as later revealed, a reference to General Leslie Groves, head of the wartime atom project. The cover note was signed "H.H.," which Jordan concluded from past encounters was Hopkins.*[2]

Jordan's 1949 testimony about all this was contested as a smear,

---

* A sidebar of Jordan's story involved a State Department official named John Hazard, an ally and friend of Hopkins. According to Jordan, when he approached Hazard to get assistance in curtailing the shipments to the Russians, Hazard would endorse the Hopkins view of unconditional aid for Moscow.

but fit with what was later learned about Lend-Lease, the nuclear program, and the views of Hopkins. At numerous other junctures, when policy toward Russia was in the balance, Hopkins invariably and emphatically came down on the side of Moscow. A notable instance was the case of Poland, which had been the casus belli of war in Europe when it was invaded by Hitler and his then-ally Stalin. Subsequently, when the Nazis invaded Russia and Stalin perforce became an ally of the West, he insisted that he be allowed to keep the Polish territory he seized in league with Hitler. In pressing this claim, he also sought to liquidate elements in Poland (as in other captive nations) that could have contested his mastery of the country. In all such disputes that we know of, Hopkins would line up with Stalin.

A striking episode to this effect concerned the fate of several thousand captive Polish officers murdered early in the war and buried in Russia's Katyn Forest—a crime we know was in fact committed by the Russians. When the Polish government in exile requested a Red Cross investigation of the murders, the Poles were denounced by Moscow and, in equally vehement terms, by Hopkins. His comment was that agitation on the issue was the work of rich landholders who owned estates in Poland—which was pro-Communist boilerplate, pure and simple.[3] (In keeping with such high-level views, proof of Soviet responsibility for the massacre would be concealed not only by the Russians but by the U.S. government, a cover-up that lasted into the Cold War era.)

The following year, Hopkins was instrumental in blocking U.S. and British aid to Polish fighters who at the instigation of the Russians had risen up against the Nazis occupying Warsaw. After encouraging the insurrection, the Soviets stood off from the battle and let the Nazis slaughter the resistance forces. It was at this time that Hopkins took it on himself to intercept cables intended for FDR that might have triggered Western efforts to aid the Polish fighters.[4] In similar vein, a key member of the Hopkins staff would hinder efforts by anti-Communist Polish-Americans to protest the communization of their ancestral country (see chapter 14).

On other European issues, Hopkins stood foursquare with pro-Soviet forces at the Treasury who conceived the so-called Morgenthau Plan for Germany, named for Secretary Henry Morgenthau Jr., which would have turned the defeated country into a purely agrarian nation. The leader of the pro-Red Treasury faction was Harry White, who had been active on behalf of Moscow in the run-up to Pearl Harbor. Now, as the war neared a conclusion, White worked with other pro-Red forces to devise draconian measures for the postwar German occupation. In this maneuvering, the records show, Hopkins was at one with the Treasury planners.[5] (This counter to the comments of Hopkins biographer Robert Sherwood, who incorrectly said Hopkins would have opposed the plans of Morgenthau and his people.)

Hopkins's endeavors along such lines would be conspicuous during the summits at Teheran and Yalta. Noteworthy at these meetings was the manner in which he turned against Churchill and the British, with whom he had earlier been cordial, and became a vocal partisan of Stalin. In this reversal, his stance matched that of Roosevelt, who adopted an increasingly hostile attitude toward London in his effort to placate Moscow. The change was even more pronounced in the case of Hopkins, who had gone to England in 1941 to size up the war situation for FDR, professing himself a friend of Britain in terms so maudlin Churchill was moved to tears of gratitude and joy.

By 1943, these pledges had apparently been forgotten, as Hopkins took to denouncing the British for "imperialism," "colonialism," and "reaction," spoke in glowing terms of Stalin, and announced in the prelude to Teheran, "we are going to be lining up with the Russians."[6] This proved an accurate forecast of American policy not only at Teheran and Yalta but of U.S. wartime diplomacy in general. An increasingly isolated Churchill would now have cause for tears of a different nature.

To read statements about these matters by Hopkins, FDR, and some historians of the era is to enter a mental world where reality counts for little and delusion is set forth as self-evident wisdom. The record is replete with comments by FDR and Hopkins about the need for the United States to stand firm against "colonialism" and "imperialism," hence to distance itself from Churchill and align with Stalin. In these assertions there appears no glimmer of awareness that Stalin and the Soviets were or could be guilty of "colonialism" or "imperialism." Such epithets were reserved by FDR and Hopkins, and their admirers, exclusively for the British.*[7]

Hopkins's pro-Soviet leanings would be on further display in the Yalta records, where his handwritten comments are available for viewing. Though seriously ill at the time of the meeting, he continued to ply his influence with FDR, who himself was mortally sick and susceptible to suggestion in ways that we can only guess at. After FDR had made innumerable concessions to Stalin, there occurred a deadlock on the issue of "reparations." At this point, Hopkins passed a note to Roosevelt that summed up the American attitude at Yalta. "Mr. President," this said, "*the Russians have given in so much at this conference I don't think we should let them down. Let the British disagree if they want—and continue their disagreement at Moscow* [in subsequent diplomatic meetings]."[8] (Emphasis added.)

One may search the Yalta records at length and have trouble

---

* Thus several decades later a biography of Hopkins would say that, at Teheran, Roosevelt "began to side with the Russians" and remarked that he "agreed one hundred per cent with Stalin in opposing Western colonialism"—with the exception of India (this for bargaining leverage with Churchill). Further, that "Churchill was still a stumbling block when it came to foreign policy," so it looked "as though the United States would wind up aligning itself with China and Russia against Britain and the other colonial powers." No hint in this discussion that Russia was or might have been a "colonial" power more deadly than the worst that was ever done by Britain.

finding an issue of substance on which the Soviets had "given in" to FDR—the entire thrust of the conference, as Roosevelt loyalist Sherwood acknowledged, being in the reverse direction.*

Even after the death of Roosevelt, Hopkins would continue in his familiar role of "reassuring" the Soviets of our compliance with their wishes. In the spring of 1945, he was sent by the newly sworn-in President Truman as a special envoy to Stalin, then pursuing the communization of Poland and other states of Eastern Europe. On this occasion, Hopkins took it upon himself to seal the doom of Poland for certain, on the off chance that it hadn't been completely sealed at Yalta.

When Stalin in his usual aggressive manner said the British did not want a "Poland friendly to the Soviet Union," Hopkins responded, also as usual, that the view of the American government was different: "that the United States would desire a Poland friendly to the Soviet Union, and in fact desired to see friendly countries all along the Soviet borders" (a formula that included, for example, Finland, the Baltic states, Rumania, and China).† To which Stalin replied, "if this be so we can easily come to terms regarding Poland."[9] Indeed they could, as the Soviets imposed a brutal Red regime in Poland and the United States stood back and let it happen.

The obvious net meaning of these episodes was that Hopkins was a zealous advocate for Stalin. That thought would gain further

---

* Some defenders of FDR have cited as an American "victory" the Soviets' willingness to take part in the United Nations, but this was on a par with other Soviet pledges that amounted to nothing—such as promises to hold free elections in Poland. Those elections never happened, there was never any prospect that they would, nor was there any likelihood that the United Nations would hinder Stalin, armed with the veto, from taking any action that he fancied. He was perfectly willing to make paper pledges for the future in exchange for solid power on the ground—knowing he could and would violate such pledges when he felt the need to.

† Also, in the Eastern/Middle Eastern regions, Afghanistan, Turkey, and Iran.

traction when the *Venona* decrypts were unveiled and other aspects of the record were made public. Among such revelations was a *Venona* entry concerning a Roosevelt/Churchill meeting in May 1943. In a report to the KGB, a Soviet contact identified as "No. 19" informed the Russians of what was said between the Western leaders in one of their private conversations. From this message, it appeared contact 19 was in the room when the leaders met, and scholars dealing with *Venona* concluded that this contact was Hopkins. As he was the main person-to-person link between the leaders, it was logical that he would have been in the room when they had their meeting. Less logical, from a U.S. standpoint, was that he would secretly report their talk to Moscow.[10]

More definite than surmises about No. 19 was the revelation of KGB defector Oleg Gordievsky that Hopkins had been named in Russia as a Soviet intelligence agent. In a book by British historian Christopher Andrew, Gordievsky was quoted as recalling a lecture by veteran KGB operative Iskhak Akhmerov, a longtime "illegal" in the United States operating under commercial cover. In this lecture, Akhmerov discussed his relationship with Alger Hiss and other American Soviet agents but said that "the most important Soviet war-time agent in the United States" was Hopkins. Akhmerov, said Gordievsky, had then discussed his contacts with Hopkins in the American capital city.[11]

These comments, while conforming to the pattern of Hopkins's behavior, were obviously contrary to accepted wisdom on such matters, and if taken in their literal meaning would have been the cause of shock and scandal. However, according to Andrew, Gordievsky later modified his account to say Akhmerov meant Hopkins was merely an "unconscious agent." This softening of the message would be repeated by Andrew and others in subsequent treatment of the matter.

In one version of this approach, it's argued that Hopkins was simply acting as a "back channel" to the Russians, maintaining informal East-West contact. But that explanation doesn't compute with the facts about Akhmerov and the workings of Soviet intelligence. If Hopkins were merely trying to maintain such contact, he could have done so through Soviet ambassadors Litvinov, Constantine Oumansky, or Andrei Gromyko, or members of the Soviet Purchasing Commission, all of whom were in the United States in legal fashion at one time or another, and with whom Hopkins could have had all the dealings that he cared to. Akhmerov, however, was an illegal operating under false cover and would not have revealed himself to Hopkins unless absolutely certain his secret KGB identity would be protected. So, whatever Hopkins's motivation, "unconscious agent" doesn't fit the picture.*

In dealing with such matters, Hopkins would be linked with other leaders of the New Deal regime who took a favorable view of Moscow. One such was Treasury Secretary Morgenthau, who was a Hopkins ally not only with regard to the postwar German occupation but on other issues involving Russia. Another, as seen in an earlier chapter, was former U.S. ambassador Joseph Davies, who continued to counsel FDR on issues relating to Russia in the war years, and along with Hopkins would play a similar role with President Truman when the latter ascended to the Oval Office.

In the White House itself, there were other staffers who shared Hopkins's regard for Stalin and whose pro-Soviet activities would earn them notice in *Venona* and other formerly secret records. The most prominent of these officials, mentioned in several places, was FDR executive assistant Lauchlin Currie, who handled the White House portfolio on China (while also dabbling in other matters) and who as revealed in now available backstage records was a Soviet spy and agent of influence for the Kremlin.

---

* Countervailing data on this subject—other than shock and outrage at the very mention of it—are few, but do exist. One is that Hopkins in 1940 was on the side of England, which in the era of the Hitler-Stalin pact wasn't the attitude of the Kremlin. It was in later years that Hopkins turned decisively against the British.

Less conspicuous than Currie, but important in his way, was Hopkins assistant David Niles, another denizen of *Venona*. The decrypts show him to have been a contact of the KGB and involved in a scheme to smuggle a husband-and-wife team of pro-Soviet illegals into Mexico. The decoded *Venona* message on this said the matter could be arranged by Niles, for a bribe of five hundred dollars. The message added that "around Niles there is a group of his friends who will arrange anything for a bribe . . . whether Niles takes a bribe himself is not known."[12] Apparently business of this sort was brisk, as the message referred to previous bribes to this group of people amounting to six thousand dollars.

In this connection a final Hopkins protégé should be mentioned, though he wasn't physically in the White House. This was Army Colonel Philip Faymonville, who at Hopkins's insistence had been posted as a U.S. Army attaché in Moscow, in charge of Lend-Lease supplies provided to the Russians. Based on what was later learned about him, Faymonville appears to have been among the most pro-Soviet of Hopkins's many U.S. helpers. The nature of his appointment, and the opposition that it sparked, are topics worthy of further notice.

10.

THE WAR WITHIN THE WAR

The pro-Soviet American policy that became dominant during World War II wasn't adopted without a struggle, though, given the powerful forces that imposed it, the odds were heavily stacked against would-be resisters. The fate of these naysayers would itself be a revealing aspect of the story.

At the outset of the war, the views of the dissenters were backed by anti-Communist laws and regulations stemming from the period of the Hitler-Stalin pact (lasting until June 1941, when the Nazis invaded Russia). During the twenty-two-month existence of the pact, Congress had viewed the two dictatorships and their agents as equal dangers, and federal law reflected this opinion. A prime example was a statute administered by the Navy that barred hiring Communists as radio operators on U.S. merchant vessels, since radio transmissions were a vital source of military data. Similar regulations involving the Army forbade commissions or access to restricted information for members of the Communist Party.

In the early months of World War II, orders began coming down from on high to overturn these standards. In May 1942, a decree was issued by the secretary of the Navy removing the radio operator ban and tying the change-over to the pro-Soviet outlook of the White House. The Navy order explained that "the President has stated that, considering the fact that the United States and Russia are allies at this time, and that the Communist Party and the United States effort were now bent toward our winning the war, the United States *was bound not to oppose the activities of the Communist Party. . . ."*[1] (Emphasis added.)

Thereafter a parallel order would be issued to the Army, saying membership in the Communist Party would no longer be a bar to commissions or access to restricted data. This edict said "no action will be taken that is predicated on membership in or adherence to the doctrine of the Communist Party *unless there is a specific finding that the individual involved has a loyalty to the Communist Party that outweighs his loyalty to the United States.*"[2] (Emphasis added.) In effect this meant that, absent proof of some overt disloyal act, there was no official taboo against having Communists in sensitive defense positions.

Officers who tried to buck these policy changes soon found they were fighting a losing battle. One such was Rear Admiral Adolphus Staton, who chaired a Navy board judging the qualifications of seagoing radio personnel in the war years. When Staton said that under the law he couldn't enforce the new decree on radio operators without a written order, others in the chain of command were reluctant to provide such a directive. The alternative arrived at was to abolish the Staton board altogether, its activities being described as "unnecessary paper work" that could be disposed of. Henceforth qualifications for radio operators would be handled directly by Assistant Secretary of the Navy Adlai Stevenson—who had proposed the changes to begin with.[3]

As for the Army, there would later be official hearings involving the notion that "mere membership" in the Communist Party was no longer a barrier to commissions. Discussing the treatment of those who objected to this reversal, Lieutenant Colonel John Lansdale, an Army security specialist, said he was the target of fierce hostility when he resisted. He was exposed, he said, to pressures "from military superiors, from the White House and from every other place, because I stopped the commissioning of 15 or 20 undoubted Communists. . . . I was being vilified, reviled and reviewed by boards because of my efforts to get Communists out of the Army and being frustrated by the blind, naïve attitude of Mrs. Roosevelt and those around her at the White House...."[4]

Lansdale's attribution of the policy switch to Mrs. Roosevelt and others at the White House would be echoed by State Department staffers who dealt with similar issues in the diplomatic service. Longtime Russia expert Charles E. Bohlen would comment in a memoir that one early purge of anti-Red officials and materials at State was imputed in the department to the influence of Mrs. Roosevelt and Harry Hopkins—though Bohlen could offer no specifics. (These and related issues at the State Department are discussed in chapter 19.)

Elsewhere in the government, the new policies would affect other civilian agencies also. Before the war, again reflecting views prevalent during the era of the Hitler-Stalin pact, Civil Service rules had barred both Communists and Nazis from holding federal office. As the Civil Service Commission explained in 1940, "if we find anybody has had any association with the Communists, the German Bund, or any other foreign organization of that kind, that person is disqualified immediately."[5] In pursuit of this decision, Attorney General Francis Biddle would circulate to federal agencies a list of Red front groups so that employee rosters could be checked for members.

In sync with the military changes then in progress, these Civil Service rules would in November 1943 be countermanded by a memo saying that not only were Communist activities and associations no longer a bar to federal employment, but that applicants henceforth could not even be asked about such matters. The memo stated, for instance, that "no reference should be made to any such organizations as the Abraham Lincoln Brigade [sponsored and manipulated by the Communist Party] or any other of the many Spanish relief groups [relating to the 1930s civil war in Spain]. Do not ask any questions about membership in the Washington Book

Shop [a Biddle-cited front group]. . . . Do not ask any questions regarding the type of reading matter read by the applicant. This includes especially *The Daily Worker* and all radical and liberal publications. . . ."[6]

While all this was going on, other strange events were unfolding that would further affect the issue of pro-Communist infiltration. As State Department security expert Ben Mandel informed the FBI, early in 1944 two Budget Bureau officials would make the rounds of federal agencies dealing with security matters—Civil Service, Office of Naval Intelligence, and G-2 of the Army—saying that their antisubversive investigations and files were no longer needed "as the FBI was already making such investigations." As with the abolition of Staton's Navy board, the rationale for the policy switch was the alleged need for greater economy and efficiency in federal operations.[7]

These recommendations were acted on promptly by both the Navy and the Army. In June 1944, antisubversive files maintained by the Office of Naval Intelligence would vanish from Navy offices in New York and Boston. That same month, orders were issued by the Pentagon to dismantle the G-2 intelligence files of the Army and disperse them to the archives, where they would have no everyday practical value. As testified by Army intelligence officer Colonel Ivan Yeaton, "the whole of G-2 was reorganized right in the middle of the war. . . . The records in every one of the branches were packed up and moved down to the basement. . . ."[8]

As would later come to view, Yeaton was a key player in many such internal battles. He was in particular knowledgeable about the Lend-Lease policies that would be testified to by Major Jordan (see chapter 9). As noted, Jordan said that colossal shipments of Lend-Lease supplies, including nuclear materials and data, were being ramrodded through to Russia, far in excess of wartime requirements, and that this was done at the instigation of Harry Hopkins. Though Jordan would be widely attacked when he made these statements, Yeaton was in a position to provide confirming testimony, and in a revealing memoir did so.

Ivan Yeaton was among the most experienced of U.S. officials on issues pertaining to the Soviet Union, having served in Russia at the era of the Bolshevik Revolution and thereafter as U.S. military attaché at our embassy in Moscow. A career Army officer, he held many other posts relevant to the Cold War, including a stint at the Pentagon intelligence shop in the early 1940s. Later he would be posted to China, where he dealt directly with Communist leaders Mao Tse-tung and Chou En-lai. In all these assignments, Yeaton specialized in gathering data concerning Communist goals and methods. His expertise was the greater since he had been professionally trained in dealing with such matters, and was proficient in speaking and reading Russian.

Yeaton's study of the Soviets and experience in Russia gave him a unique perspective on the wartime alliance with Moscow and would place him in direct and jarring conflict with Hopkins. The first episode to this effect occurred in July 1941, when Yeaton was serving in Russia and Hopkins traveled there to assure Stalin of U.S. support against the Nazis. Yeaton's job as attaché involved trying to get information on the progress of the war, the nature of German weapons and tactics, and other military data relating to the Nazis that would have aided the Soviets themselves if we were to help them in effective fashion.

However, like others who served in Moscow (Admiral William Standley, Major General John R. Deane), Yeaton said he could get no Soviet cooperation on such matters and was thus unable to perform his duties in proper fashion. Accordingly, when he met with Hopkins, he suggested that U.S. assistance be offered quid pro quo—American aid in exchange for Soviet information about the Germans. In Yeaton's telling, Hopkins turned this down flat.

In terms virtually identical to those FDR would later use with William Bullitt, Hopkins told Yeaton we would give the Soviets everything they wanted but for ourselves ask nothing. As Yeaton paraphrased the President's adviser: "We would furnish the Russians all possible military and economic assistance, *but* Lend Lease would never be used as a bargaining agency."

Yeaton then got further crossways with Hopkins when he voiced skepticism concerning the motives of Stalin. As the colonel recalled it, when he spelled out his negative view of Red behavior, Hopkins "suffered my monologue in silence, but when I impugned the integrity and methods of Stalin he could stand it no longer, and shut me up with an intense 'I don't care to discuss the subject further.'"[9]

A subdivision of the Lend-Lease dispute was the earlier-noted case of Philip Faymonville, an Army officer well-known to Yeaton and a favorite of Hopkins. Faymonville had preceded Yeaton as Moscow military attaché, and the two had much in common as students of the Russian language and Soviet affairs in general. The difference was that Faymonville was an avid fan of Stalin, worked closely with the commissars in the manner of Raymond Robins and Armand Hammer, and was withal a conduit for Soviet views and alleged data purveyed to U.S. officials as "intelligence" from Moscow.

As we now know, and seems to have been known at the time to Yeaton (though he didn't explicitly say so), Faymonville had been compromised in a "honey trap" scheme by the KGB and forced to serve the purposes of the Kremlin. (Whether these differed materially from his private purposes is uncertain.) Yeaton's references to Faymonville strongly hinted at this background, and said Faymonville was "irrefutably a captive of NKVD [KGB]." As Yeaton further noted, and would be confirmed by others, Faymonville was widely mistrusted in military circles because of his pro-Soviet opinions.[10]

All this made it the more significant that Hopkins was committed to Faymonville and would insist on sending him back to

Russia to handle Lend-Lease affairs at that end of the pipeline. Army Chief of Staff General George C. Marshall, who had made inquiries about Faymonville resulting in a lengthy and unfavorable FBI report, objected to the posting—thus placing the general in opposition to Hopkins, in most other cases his intramural ally. Hopkins, as he usually did, prevailed, and Faymonville would return to Russia, where according to then–U.S. ambassador Standley, he regularly undercut the admiral in dealings with the Moscow bosses.*[11]

A second major episode in which Yeaton ran afoul of Hopkins was the dismantling of the G-2 intelligence files, concerning which Yeaton would testify to Congress. As shown by FBI reports, this dismantling or "reorganization" was attributed by Army spokesmen to the influence of Hopkins. The dismantling would later be confirmed to members of the Senate by Lieutenant General Joseph McNarney, identified by Yeaton as another favorite of Hopkins.[12] Yeaton thus was opposed to Hopkins on two major issues—unlimited and unconditional aid to Moscow and the dismantling of antisubversive records of the Army. For officials of that era, such opposition to the most powerful member of the government under FDR was not a career enhancement.†

As will be seen hereafter, Yeaton was also a leading member of a group of Army intelligence experts who in 1945 put together

---

* As Faymonville was mistrusted by his military colleagues, reports to this effect were made known to Marshall, prompting the FBI investigation. The colonel undercut Ambassador Standley by dealing directly in Moscow with the Soviet bosses, without Standley's input or knowledge. This was also reminiscent of the role of Raymond Robins at the era of the revolution.

† In his memoir, Yeaton contended that his conflicts with Hopkins meant he would never rise above the rank of colonel—which he didn't. Others who suffered in similar fashion, as discussed by Yeaton, included Colonel John (Mike) Michela, who also served in the Moscow embassy and would try to combat the pro-Soviet influence exerted by Faymonville on American policy toward Russia.

an in-depth assessment of the war in Asia, the question of Soviet involvement there, and the wisdom of U.S. policy adopted at Yalta granting concessions to Stalin as the price of such involvement. However, in keeping with other episodes to be noted, this estimate would never make its way to policy makers, and for a considerable time would disappear entirely. (Nor was it evident, had the report reached higher levels, that it would have made much difference. As Yeaton commented, based on his G-2 experience: "The White House would tolerate no hint of disapproval of its U.S. Soviet policy. Critical papers [on] this subject would surely end in the waste basket.")*[13]

Yeaton's wartime intelligence duties at the Pentagon also brought him into direct contact with Marshall, resulting in a description of the chief of staff sharply different from that appearing in most histories of the era. In the usual treatments, Marshall is depicted as a man of sterling character, great intellect, and inspirational leadership qualities impressive to all who knew him. The Marshall described by Yeaton is far distant from this portrait—inattentive to intelligence data, rigid in preconceived opinions, imperious in dealings with subalterns.

Most to the point, the Marshall sketched by Yeaton is different from the strategic mastermind featured in other essays. Yeaton said he could never figure Marshall out or know whether intelligence briefings of the general meant a great deal or little, as Marshall's reaction to them seemed torpid and indifferent. The Yeaton memoir

---

* In addition to testifying about the G-2 imbroglio, Yeaton in his memoir would discuss other intelligence issues significant in the history of the Cold War. He noted the rise to eminence in Army intelligence ranks of Alfred McCormack, a civilian ally of Assistant War Secretary John McCloy who was given the rank of colonel in the war and assigned to high-level intelligence duties. Yeaton considered McCormack an example of the politicization of the Army, a concern highlighted in the postwar era when McCormack was transferred to the State Department to handle intelligence matters there. In this role he would attract the hostile notice of State Department security staffers in terms similar to those employed by Yeaton.

does, however, quote Army intelligence chief General George Strong as exclaiming, after one such session with Marshall: "That is the dumbest man I ever briefed." [14]

This background would become acutely relevant in 1946, when Yeaton and Marshall were both in China and civil war was raging between the regime of Chiang Kai-shek and the Communist forces based at Yenan, in a far northwestern province. Yeaton was sent to Yenan to wrap up the so-called Dixie Mission of U.S. observers stationed there, concerning whom more later.* Marshall's task was to work out some kind of coalition between Chiang and the Communist rebels. And though it gets a bit ahead of the wartime story, brief notice of Yeaton's comments on postwar China is offered here as a significant aspect of his memoir.

Fact one as conveyed by Yeaton—confirmed by his immediate boss in China, Lieutenant General Albert Wedemeyer—was that Marshall's indifference to intelligence briefings would persist while he was in Asia. Yeaton recalled telling Marshall that the goal of uniting the Communists with Chiang Kai-shek was impossible, given the war to the death being waged by the opposing forces. As Wedemeyer would likewise recall, he told Marshall the same when the former chief of staff arrived in China. In neither case did Marshall accept the counsel he was given, instead preferring the views of Lieutenant General Joseph "Vinegar Joe" Stilwell, former commander of U.S. ground forces in China and a protégé of Marshall.

This Marshall-Stilwell linkage would prove fatal for Chiang Kai-shek, as Stilwell was a bitter enemy of the Nationalist leader and made no secret of his feelings. Yeaton noted that Stilwell's anti-Chiang opinions seemed to be shared in full by Marshall, and, since Marshall to a large extent held the fate of the country in his hands, this portended ill for China. As Yeaton remarked

---

* The term "Dixie Mission" was applied to U.S. officers assigned to Yenan as envoys to the rebels, in reference to Confederate rebels of the American Civil War.

to an associate at the time, "if Marshall ever had a chance to do Chiang in, God help him."[15]

In related comment, Yeaton discussed another Hopkins protégé (and friend of Philip Faymonville), John Hazard of the State Department. This was the official who reportedly dismissed the Lend-Lease concerns of Major Jordan, as noted in chapter 9, in essence preaching the Hopkins line that aid to Moscow should be unstinting, with no embarrassing questions asked about it. Hazard would voice similar views to Yeaton, confirming the latter's unfavorable view of Hopkins and those linked closely to him.*

From his dealings with numerous U.S. officials of pro-Soviet persuasion, Yeaton pieced together a diagram of the principal forces promoting Soviet interests in the guise of U.S. policy overseas.[16] This network, as he saw it, consisted of various individuals cited above, plus ambassador to Moscow Averell Harriman, who according to Yeaton acknowledged the evils of the Stalinist system but never would deal with Moscow in effective fashion. The Yeaton chart of pro-Soviet influentials under Hopkins appears as follows:

FDR

H.H.

John J. McCloy[†]	W. Averell Harriman
George C. Marshall	General "Cid" Spalding[‡]
Joseph T. McNarney	Philip Faymonville
	John Hazard

---

* Hazard would also figure in the China story as he was one of those assigned to accompany Vice President Henry Wallace on a Far Eastern journey that presaged the Marshall mission.

† As above noted, Assistant Secretary of War.

‡ An Army Lend-Lease official.

Based on his observations of this group, and his dealings with Hopkins on Lend-Lease issues, Yeaton reached a harshly negative judgment on the President's top adviser. "The Harry Hopkins mission to Moscow in July of '41," Yeaton wrote, referring to Hopkins's asserted refusal to stand up for U.S. interests, "gave me the greatest shock of my entire career. . . . From our first meeting I considered him disloyal to the trust that had been imposed on him. After learning of the manner in which he high handedly handled security at our end of the Alaska Siberian [Lend-Lease] pipeline, I changed it to perfidious or traitorous, if you like." [17]

This view was obviously congruent with the statement of Iskhak Akhmerov, quoted by Gordievsky, that Hopkins had functioned during the war as Moscow's principal "agent" in the United States. Whatever his motives, and whether he could plausibly be described as an "unconscious" agent, the pro-Soviet policies advanced by Hopkins would be of the same effect, and as calamitous for free-world interests.

11.

THE MEDIA MEGAPHONE

A main focus of this study has been the oft-neglected link between pro-Communist infiltration of the federal government on the one hand and calamitous policy outcomes on the other. As suggested in preceding chapters, both the infiltration and the policy impact in many cases were substantial.

The problem of official infiltration can't, however, be considered in a vacuum. There were other factors operative in the war years and Cold War era that affected American policy overseas, though the people wielding influence weren't then serving on official payrolls. (Some did serve in public office later.) These were chiefly members of the press corps, but also included significant players in academic institutions, lobby groups, civic organizations, and think tanks that exerted leverage on U.S. officials, members of Congress, and the attitudes of the public.

The importance of this outside activity was that it helped create a climate of opinion and set forth an alleged body of empirical data that prepared the way for pro-Red policy makers in federal office. Likewise, once a policy of such nature was adopted, sympathetic media spokesmen could help publicize and promote it, while attacking the views and reputations of people who wanted to move in other directions. On a host of issues, pro-Soviet elements in the government and their allies in the press corps thus worked together in effective fashion.

This relationship was in one sense natural, apart from ideological factors, as journalists and secret agents on official payrolls, viewed in purely procedural terms, had much in common. Both were in the information business, inquiring into esoteric matters, ferreting out data that were supposedly confidential, and sharing the results with outside parties. Such behavior on the part of journalists has usually been considered not only normal but praiseworthy, which meant that cover as a member of the press corps was made to order for Moscow's agents. It's noteworthy indeed that many Communist apparatchiks—including such notorious figures as Kim Philby and Richard Sorge—were ostensibly journalists by profession.

Likewise, when pro-Red government staffers were exposed for having passed information to Communists or Soviet handlers, a frequent alibi was that the officials thought the pro-Moscow contact was simply a journalist seeking "background." Such was the explanation provided, for instance, by Bentley suspect William Remington who allegedly thought he was merely sharing data with a member of the press corps. A similar rationale was offered by Alger Hiss in describing his linkage to Whittaker Chambers and by John Stewart Service in explaining why he passed official documents to pro-Red editor Philip Jaffe in the *Amerasia* scandal. (See chapter 18.)

In the related but more subtle matter of policy influence, there were explicitly Communist newspapers and periodicals that sought to affect the course of U.S. conduct on issues of concern to Moscow. The *Daily Worker* and *New Masses* were prominent cases, but there were others, including periodicals published by front groups such as the League for Peace and Democracy, American Friends of the Chinese People, and many more of like persuasion. The degree of influence exerted by the Communist media would have of course been doubtful, though the disguised nature of the front group publications arguably made them more persuasive than overtly Communist outlets.

More effective still were media figures in mainstream circles whose connections to the Communist Party and Soviet interests were totally unknown to the public, or if suggested by anti-Communist critics were discounted as smears and libels. Today we have a considerable body of information about such people, indicating that Communist and pro-Soviet penetration of the media was indeed extensive, and as in the case of government bureaus reached up to significant levels. It now appears that literally scores of allegedly non-Communist journalists were secretly connected to the Communist Party, the KGB, or Soviet propaganda organs. What follows is a sampler from this record.

While revelations about pro-Red journalists concern some of the major media of the era, the writer whose case has recently attracted the most attention, though famous in his way, was not for most of his career a big-media figure. He was the columnist who wrote under the name of I. F. Stone, whose doings have become an object of contention among authors dealing with Cold War issues. In the 1930s, Stone had been on the staff of the then-leftward *New York Post*, thereafter moving to the radical daily paper *P.M.*, and ultimately founding his own publication, *I.F. Stone's Weekly*. He was also the author of several books advancing leftward notions on Cold War matters. It was in his self-publishing incarnation that he became best known, developing something of a cult following in left-wing circles.

Decades later, in 1992, defecting former KGB general Oleg Kalugin revealed that Soviet intelligence had had "an agent" in the U.S. press corps—"a well known American journalist"—who had broken with the KGB on two occasions but had then resumed contact with Soviet handlers. Kalugin would confirm to Herbert Romerstein, coauthor of this study, that Stone was the agent referred to. That revelation matched closely with Stone's journalistic output, which included panegyrics to the Soviet dictator Stalin and other pro-Red disinformation—including the thesis that the Korean War of the early 1950s was instigated by the anti-Communist South rather than the Communists of the North, plus similar propaganda salvos in the 1960s during the war in Indochina.[1]

Kalugin's disclosures would later be confirmed in major part by data from *Venona* and the Vassiliev papers, which show Stone in contact with the KGB, discussing his off-and-on relationship with the Soviet bosses, including comments about possible financial compensation for his efforts. One KGB message said that, after such an episode in the 1930s, relations with him had "followed the channel of normal operational work," the meaning of which was that Stone was then functioning as a Soviet intelligence asset.[*2]

A second instance of secret KGB connection involved a periodical more prestigious than Stone's *Weekly*, and also longer lasting, since it is with us still today. This was the *New Republic*, a left-liberal magazine with a modest subscription base but read by many influential people in government and elsewhere. The journal was cofounded and in part owned by the affluent Willard and Dorothy Straight, prominent in early-twentieth-century progressive causes in the United States and England. Their role in launching the *New Republic* led to the employment there of family scion Michael, who would become editor of the journal and thus a somewhat consequential figure in political discourse of the late 1940s and early '50s.

Michael Straight's background of privilege made him distinctive in journalistic circles, where inherited wealth and social standing weren't, generally speaking, met with. Underscoring the difference was that Straight in the 1930s had attended England's venerable Cambridge University, where he was known for the comfortable income he enjoyed and the generosity of his spending.[†] Even more distinctive, as would later be revealed, he had also been recruited

---

[*] Stone would be identified as a contact of the KGB in both the *Venona* decrypts and the records transcribed by the defector Vassiliev. *Venona* shows Stone to have been engaged in discussions with KGB operatives about possible "supplementary income" for the propaganda services he rendered.

[†] Straight in the 1930s figured his annual income at fifty thousand dollars—an enormous figure in that era—from which he would contribute thousands of dollars to the Communist Party in both Britain and the United States.

there as a member of the Communist Party and Soviet agent, thus becoming a confrere of Guy Burgess, Donald Maclean, and Anthony Blunt, all also Communists and all also eventually revealed as Soviet agents. Straight had been enrolled in 1937 by spy king Blunt as an operative of the KGB, then sent back to the United States to do the Kremlin's bidding.

We know all this for sure because Straight would one day disclose it in a memoir, though there is reason to think his confession in many respects was less than candid. In it, he acknowledged his party membership and KGB recruitment, but indicated he had broken with the Soviets around the time of the Hitler-Stalin pact—exact date of his break uncertain—a claim some writers have accepted at face value, though there is documentary evidence to the contrary. More to the point, despite his allegedly early break with Moscow, Straight for years neglected to tell anyone about the Cambridge comrades, specifically about Guy Burgess, whom Straight knew to be working at the British embassy in Washington during the Korean War and undoubtedly sharing Anglo-American military secrets with his Soviet bosses.

It was only in 1963, when Straight was up for a federal job he knew would be vetted by the FBI, that he went to the authorities and told them of his Communist/Soviet agent background—an episode that led in turn to the identification of Blunt in England (whose Red connections weren't, however, made public until 1979). Add to this the fact that Straight was related by marriage to two other certified Soviet agents—Louis Dolivet and Gustavo Duran—concerning whom again he was not conspicuously forthcoming. Such was the backstage record of the respected editor of the *New Republic*, who regularly instructed its liberal readers on Cold War issues.[3]

At the opposite end of the journalistic spectrum, at least in terms of circulation numbers, was famed newspaperman Drew Pearson, whose sensational exposés in his syndicated column, appearing in hundreds of papers and widely broadcast radio show, made him a prominent and powerful figure. A Pearson specialty was attacking anti-Communist spokesmen of the day in the executive branch and Congress—though his targets included political figures in other disputed areas also. He was in a sense an equal-opportunity scandalmonger, though the ideological tilt of his column was markedly to the left.*

This ideological aspect is perhaps explained by the fact that not one but two of his legmen/reporters turned out to have been Communist Party members, according to sworn testimony and other official records. The better-known member of this duo was David Karr, who before his employment with Pearson had been a staffer at the *Daily Worker* and then at OWI—a sequence that, in view of material reviewed in chapter 8, may not be surprising to the reader. Karr's Communist connections would be confirmed by the disclosures of *Venona* and the testimony of former *Daily Worker* editor Howard Rushmore, who said he knew Karr at the *Worker* and had there given him assignments, and that Karr was a party member.[4]

Later in his career, Karr would be linked with the remarkable Moscow front man Armand Hammer, discussed in chapter 5, and in this phase of his activity continued to function as a contact of the KGB. Specifically, as reported by Russian sources, Karr in the 1970s was identified as a go-between linking the Soviet bosses in the Kremlin to then-senator Edward Kennedy and former senator John V. Tunney of California, the latter allegedly in search of business opportunities via Moscow.[5]

The second Pearson staffer to be revealed as a Communist Party member was less publicized than Karr, but named in equally definite fashion. This was Andrew Older, identified by FBI undercover operative Mary Markward as a member of the Communist Party in the District of Columbia—an identification later confirmed by yet

---

* Pearson was arguably the most famous journalist of his day, gauged in terms of total audience reached in print and via the airways, but was also one of the least respected in polite political-media circles.

another Pearson staffer, Jack Anderson, in his own memoir of the era. At one remove, Older also had an OWI connection, since his sister Julia, who took the Fifth Amendment when asked if she was a Communist Party member, had worked there before moving on to the United Nations. So exposé specialist Drew Pearson had at least two exposé-worthy skeletons in his closet, in the form of twin identified Communist agents Karr and Andrew Older.[6]

In the daily newspaper field, less widely read than Pearson but generally considered more reliable and dignified was the *New York Herald Tribune*. Now defunct as an American domestic journal (there remains a vestige in the *International Herald Tribune* overseas), the paper in its heyday ranked second only to the *New York Times* as a must-read for upscale New Yorkers. Of moderate Republican editorial outlook, the paper strove to keep up with or outdo the *Times* in its coverage of foreign issues.

What made all this significant in context was that, for several years, the foreign editor of the *Herald Trib* was Joseph Barnes, another one-time official at OWI, who as noted in a preceding chapter was involved in the complex maneuvers by which alien staffers were in effect placed on that agency's payroll. His main journalistic fame, however, occurred at the *Herald Trib*, where he would be a highly influential figure. Of interest therefore is that Barnes too would be identified under oath in congressional hearings (by ex-Communists Whittaker Chambers and Louis Budenz) as a Communist Party member.

Subsequently, Barnes would be named as well by Soviet defector Alexander Barmine as someone singled out in Russia as an agent of the Soviet GRU (military intelligence) by the head of that unit. All these identifications occurred in 1951 hearings of the Senate Internal Security Subcommittee concerning the previously noted Institute of Pacific Relations, a heavily infiltrated "agent of influence" operation dealing with affairs of Asia, where Barnes had worked before obtaining his media assignments. (Named by Barmine also as a Soviet intelligence asset was Barnes's IPR and OWI colleague Owen Lattimore, who though not a journalist by profession did for a period write a syndicated newspaper column.)*[7]

As suggested in our earlier treatment of IPR, there were other journalists connected to it in one way or another who helped advance pro-Communist interests. One such was Guenther Stein of the *Christian Science Monitor*, who as has been seen was a member of the Sorge ring in Shanghai and like Barnes an identified agent of Red intelligence. Yet another was Israel Epstein (married to Communist IPR staffer Elsie Fairfax-Cholmeley), who served as a stringer for the *New York Times* and was also identified in sworn testimony as a Communist/Soviet agent. Stein and Epstein would have more than journalistic influence on events, since both functioned as contacts and information sources for the diplomat John Service, who played an official and pivotal role in promoting the Communist cause in China.

Yet a third journalist with linkage to the IPR—and Service—was Mark Gayn, a Manchurian-born correspondent who wrote for *Collier's*, a mass-circulation magazine of the era. Gayn would later figure in the *Amerasia* scandal, as he consorted with that journal's pro-Communist editor Philip Jaffe, receiving confidential government data from Service. (In June 1945 Jaffe, Gayn, Service, and three others would be arrested by the FBI in connection with this data traffic, in what would be in some ways the most mysterious U.S. spy scandal of the Cold War. See chapter 18.)

Also part of the pro-Red media network, and perhaps the most influential of them all, was Edgar Snow, who wrote on Cold War–related matters for the *Saturday Evening Post*. Despite the conservative editorial stance of this popular periodical, Snow was able to disseminate through its pages a good deal of propaganda in favor of pro-Red causes. His most famous journalistic effort, and basis for

---

* Barmine testified that he had been told by General Ian Berzin, head of Soviet military intelligence, that Barnes and Lattimore were "our men," meaning operatives of the GRU, then called the Fourth Bureau of the Red Army.

his reputation, was his 1938 book, *Red Star Over China*, which was for the most part an unabashed commercial on behalf of the Communist Mao Tse-tung and his Yenan comrades.

As would later be revealed, Snow in revising this bestselling volume made editorial changes at the behest of the American Communist Party. This was first disclosed during the Senate hearings on IPR by ex-Communist Budenz, a former managing editor of the *Daily Worker*. Budenz discussed before the Senate the role of Snow and his wife, Nym Wales, identified by Budenz as a Communist Party member, in promoting the Communist line on China. In this connection, said Budenz, Snow made alterations in the text when the Communists criticized it for ideological deviation. For his testimony on these and related matters, Budenz would be excoriated as a liar and "paid informer."

Years later, researchers would uncover correspondence between Snow and leaders of the Communist Party concerning the manuscript changes to which Budenz alluded. In these letters, Snow acknowledged the party's criticism of his performance, asked forgiveness for his sins, and promised to make amends by removing the offending passages from the next edition. As comparison of the two versions showed, he made good on this promise, as various items deemed unacceptable from a pro-Moscow standpoint were deleted. Snow thus showed his subservience to the party, while incidentally confirming the veracity of Budenz.[8]

One further example in this vein was the case of *Time* magazine Moscow correspondent Richard Lauterbach. He would be identified by Whittaker Chambers, a former editor at *Time*, as one of those on the magazine's staff most hostile to Chambers himself and his efforts to inject some realism into coverage of what would be known as Cold War issues. The Chambers comments to this effect in *Witness* would be confirmed when the *Venona* decrypts were made public. These revealed that Lauterbach was a secret member of the Communist Party, something

Chambers probably suspected but didn't say explicitly in his memoir.[9]

Though only a sampling, this was a fairly impressive lineup of writers at major media outlets who were or had been Communists or Soviet intelligence contacts and were well placed to advance pro-Red causes in their writings. *Time,* the *Saturday Evening Post, Collier's,* the *Herald Tribune, Christian Science Monitor,* etc., were important media outlets, while even smaller publications like the *New Republic* and Stone's *Weekly* had leverage in certain circles. Add to these a penumbra of correspondents who advanced the Red agenda on Russia or China—Walter Duranty providing the premier example—and journalistic firepower on behalf of pro-Red causes was extensive. Wielded in concert with the work of secretly pro-Red officials, it was a powerful force in favor of the Communist program.

Worth emphasizing also is that many of these pro-Red operatives were working in the Communist-friendly atmosphere of World War II, or its immediate aftermath, which made their efforts the more persuasive. All of this in turn built on the considerable body of pro-Soviet writing of the 1930s, when such as Duranty, Lincoln Steffens, Anna Louise Strong, and a host of others were spreading Stalinist disinformation to the reading public. In this setting, the pro-Communist media message often found ready acceptance, with dire effects for free-world interests.

Noteworthy also was the considerable concentration of these journalists on the subject of China, which in the latter 1940s became a major battleground between Communist and anti-Communist forces. By their reportage and advocacy, Snow, Stein, Epstein, and others helped create a U.S. political climate intensely hostile to Nationalist Chinese leader Chiang Kai-shek in his struggle with the Communists at Yenan, while lavishly praising the alleged virtues of Mao and Red China's Army. All this in turn would link up, again, with the policies being pursued by certain U.S. officials, whose backstage maneuvers in some cases were even more hostile to Chiang than the views advanced by pro-Red writers.

12.

THE PLOT TO MURDER CHIANG KAI-SHEK

Understanding who stood where in the often confusing propaganda battles of the Cold War depends on knowing what the interests of the Soviet Union were at any given moment and how these could abruptly change when the global balance of forces shifted.

The most famous instance of such change was the sudden reversal of the Communist line at the outset of World War II, after Moscow had been aligned with Hitler and U.S. Communists had loudly argued that Nazi aggression in Europe was nothing that should alarm us. This stance was instantly altered in June 1941 when Hitler invaded Russia, at which point the comrades dropped their "isolationist" pose and came out as fervent war hawks against the Nazis. Watching these gyrations, one could easily tell the faux isolationists from the real ones like Colonel Robert McCormick, Herbert Hoover, and Senator Robert La Follette Jr., whose views didn't change overnight to match the policy of the Kremlin.

Less often noted but equally telling was the zigzagging Communist line on China. As seen, a main Soviet concern of the later 1930s was the danger of invasion from Japan, then on the march in Asia and long hostile to the USSR. This threat dictated a temporarily friendly view of China's Chiang Kai-shek, then pinning down a million or so Japanese who might otherwise have invaded Russia. The same Soviet interest meant blocking an American modus vivendi with Japan concerning China, as this too could have freed up the empire for an assault on Soviet Asia. In both respects, Chiang's then-high standing with U.S. opinion trumped notions of accommodation with Tokyo in the Pacific.

By the summer of 1943, with world war raging at full blast, the strategic picture as seen from Moscow had changed greatly for the better. In Europe, the Soviets had survived the siege of Stalingrad and moved to the offensive. In Asia, thanks to the U.S. Navy and Marines and General MacArthur's steady advance in the South Pacific, Japan was in retreat and in no position to threaten Russia. From which it followed that Chiang Kai-shek was no longer of any particular value to the Kremlin. He would accordingly be portrayed from this time forward not as gallant ally, but as corrupt, despotic, and—most important in wartime context—a collaborator with the very Japanese he was previously lauded for resisting.

This rhetorical switch would occur in July and August of 1943, explained in propaganda broadsides issued to the Communist Party and fellow-traveling faithful. The new direction was signaled by Soviet asset T. A. Bisson in the IPR's *Far Eastern Survey*, and by Moscow publicist Vladimir Rogov in a Red propaganda journal. The composite meaning of these essays was that Chiang was now the bad guy in China, and that the only reliable U.S. allies in the country were the Communists serving under Mao. According to Bisson, the regions controlled by Chiang should be described henceforth as "feudal China," while those run by Mao were more properly called "democratic." Rogov's message was that Chiang was colluding with the Japanese, and that the only people fighting the invaders were the Red guerrillas at Yenan. In the months succeeding, these themes would be repeated many times by many voices, eventually forming a mighty chorus.[1]

Such was the changing background of American Far Eastern policy in the latter part of 1943, a crucial time for Chiang and his quest for greater U.S. assistance in his war with Japan and the still deadlier combat with the Reds he knew was coming. In mid-November, he would stake his chances of success on a summit meeting with Roosevelt and Churchill to be held in Cairo, Egypt. Chiang's hope was that this might be a watershed in his wartime and postwar fortunes. It would be a watershed indeed, but not the kind that he had wished for.

On hand at Cairo, shortly before or during his summit with the Western leaders, were four bitter enemies of Chiang, all working for the U.S. government that was professedly his ally. These were Lieutenant General Joseph Stilwell, Allied Army commander in China; Stilwell's State Department adviser, John Paton Davies, a senior diplomat and China expert; Assistant Treasury Secretary Harry White, whose various backstage doings have been noted; and White's Treasury colleague Solomon Adler, then serving as the department's attaché in China. All were adamant foes of Chiang and promoters of his Red opponents. All would in due course echo the notions advanced by Bisson-Rogov, and all had the political/economic muscle to enforce those notions in practical fashion.

This was most obviously true of Stilwell, who under the hybrid arrangements then prevailing was Chiang's top military officer in China as well as U.S. commander in the theater. He was at best an odd selection for this role, as he had an abiding hatred for Chiang and expressed this violently and often, while praising the Red Chinese in extravagant language.* These attitudes were shared by Davies, who would denounce Chiang in dispatches and tout the Reds as the hope of China.

The case was, if anything, even worse with Treasury staffers White and Adler, who arrived in Egypt a few weeks before the summit opened. Their animus toward Chiang in fact was part of their secret daily mission, as both were veteran Soviet agents serving the interests of the Kremlin. They too were well positioned

---

* Stilwell was an intrepid soldier but politically naïve and obviously guided by both his aversions and his advisers. He disliked the British as much as he disliked Chiang Kai-shek, and was also no admirer of FDR, whom he criticized in scathing fashion.

to injure Chiang, as they controlled the flow of U.S. aid funds to China—White as a top Treasury official in Washington, Adler as the Treasury's man in Chungking. Between them they had both ends of the money pipeline covered.

A curious aspect of all this was the way White and Adler turned up in Cairo, though neither had any official role in the China summit. In mid-October 1943, White and Treasury Secretary Morgenthau would set out from Washington for Egypt, in what proved to be a fleeting visit. On leaving D.C., White cabled Adler in Chungking, telling him to start moving the other way so that they could meet up in Cairo. These two Soviet agents thus traveled ten thousand miles between them to have their tête-à-tête in Egypt. Such a prodigious effort in the midst of the global war then raging would on the face of it seem to indicate some important purpose to the journey.[2]

Studying this background in preparing the Cairo diplomatic papers for publication, State Department historian Donald Dozer wondered what connection the White-Adler trip might have had to the Anglo-American meeting with Chiang a short time later. As Dozer would recall it: "When I inquired from Treasury Department officials what was the reason for this Morgenthau mission to North Africa I was told that White and Morgenthau had gone to Cairo to meet with Solomon Adler to start a war bond drive." Dozer thought this unlikely and would so indicate in a monograph about the handling of diplomatic records.[3]

Based on what we know today, Dozer's skepticism seems justified, and then some. We know, for instance, that both White and Adler were Soviet agents, and had been for years before this; we also know that, when they returned to their respective posts from Cairo, they would collaborate in a disinformation scheme to vilify Chiang, while talking up the Communists under Mao. This campaign consisted of memos and dispatches echoing the Bisson-Rogov line that aid to Chiang should be suspended, and that the

United States should look to the rebels at Yenan as our new friends in China.

These views would be expressed by Adler in a series of dispatches to Washington, which White would circulate to others. Typical was a December 1943 letter attacking Chiang as corrupt, despotic, and militarily useless. This contained the soon-to-be-familiar charge of "fascism" against Chiang, plus the supremely damaging wartime comment that "the government has lost any interest it ever had in doing anything effective to fight the Japanese." It added that "Chiang no longer fulfils the function of being the unifying factor in China"—which meant, as other comment made clear, the need for U.S. policies to make such "unifying" happen. "The central government," said Adler, "survives in its present form only because of American support and influence and Japanese collusion." The cure for such failings, he concluded, was to use the lever of U.S. aid to force Chiang into a coalition with the rebels.*[4]

As a pro-Soviet operative himself, White didn't need Adler to tell him Chiang should be reviled or the Reds promoted. He did, however, need such memos to show to Washington higher-ups as on-the-scene reports from China supposedly documenting the evils of the anti-Communist forces. The Adler dispatches were in particular shared with Morgenthau, who accepted them as authentic (his diaries show him exclaiming, "I love those letters from Adler"). Since Morgenthau had ready access to FDR, his friend and neighbor from New York's Hudson Valley, the White-Adler pro-Soviet combine thus had, at one remove, a line into the Oval Office.[5]

A specific target of this Adler-White disinformation scheme was a loan of $200 million in gold the United States had pledged to Chiang to help combat wartime inflation. By foot-dragging methods, White

---

* "Our China policy," Adler explained, "must be given teeth. It should be made clear to the generalissimo that we will play ball with him . . . if and only if he really tried to mobilize China's effort by introducing coalition government."

and company succeeded in delaying and whittling down deliveries (as White made plain in later comment). When the Nationalist Chinese protested the slowdown, Morgenthau quizzed his aides as to why the gold wasn't being delivered. At a series of Treasury meetings, White, Adler on a visit to the capital, and their colleague V. Frank Coe patiently explained to the secretary that there were technical issues, transportation problems, and other complications. And, anyway, Chiang and his cronies would simply steal or squander the gold if they received it. As shown by *Venona* and other security records, all three of the Treasury staffers thus advising Morgenthau to undercut the Nationalist leader were Soviet secret agents.[6]

These were just a few of many such meetings transcribed in then-confidential Treasury records. Others would feature a memorable cast of characters called in by Treasury higher-ups to confer about the fate of China. These included not only the Soviet assets White, Coe, and Adler but other prominent Cold War figures such as Alger Hiss, Harold Glasser, and Lauchlin Currie—all also as noted Soviet agents of influence, and all helpfully advising the Treasury on how to handle events in Asia.

The Treasury was further important as it had a part to play in the internal affairs of China. Among his duties there, Adler was a member of a Sino-Anglo-American "currency stabilization board" supposedly combating the ravages of the inflation. Here he served with yet another Soviet undercover agent, the U.S.-trained Chinese economist Chi Chao-ting, an alumnus of the IPR, veteran Communist, and secret Maoist inside the government of China. Making the Chi-Adler linkage still more cozy, these two Red apparatchiks in 1944 were living together at a house in Chungking.

All this would have been significant in itself, but it became the more so as Chi-Adler had a third housemate—one of the most important American diplomats in China, and arguably the most famous U.S. civilian to serve in wartime Asia. This was Foreign Service officer John Stewart Service, later posted to Yenan as an "observer" of the Chinese Reds with the so-called Dixie Mission, a job for which he had ardently lobbied, sending back glowing reports about their alleged virtues. Later still he would be arrested in the *Amerasia* scandal (see chapter 18), a cause célèbre that made him in some historical treatments a Cold War victim of the 1950s. In mid-1944, at a flat in far-off Chungking, he was living and working at close quarters with two case-hardened Soviet agents.*

Like his roommate Adler, Service was a bitter foe of Chiang and admirer of the Red Chinese, and like John Davies conveniently assigned to Stilwell. Since "Vinegar Joe's" hatred of Chiang was epic, this posting gave Service, Davies, and others like them license to be as hostile to the Chinese leader as they wished, and they would exploit the privilege to the fullest. Service would thus join with Adler, Davies, and other U.S. officials in China in drafting dispatches attacking Chiang for all manner of alleged evils, while depicting the Communists at Yenan in terms of rapt approval.

In these memos Service expanded on the Bisson-Rogov themes, but went beyond them in the volume of his comments. He depicted Chiang as a tyrant who did nothing to combat Japan while running a corrupt regime that oppressed the people. The Reds, meanwhile, in Service's telling, were democrats and reformers whose ideas were more American than Russian. ("The Communist program is simple democracy. This is much more American than Russian in form and spirit.") Dispatches to this effect, numbering more than a thousand pages, went to the Army, State Department, and White House, where Service had a high-level contact of his own in Currie—who, as seen, was yet another pro-Soviet asset well placed to promote the Reds of Asia.[7]

---

* Like his friend and fellow diplomat John Davies, Service was the son of American missionaries in China, born and schooled there before coming to the United States to attend high school and go on to Oberlin College in the 1920s. Also like Davies, he was fluent in Chinese, and thus a natural choice for assignment with Stilwell and later posting to Yenan.

As the records further show, Service worked closely with Adler in drafting reports adverse to Chiang and helpful to the Communist forces. In these dispatches, the roommates generously praised each other, Service citing Adler as economic expert, Adler citing Service as the foremost authority on the politics of China—all to the detriment of Chiang. These efforts reached a crescendo in June 1944, when the duo combined on a sixty-eight-page report denouncing Chiang, given to Vice President Henry Wallace on a trip to Chungking—a trip that proved to be of key importance in promoting a U.S.-Yenan connection, thus easing the way toward a pro-Red American policy in China.[8]

Advices from the Chungking roommates would also make their way to U.S. policy circles by other channels—each set of memos providing confirmation of the other—and help induce a total cut-off of aid to Chiang, military as well as economic. Thereafter, when the Chiang government collapsed and the Communists took over China, Service housemates Chi and Adler would abscond to Beijing and work for the Red regime there (as would Frank Coe and some other U.S. officials involved with China). So, looking back at the events of Cairo, it does seem unlikely that when Soviet agents White and Adler met there in the fall of 1943, they had traveled ten thousand miles between them to discuss the sale of war bonds.

Nor was that all of the plotting that would develop after Cairo. Still other events set in motion there are useful in understanding the fall of China. As might be guessed, the attitude of some U.S. officials was that Chiang should be not only forced into a coalition with the Reds but removed from power entirely—a view made increasingly explicit as the war unfolded.* Such thoughts were bluntly voiced by Stilwell, who said, "the cure for China's trouble is

---

* By late 1944, Service was saying "we need not fear the collapse of the Kuomintang [Nationalist] government. . . . There may be a period of some confusion, but the eventual gains from the Kuomintang's collapse will more than make up for this."

the elimination of Chiang Kai-shek," and "what they ought to do is shoot the G-mo [Chiang] and the rest of the gang."[9] Which sentiments, given Stilwell's reputation for invective, might be discounted as dramatic license. But considering what happened after Cairo, these comments don't seem to have been overstated.

On two occasions at Cairo, Vinegar Joe met with FDR, and at one of these had John Davies with him. Judging by the account of Roosevelt's son Elliott, who sat in on these meetings, Stilwell's views made a strong impression on FDR. In Elliott's telling, the President at Cairo would parrot the Stilwell line on China (for instance, "Chiang would have us believe that the Chinese Communists are doing nothing against the Japanese . . . we know differently"). FDR further said, according to Elliott, that Chiang needed to create a "more democratic" regime by forming a "unity government . . . with the Communists at Yenan." This was vintage Stilwell-Davies.[10]

All of this was merely prelude. After the Cairo meeting, Stilwell returned to Asia and met with his top assistant, Lieutenant Colonel Frank Dorn. According to Dorn, the news Stilwell brought back from Egypt was even more startling than the anti-Chiang invective that suffused the memos of Adler-Service-Davies. Stilwell, Dorn reported, had been told to plan not merely the abandonment of Chiang, but his elimination from the scene in China by way of outright murder.

Such a plan, said Dorn, was to be devised by U.S. officials and held in readiness for the proper moment. "I have been directed," he quoted Stilwell, "to prepare a plan for the assassination of Chiang Kai-shek. . . . The order did not say to kill him. It said to prepare a plan." When the time came for action, Stilwell was further quoted, "the order will come from above and I will transmit it to you personally." There was, understandably, to be nothing about the scheme in writing.

As to who exactly said this, Stilwell's language as relayed by

Dorn wasn't clear, though the quotes suggested that Roosevelt personally gave the order: "The Big Boy's fed up with Chiang and his tantrums. In fact, he told me in that Olympian manner of his: 'If you can't get along with Chiang and can't replace him, get rid of him once and for all. You know what I mean. Put in someone you can manage.'" Based on these comments, Dorn speculated that the edict came direct from FDR, though it also "could have come from Hopkins or one of the senior officers in the Pentagon."[11]

Though Dorn and Stilwell expressed misgivings about plotting to kill the leader of a friendly nation, they set out to do what had been ordered. Dorn described various plans for murdering Chiang discussed with Army officials before settling on a scheme to have him die in a plane sabotaged by U.S. technicians. (Mme. Chiang was to be included in the plane crash also.) In the event, while this plot would be developed, the top-down order wasn't given, so the plane wreck didn't happen.

Dorn added that there were other schemes to have Chiang overthrown or murdered, the most serious of which occurred after his regime collapsed and he sought refuge on Formosa (Taiwan). This plot sought to foment an uprising in favor of a dissident Nationalist general named Sun Li-jen. In this scenario, Chiang and family would be taken into "protective custody," from which, however, they would not emerge alive. (This also came to naught, as Chiang found out about it—allegedly causing at least one U.S. official to flee Taiwan because of supposed complicity in the plotting.)

Despite Dorn's closeness to Stilwell, the existence of these bizarre conspiracies would be hard to credit if we didn't have independent confirmation that such things happened. Confirmation, however, does exist. In the case of the World War II assassination plot, development of such a project would be confirmed in 1985 by Office of Strategic Services archivist Eric Saul, who said Stilwell thought Chiang was bad for China and gave OSS the task of "taking him out of the picture." This could have been the plan referred to by Dorn, or perhaps a successor, as it involved OSS, which Dorn hadn't mentioned.[12]

Also, we know that the State Department in 1950 was in fact encouraging a coup by Sun Li-jen, since this is spelled out plainly in diplomatic records. In this instance, it appears events again outran the planners, as in June 1950, Communist North Korea launched its invasion of the South, seemingly not a good time for the U.S. government to be promoting the overthrow of an anti-Communist Asian leader. Amazingly, however, a similar plot would in the latter phases of the war be concocted against Syngman Rhee, the anti-Communist president of South Korea, considered a source of trouble by American peace negotiators. So perhaps that plan took precedence over State Department scheming against Chiang.*

As with the plots to topple Chiang, the Rhee overthrow didn't happen, but official U.S. efforts along these lines at last succeeded in November 1963, when State Department officials and other agencies sponsored a coup against anti-Communist South Vietnamese leader Ngo Dinh Diem, resulting in his overthrow and murder (along with the murder of his brother). Thus the scheme Stilwell brought back from Cairo did, after a span of twenty years, achieve fruition in the Kennedy era against one of our anti-Communist Asian allies.

---

* The contemplated coup against Rhee was prompted by his action in releasing North Korean POWs who would otherwise have been turned over to the Communists by U.S. negotiators. This outraged American officials, including those of the Eisenhower administration, who feared Rhee would take still other such unilateral actions. In this context, on June 17, 1953, according to minutes of the National Security Council: "The President said that he too was concerned, and that in certain contingencies perhaps the only quick way to end the danger was the *coup d'état*. Certainly he added, this course of action deserved consideration. [deleted] The president continued on to say that of course 'we ourselves don't actually do it; we merely assure immediate recognition to those in Korea who would bring the thing off.'"

13.

BETRAYAL IN THE BALKANS

O n Saturday morning, November 27, 1943, immediately following his Asia policy talks with Chiang, FDR took off from
Cairo for a 1,300-mile air journey to Teheran, the capital
of Iran, where he and Churchill would have their first Big Three
meeting with the mysterious Stalin.

The Cairo and Teheran summits were scheduled back-to-back in
this inconvenient way because there were two separate wars being
fought under a single heading. China was our ally in the Pacific,
but the Soviet Union—though an Asian power once aligned with
China against Japan—was not. In emulation of his earlier deal with
Hitler, Stalin in April 1941 had signed a neutrality treaty with the
Japanese, which he would observe until the summer of 1945, scant
days before Japan's surrender. In deference to this pact (which he
would break when he found that useful), the Soviet leader wouldn't
meet with Chiang, who also wasn't eager to meet with Stalin. So
Chiang and Stalin had to be met with in different places.*

Accordingly, Roosevelt and Churchill with their official retinues
now proceeded by air convoy to Iran, a site insisted on by Stalin
as it was adjacent to the USSR and he refused to travel farther
than that beyond its borders. The fact that the meeting was at
this remote locale, despite Roosevelt's pleas for some place more
accessible to the United States, set the tone for the discussions.

---

* Further complicating matters, Roosevelt and Churchill would return to Egypt in
December for a second, post-Teheran conference in Cairo.

Having played hard-to-get for months, Stalin now made the Western powers come to him (as he would again at Yalta). He was the sought-after party, they the ardent suitors. He would build skillfully on this advantage at the meeting, maintaining the initiative throughout, while Churchill and Roosevelt were generally hesitant and defensive.

Predictably, Stalin's chief emphasis at Teheran was on the need for a "second front" in Europe to relieve pressures on the Soviets in their combat with the Nazis. In this context he spoke bitterly of Poland as a staging ground for Germany's attack on Russia, and of the French for having succumbed so quickly to the Wehrmacht. Neither Roosevelt nor Churchill was impolitic enough to note that when Hitler invaded Poland he notoriously did so in alliance with Stalin, or that when the Germans conquered France they were still in league with Moscow.* (Nor, as seen, did the Anglo-Americans make the point that, while demanding a "second front" in Europe, Stalin would launch no such front in Asia, where British and American forces had been fighting for two full years before this. See chapter 17.)

While military matters were the immediate topics at Teheran, postwar political and diplomatic issues would be considered also. Of special interest were the states of Eastern Europe that lay in the path of the Red Army advancing west from Russia, and what would happen to them when they were "liberated" by Soviet forces. Foremost among the nations getting notice in this context were Yugoslavia and Poland, the first the subject of extended comment by Churchill, the second stressed by Stalin as a security issue for Moscow.

In both states, fierce internal conflicts were developing between Communist and non-Communist factions for supremacy when the war was over, identical in key respects to the struggle shaping up

---

* While the French Communist Party, obedient to the Kremlin, undermined resistance to the Nazis.

in China. At the era of Teheran, the Yugoslav battle was the more advanced, though Poland wasn't far behind it. Making the Yugoslav contest still more distinctive, the case for Communist victory there would be not merely accepted by the Western powers, but promoted by them, with Churchill incongruously in the forefront. The way this was accomplished provides a classic study in disinformation tactics and the vulnerability of the Western allies to such deceptions.

The battle for postwar Yugoslavia pitted the Communist Josip Broz, who took the nom de guerre of Tito, against the pro-Western Serbian General Draza Mihailovich, who at the outset of the fighting assumed the mantle of anti-Nazi leadership in the Balkans. When Hitler attacked Yugoslavia in the spring of 1941, the Belgrade government collapsed, and Mihailovich led a breakaway group of officers into the mountains to carry on resistance. These guerrilla fighters, in the jargon of the war called Chetniks, were among a handful of forces in Europe then actively opposing Nazi power, and thus would for a while be much admired in the United States and Britain.

However, such anti-Nazi activities weren't at that time admired by Stalin, still observing his pact with Hitler, as he would continue to do until his totalitarian partner double-crossed him. Significantly, in view of what happened later, it was only after Hitler invaded Russia that the Yugoslav Communists led by Tito would join the fray against the Nazis, making it clear that their allegiance was to Moscow.[1] This common alignment against the Wehrmacht would last for a year and a half after the Russo-German fighting started, as all the Allies now looked with favor on the Chetniks. Tito, still assembling his own guerrilla forces (who took the later familiar "Partisan" label), was at this period little heard from.*

---

* *Chetnik* and *Partisan* were both generic terms for resistance fighters, the first suggesting home-based citizen militias, the second mobile guerrilla units.

By late 1942, however, as the Red guerrillas began to come on line, Mihailovich was no longer the only Balkan military leader in the field to oppose the Germans. At this time, Communist and pro-Soviet propaganda outlets suddenly began portraying him not as gallant ally but as a collaborator and traitor. The previously unheralded Tito would be acclaimed instead as the only Yugoslav commander carrying the fight against the Axis. Mihailovich would thus be converted virtually overnight from freedom fighter to pro-Nazi villain.[2]

By early 1943, this new message was being broadcast by a short-wave service called Radio Free Yugoslavia (based in Russia) and pro-Red spokesmen in the West, demanding that Allied support be denied the Chetniks and switched to Tito. In the United States, this line was promoted by the writer Louis Adamic, Communist novelist Howard Fast, and a subsequently cited Communist front called the American Slav Congress, which advocated a pro-Red stance on issues of Eastern Europe.

Aiding the pro-Tito cause in the United States was the fact that in these matters the Americans played second fiddle to the British, who had long-standing interests in the region and were much better versed than we in the ways of secret warfare. Significant in this respect was a British intelligence unit based at Cairo, wielding influence on Yugoslav affairs even as FDR and Churchill were coincidentally meeting there to weigh the fate of China. Cairo was the British "special operations" hub for the Mediterranean and the Balkans, whence Allied agents were dropped into Yugoslavia to harass the Nazis, assist guerrilla forces, and send back reports about what was happening in country.

These reports would have great impact on Allied policy in the region. By the latter months of 1943, Cairo intelligence was portraying the Yugoslav Communists as heroic anti-Nazi fighters, while Mihailovich, as in the broadcasts from Russia, was derided as a collaborator and traitor. Typical of such dispatches was a Cairo update from November 1943, a few weeks before the Teheran summit. This said that "General Mihailovich does not represent a fighting force of importance West of Kopaonik [a mountain in Serbia] . . . his units in Montenegro, Herzegovina and Bosnia are already annihilated or else in close cooperation with the Axis. . . . The Partisans represent a good and effective fighting force in all parts whereas only the Quislings [collaborators] represent General Mihailovich."[3]

Other like dispatches said the Partisans were vast in number (200,000 being a commonly cited figure) and were tying down twenty to thirty Nazi divisions in Yugoslavia, while Mihailovich had only ten to twenty thousand men at his disposal. Also relayed to London were accounts of the supposedly tremendous damage inflicted on the enemy by Tito, while the Chetniks allegedly did nothing or worked in tandem with the Nazis.

Based on a steady stream of such reports, London turned decisively toward Tito. By the end of 1943, the British Foreign Office concluded that "there is no evidence of any effective anti-Nazi action initiated by Mihailovich," and that "since he is doing nothing from a military point of view to justify our continued assistance," a cutoff of material to the Chetniks was in order.[4] A few months later, this would in fact be the policy adopted by the Western allies.

In all of this, the Yugoslav case obviously paralleled events in China. One parallel was that accounts of valiant Communist fighting in both countries frequently proved to be fabrications. Thus Tito for a considerable period sought a neutrality agreement with the Nazis—the very thing the Reds accused Mihailovich of doing. Likewise, contrary to tales of Tito's military prowess, the Nazis in May 1944 routed him from his headquarters and ran him out of the country; he would thus unheroically spend the rest of the war under the protection of the British and the Russians. Only when Soviet troops rolled into Belgrade would he go there to stake his claim to power.

Yet another parallel, in some ways the most important, was the way disinformation on these topics was conveyed to top Allied officials. As is now well-known, British intelligence and information agencies in the war years were riddled with Soviet agents, Communists, and fellow travelers, who among other things made it a project to attack Mihailovich and build up Tito. (We need only note in this connection, as recorded by Rebecca West, that among those spreading the pro-Tito line was Guy Burgess, the now notorious Soviet agent, then working with the BBC.)[5]

At the Cairo station, the available data suggest an overall tendency to the left, with officials naïvely accepting as authentic the claims of Tito and the downgrading of the Chetniks. However, we know that at least one Cairo staffer wasn't naïve at all, and was arguably the most important person at the post. We also know, by his own account, how he crafted intelligence data in favor of the Tito forces while ensuring that dispatches creditable to the Chetniks didn't get through to London.

This officer was Cambridge graduate James Klugmann, a bookish, reportedly brilliant individual who worked Yugoslav issues at the Cairo station. While there were other actors in the drama, Klugmann was the longest serving and most experienced staffer there, renowned for his knowledge of the Balkans and diligence in sharing his expertise with others. Briefing agents going into Yugoslavia and receiving their reports when they came back, then writing, editing, and otherwise shaping dispatches sent to London, he was the intelligence gatekeeper for the region. In still another parallel to China, he was also, we now know, a Soviet agent.

Though less famous than some other British Cold War figures, Klugmann was an important member of the Cambridge circle of the 1930s, a confrere of Burgess, Donald Maclean, Kim Philby, Anthony Blunt, and the American Michael Straight, all of whom would become Soviet agents also. That Klugmann wound up in a pivotal intelligence job with the British army is testimony to the kind of security measures that prevailed in wartime England (though no worse than those in the United States). British security screeners had in fact recommended against his employment, but officials in charge of hiring ignored the warnings.

The methods by which Klugmann and others doctored the intelligence product have been discussed at length by British writers Michael Lees and Nora Beloff, and by the Americans Gregory Freeman and David Martin.* The main technique was to sidetrack dispatches that told of what Mihailovich was doing against the Nazis, while passing on Partisan reports accusing him of collaboration. Even more audacious, Cairo would attribute action by the Chetniks to the Communists under Tito. A variation on this practice, discussed at length by Lees (who himself served in the Balkans), was to display a map festooned with pins allegedly showing the exploits of Tito, again attributing achievements of the Chetniks to their Red opponents.[6]

The findings of these researchers would one day be confirmed by materials from the British archives—in the words of none other than James Klugmann. Toward the conclusion of the war, MI5, the English equivalent of the FBI, secretly recorded a talk between Klugmann and an official of the British Communist Party, discussing what had gone on at Cairo. His goal, said Klugmann, had been precisely to switch British support from Mihailovich to Tito. In this respect, he added, his position at the intelligence hub was of key importance. As MI5 summed up his comments:

> In the first place, he was able to control the selection and destination of agents [bound for Yugoslavia]. Secondly, he was responsible for briefing agents prior to their dispatch to the field. As he says . . . "everybody who went into the field had to go through me and I

---

* Of this foursome, Martin was the pioneer researcher and mentor to the others, as all of them acknowledged. He was the author of three books about the subject: *Ally Betrayed* (1946), *Patriot or Traitor* (1978), and *The Web of Disinformation* (1990).

had to tell him what to find, and you know people find what they expect . . ." Thirdly, he directed his efforts to secure only intelligence from the field which supported his policy of recognition for the Partisans and discrediting of the Chetniks. . . . [7]

The pro-Tito message thus supplied to London proved so convincing that Churchill would repeat it at Teheran, citing alleged statistics about the vast number of Tito's forces and the twenty-plus Nazi divisions pinned down by their resistance. This led to one of the more curious incidents at the summit, as Stalin replied that Churchill's figures were wrong, that there were no more than eight Nazi divisions in Yugoslavia. Why Stalin thus corrected Churchill is a bit of a puzzle, but may have stemmed from the dictator's concern that credit for routing the Nazis in the Balkans go to the Soviets themselves, not one of their minions.*[8]

The American role in all this, though subordinate to the British, also contributed to the Tito buildup. A key player was the Office of Strategic Services (OSS), which worked closely on such matters with British forces. Accentuating U.S. reliance on "the cousins" was the close relationship that existed between OSS chief William "Wild Bill" Donovan and Churchill's North American intelligence chief, the Canadian William Stephenson. A main project of the Donovan-Stephenson team was a Canadian training site called "Camp X," in essence a school for spies, saboteurs, and guerrillas. (One of the

---

* This was an issue that later arose between the two Communist bosses when Tito was thought to be getting out of hand and in need of Soviet instruction. Among the items annoying Stalin was the Partisans' claim that they had "liberated" their country unaided (a claim echoed in some Western histories). As noted, it was only when the Soviets took Belgrade that Tito would be installed there, a fact Stalin pointed out to Tito's forces. "After the headquarters of the Yugoslav Partisans had been routed by the German paratroops," said Stalin, it was the Soviet army that "routed the German occupiers, liberated Belgrade and thus created the conditions indispensable for the Communist Party taking power." If Tito and company would recall those facts, Stalin concluded, "they would clamor less about their merits."

Britons stationed there was Ian Fleming, who would recall various Camp X tricks and gadgets in writing the James Bond novels.)

At this location, some thirty to forty Croatian Communists who had been working as miners in Canada were brought in to train for action in the Balkans. The group would thereafter be flown to Cairo, turned over for briefing to Klugmann, then dropped into Yugoslavia as intelligence spotters to report what was occurring in the country. Given Klugmann's explanation of what he was up to, and the Communist pedigree of these recruits, it's not hard to guess what kind of intelligence they would have provided about Mihailovich and Tito.[9]

Nor would that be the only contribution of Camp X to Yugoslav subversion. A further instance was provided by the American Milton Wolff, a veteran of the Communist-sponsored International Brigade in the Spanish Civil War of the 1930s (who took the Fifth Amendment when asked if he were a Communist Party member). Wolff would be approached by Donovan in 1941 to sign up alumni of that unit for Camp X training and service in Yugoslavia, on the theory that they would be good fighters against the Nazis. A number of these inductees would surface in later chronicles of the Cold War, when they likewise took the Fifth on the subject of Red allegiance.[10]

One further example of OSS policy tracking with that of London was perhaps the most decisive of them all. This was the case of OSS officer Linn Farish, who parachuted into Yugoslavia in September 1943 to work with the Partisans and the British. Like others who uncritically accepted what the Partisans and British told them, Farish would quickly absorb the pro-Tito message and as quickly repeat it, thus striking the most lethal blow against Mihailovich inflicted by any American in the struggle.

After being in country for six weeks, Farish would file a report lavish in its praise of Tito and bitter in its denunciation of the Chetniks. This dispatch, matching the reports of John Service out of

China, compared the Communists to the American Revolution, said they believed in democratic freedoms, and claimed they were doing a magnificent job against the Nazis. The Chetniks were conversely described once more as collaborators with the Axis and traitors to the Allies (disinformation Farish may also have received from a KGB officer with whom, according to *Venona*, he was in contact).

This memo praising the Communists of the Balkans might have been just another random message from countless agents in the field, except that it somehow turned up at the highest levels in Teheran a few weeks later. Farish filed his report on October 29; just one month thereafter, on November 29, it was in the hands of President Roosevelt in Iran. FDR on this day had a one-to-one meeting with Stalin, and the first thing he did was to give Stalin, as a kind of goodwill gesture, a copy of Farish's memo praising the Yugoslav Communists and attacking their anti-Red opponents. (How this memo got picked up and passed so quickly to FDR is another Cold War mystery, but becomes more comprehensible when we note that Donovan's top assistant at OSS, keeping an eye out for data useful to Moscow, was the Soviet agent Duncan Lee.)[11]

That Roosevelt or (more likely) someone in his entourage thought enough of this OSS memo to present it to Stalin indicates that the pro-Tito message had penetrated to the highest U.S. levels, as it had in England, thus making the Yugoslav outcome a foregone conclusion. When the Teheran meeting ended, the Big Three would issue a statement promising generous aid to Tito, while Mihailovich was nowhere mentioned. It would be only a matter of weeks before the anti-Communist leader was abandoned outright, the support of all three major powers going exclusively to the Communist forces. Thereafter, in 1946, Mihailovich would be hunted down, given a Red show trial, and put to death by Tito. The Soviet strategy of disinformation in the Balkans—aided by the United States and Britain—had succeeded. It would be the first of many such successes in the rapidly looming Cold War.

14.

THE RAPE OF POLAND

The political outcomes of World War II were disastrous not only for the defeated nations, but also for many who sided with the victors. Nowhere was this more obviously so than in the case of Poland. The war in Europe was ostensibly fought for Polish independence, but would end in the country's total subjugation. Poland thus embodied the tragedy of the conflict as described by Churchill: the democracies at terrible cost had won the war, then lost the peace that followed.

Poland became the proximate cause of fighting by the Western powers in September 1939, when it was invaded first by Hitler, then by Stalin, and the dictators divided up the country between them. Hitler's invasion triggered a guarantee from England and her ally France to come to the aid of Poland in the event of such aggression. However, neither the British nor the French had the means of enforcing these brave pledges, so that Poland quickly fell to the invaders (as France herself would fall some nine months later).

Subsequently, when the United States entered the war as well, the Anglo-Americans would make further vows to Poland, as to other nations conquered by the Nazis. Such pledges were implicit in the Atlantic Charter of 1941 and related statements by the Allies about self-government and freedom, reinforced in comments to Polish exile leaders about the reign of liberty that would follow when the war was over. But these promises too would not be honored. Rather, when the fighting ended, Poland would again be conquered and dismembered—this time with the explicit sanction of the Western powers.

The reason for this reversal was that, between the beginning of the war and its conclusion, the Soviets had been converted from foes to allies, and in this new guise continued to press their claims on Poland. When Hitler invaded Russia, the Communists were thrown willy-nilly into alliance with England. Grateful for backing from any quarter, Churchill embraced them as newfound friends and praised them in extravagant fashion. As has been seen, similar notions would prevail at the Roosevelt White House, in terms exceeding the views of Churchill. The pro-Soviet attitudes now suffusing Western councils would spell the doom of Poland.

Among the most striking features of wartime diplomatic history was the oft-repeated belief of the Western leaders that they had to make concessions to Moscow, while asking little or nothing in return from Stalin. The rationale for this would vary from one case to the next: to keep the Soviets from making a separate peace with Hitler, to build up their confidence in our intentions, to reward them for "killing the most Germans," to placate them because of their great military power. Whatever the stated purpose, the result in nearly all such instances was the same: to give Stalin things that he demanded.

Foremost among such demands was that the Soviets keep the part of Poland they had seized in 1939 in common cause with Hitler. Despite efforts by some in the State Department to oppose this, and occasional statements to the contrary by FDR, the Americans and British would concede the point early on, with virtually no resistance. Tentatively at Teheran, more definitely at Yalta, they agreed to bisect the prewar territory of Poland and consign roughly half of it to Russia.

Nor was that the total story. When the Red Army rolled back into Poland, the Soviets would control not merely half the nation but all of it. They would then set up a puppet regime in the city of Lublin for the part of the country still called "Poland," plus a sector of Germany awarded the Poles in compensation for what was given Russia. To this further demarche the Americans and British consented with misgivings, but consent they did, covering their retreat with pro forma protests and never-to-be-honored Soviet pledges to provide for Polish free elections.

The scenes at Teheran and Yalta where these matters were discussed would read like a comedy of errors if they hadn't been so tragic. Stalin's posturing on the danger of invasion via Poland—a country he had himself invaded—has been noted. Equally bizarre were his objections to having outside observers monitor Polish elections, on the grounds that this would be offensive to the independent-minded Poles. This was said by Stalin with a presumably straight face, even as his agents were imposing a brutal dictatorship in Poland that would crush all hope of independence. All this was known by the Western allies to be bogus, but in the end they would swallow the whole concoction.

Noteworthy in these events was the performance of FDR. One suggestive episode occurred at Teheran, when the President told Stalin the United States was willing to go along with the Soviets on Poland, but that he had political realities to deal with. "[T]here were six to seven million Americans of Polish extraction," Roosevelt said, according to the official Teheran record, "and, as a practical man, he did not wish to lose their vote [in the 1944 election]. He hoped . . . that the Marshal would understand that, for the political reasons outlined above, he could not participate in any decision here in Teheran . . . and could not take any part in any such arrangement at the present time." The magnanimous Stalin replied, now that FDR had explained it, that he understood the President's problem.[1]

Having thus clearly signaled his willingness to cave in on Poland, Roosevelt then proceeded to do the same concerning the Baltic states on Russia's northwestern border. The United States, he told Stalin, was certainly not "willing to go to war" with Moscow over the fate of these small nations; FDR added that he was sure they would gladly be absorbed by Russia but hoped there might be some manifestation of the popular will to show this. To this Stalin curtly answered that such opinion would be expressed according to the tenets of the Soviet constitution. Case closed, with nothing further to be said about it.[2]

Soviet policy in Poland and other captive countries should have been no surprise to either Roosevelt or Churchill, and certainly not to those of their advisers who had followed events in Europe. Stalin had made his intentions plain from the beginning, not only through his invasion of Poland, but in numerous other instances in the fighting.

At the time of the Hitler-Stalin pact, to take an example earlier noted, the Soviets captured a million-plus Poles and shipped them off to Russia, some to become slave labor in the Gulag, a few recruited as agents, others who disappeared entirely. One vexing question was the fate of fifteen thousand Polish officers who couldn't be found when efforts were made to form an army-in-exile to fight the Nazis. Nobody could get the facts about these captives, who had in fact been murdered by the Soviets and buried in mass graves in Russia's Katyn Forest. The truth about the murders would be denied and covered up for years, not only by the Soviets but by Western leaders who knew the facts but kept discreetly silent.[3]

Similarly, in 1941, the Soviets arrested Polish labor leaders Henryk Ehrlich and Victor Alter, who had been trying to organize an anti-Nazi resistance among Polish workers. The pretext for these arrests (and subsequent murders) was that Ehrlich and Alter, both Socialists and both Jewish, were pro-Nazi saboteurs. These accusations were doubly incredible as Ehrlich and Alter had not only been anti-Nazi activists but were running a Jewish labor committee at the behest of Moscow. (The episode presaged many instances of Soviet anti-Semitism that would eventually surface.) The charges were denounced by American labor leaders, including AFL president William Green, CIO president Philip Murray, and David Dubinsky of the International Ladies' Garment Workers Union. These protests were predictably unavailing and the whole subject, as with Katyn, would be swept under the rug by Moscow and the Western powers.[4]

In August 1944 there occurred at Warsaw one of the most horrendous massacres of the war, conducted by the retreating Nazis but with the complicity of the Russians. As discussed in chapter 9, with the Red Army at the gates, Russian broadcasts had urged the Poles to rise up against the Germans and battle for their freedom. When the people of Warsaw did so, the Soviets stood off from the fighting and refused to help them. As the Nazis slaughtered tens of thousands of outgunned civilians, Churchill and Roosevelt pleaded with Stalin to allow airlifts to the resistance, pleas that met with stonewalling Soviet answers. Only at the end, too late to affect the outcome, would supplies be dropped into Warsaw, which by then had become a house of horrors and graveyard.[5]

A fourth atrocity occurred in the spring of 1945. With the war winding down and the defeat of Hitler certain, sixteen Polish leaders were summoned to Moscow to negotiate postwar arrangements for their country. A promise of safe passage was given, but in the familiar Soviet manner broken, as all sixteen were arrested and imprisoned. Again, the common feature, beyond the usual treachery and deception, was the meaning of such episodes for postwar Poland. By these actions, the Soviets were systematically liquidating Polish leaders who could have resisted the Red takeover of their country.

Of chief concern to Moscow in this respect was the exile regime in London, recognized by the Americans and British as Poland's rightful rulers. As with Ehrlich, Alter, and other arrestees, the Soviets would brand the London Poles as collaborators and traitors—charges identical to those lodged against the anti-Communists of

Yugoslavia and China. Like Mihailovich and Chiang, the London Poles would be assailed as "reactionary," "feudal," and unworthy of Allied backing. More representative of Poland, said Stalin's agents, was the pro-Red regime they had set up in Lublin.[6]

As in other cases, the Soviets in pursuing this line had Western helpers. Among these was the previously noted Oscar Lange of the University of Chicago, a Polish-born naturalized American with numerous official contacts, who was on the watch list of the FBI as a player behind the scenes in shaping attitudes toward Poland. Teamed with him in pro-Red ventures was Leo Krzycki, also prominent in such agitational efforts. He ran the Communist-front American Slav Congress, headed a pro-Communist labor union, and later advised the Lublin delegation at the founding of the United Nations.

Another significant figure tracked by the FBI was economist Ludwig Rajchmann, active in matters pertaining to Poland, and also, as a sideline, those of China. Like Lange, Rajchmann had many U.S. contacts and was a familiar figure in official policy circles. Assisting these pro-Red operatives was Boleslaw "Bill" Gebert, also a Polish-born naturalized citizen and a leader of the American Communist Party.[7]

These pro-Lublin forces had numerous dealings with U.S. media figures and officeholders that were monitored by the FBI. A notable instance occurred in 1945, when confidential data pertaining to Poland were leaked to newspaper columnist Drew Pearson. In tracking down this leak, the Bureau compiled a lengthy report discussing possible suspects among pro-Lublin forces in the United States and their official contacts.

Among the cast of characters thus identified were Pearson reporters David Karr and Andrew Older, both as earlier noted named in sworn testimony as members of the Communist Party. The FBI paid particular notice to Karr, the better known of the duo (more would later be learned of Older). As a onetime staffer at OWI, Karr had many official connections.[8] Among these was White House staffer David Niles, aide to Harry Hopkins and denizen of *Venona*. Another was Lauchlin Currie, the pro-Soviet White House staffer appearing frequently in these pages.

The FBI report also spotlighted New Deal officials Thomas Corcoran and Benjamin Cohen, law partners and longtime insiders in the capital. The Bureau noted that both had intervened to help the pro-Soviet Rajchmann when he was having immigration problems. Cohen was of further interest as a possible source of confidential data since he was, like Niles and Currie, a White House staffer. (Corcoran and Cohen would also have roles to play in one of the most significant espionage cases of the Cold War. See chapter 18.)[9]

Still other investigations by the FBI and members of Congress would lead to U.S. officials working behind the scenes to discredit the anti-Communists of Poland and advance the cause of Moscow. Among these were staffers at OWI, OSS, and intelligence units where efforts were under way to circulate disinformation helpful to the Reds and suppress facts harmful to the Kremlin.

Exhibit A in this respect was the case of the officers buried at Katyn. As seen, this crime was committed by the Soviets, but since the territory in question had alternately been controlled by the Russians and the Germans, each side could plausibly accuse the other as the guilty party. The Polish exile government accordingly issued its call for a Red Cross investigation of the matter—thereby provoking the wrath of Moscow, but also of the Americans and British, who wanted no such investigation involving their wartime partner.

This episode became the pretext for the Soviets to break relations with the London Poles and switch recognition to the Lublin puppets. It became the pretext as well for a multilayered cover-up by U.S. officials that extended past the war years. As it happened, an American Army officer was on the scene as a POW when the

Germans discovered the Katyn grave site. Examining the bodies and papers pertaining to them (dated letters and newspaper clippings), he concluded the Soviets were in fact the culprits and on his return to the United States filed a report to this effect with his superiors in the Army. This report, however, would never see the light of day. It would instead be concealed from view, labeled "top secret," then disappear entirely.

These events would in turn become the focus of a House of Representatives investigation conducted in 1952 by Representative Ray Madden (D-IN). The Madden committee likewise found the Soviets were responsible for the Katyn murders and concluded that evidence to this effect had been suppressed by U.S. officials. As the committee further stated, three Army officers had testified in executive session that "there was a pool of pro-Soviet civilian employees and some military in Army intelligence . . . who found explanations for almost anything the Soviets did. These same witnesses told of the tremendous efforts exerted by this group to suppress anti-Soviet reports."[10]

Similar charges would be leveled at OWI, whose broadcasts concerning Poland (and other matters) were denounced in Congress as pro-Communist propaganda. Particularly vocal was Representative John Lesinski (D-MI), who took the floor to address issues involving Poland, Yugoslavia, and Eastern Europe in general. Lesinski said the facts about Katyn had been concealed through "the censorship imposed by the handpicked personnel of the Office of War Information," and that "the newspapers of the United States were told by the Office of War Information" to lay off the story.[11]

Giving credibility to these charges was an OWI project run in tandem with the Federal Communications Commission to crack down on Polish-American radio broadcasts deemed adverse to Moscow. In this venture OWI official Alan Cranston (later a U.S. senator from California) and an aide would inform radio executives as to what was acceptable comment, who should be on the air, and who should not—advice implicitly backed by the FCC with its power over the broadcast license. In one episode described to Congress, Cranston and an FCC staffer visited a Midwest radio station to express concern about broadcasts relating to the Polish-Russian border. A Polish-language commentator at the station had voiced "a rather negative attitude toward Russia" that "was inimical to the war effort." Following which word to the wise, the broadcaster was suspended.*[12]

A kindred project was an OWI questionnaire testing Polish-American attitudes toward the London exile government vis-à-vis the Soviet Union. This contained such questions as "Do you think the Polish government in exile really represents the Polish people, or do you think it represents only a certain group of Poles?" And: "Do you think the United States should guarantee a fair territorial settlement for Poland, even if it means fighting Russia?"[13]

A parallel survey was conducted by OSS, with the asserted aim of ensuring American "unity" with Moscow. A key feature of this inquiry was a finding that Polish-Americans backing the London government were themselves unrepresentative of Poles in Poland, since the U.S. Poles were allegedly too Catholic, as well as anti-Semitic and anti-Soviet, and hence a threat to unity with the Kremlin. Especially bothersome to OSS investigators were "reports of Catholic and Polish agitation against the alliance with Russia."[14]

A further instance was a report by OSS staffer Adam Kulikowski, submitted to Cranston of OWI. This said, echoing the earlier noted strategy memo carried around by Harry Hopkins, that Russia in the postwar era would be the dominant power in Europe and that Poland would fall naturally into the Soviet orbit.

---

* Quizzed about this by the Madden panel, Cranston denied any responsibility either for censorship or for firings. He and his office, he said, would simply make a "recommendation" and any action subsequently taken was the doing of the station. As members of the committee noted, such a "recommendation" backed by the power of the FCC was in effect an order.

However, the memo added, there were some Poles, "remnants of a feudal pattern of life," who refused to recognize this significant fact and make a "realistic adjustment to inescapable historical trends." These backsliders had been conducting a "systematic anti-Soviet campaign" and "sabotaged" hopes for cooperation with Russia.*[15]

These blatantly pro-Soviet effusions, to repeat, were contained in *official documents of the U.S. government*, pressing for a policy congenial to Moscow and inimical to our Polish allies. Two other such cases may be briefly cited. One occurred in 1943, when relatives of the slain officers at Katyn were trying to ascertain their whereabouts and seeking assistance from U.S. officials. An inquiry from the wife of one victim was sent to Vice President Henry Wallace, providing a list of missing officers and asking if the United States could help to find them. Wallace forwarded this to the State Department, where it would by a fatal mischance be handled by the pro-Soviet operative Laurence Duggan. The State Department answer to this request: "Mr. Duggan feels that no reply should be made to it." There would be no help for Moscow's victims from the likes of Laurence Duggan.[16]

A replay of this episode occurred some two years later, this time involving Hopkins assistant David Niles. In this case, the FBI uncovered a scheme by pro-Communist forces to abort a Chicago rally planned by Polish-Americans to protest the communization of their ancestral country. Scheduled to address this meeting was Chicago Democratic mayor Edward Kelly, a prospect that greatly bothered pro-Red apparatchiks Oscar Lange and Krzycki of the Slav Congress. They thus planned an appeal to the White House to pressure Kelly into skipping the rally.

---

* Against these "feudal remnants," said Kulikowski, was a promising new group of leaders—the pro-Soviet regime in Lublin. His memo said that this government was in fact representative of Poland, and that in the United States it had the backing of such worthy leaders as Oscar Lange, Leo Krzycki, and the American Slav Congress, who understood the need for unity with Moscow.

Maneuvering to this effect was monitored by the FBI, which called it to the notice of Hopkins, who in turn referred the matter to Niles. The outcome duplicated the case of Duggan and Katyn. The Niles office soon reported back that the problem involving Mayor Kelly had been dealt with. As relayed by Niles's secretary, "Mr. Niles has handled this and asked me to tell you that the mayor would not make the speech referred to"—which of course was the very pro-Communist outcome about which the FBI was warning. Thus were matters pertaining to Poland—and many others—"handled" in sectors of the wartime State Department and White House.[17]

With so many pro-Lublin and pro-Soviet influences threaded throughout the U.S. government, and so much inclination to kow-tow to Moscow, the demise of Polish freedom was all but certain. By mid-1945, it was clear that a Communist despotism was being imposed on Poland, with scant effort by the Soviets even to conceal this. Despite which, on July 3 the United States would extend official recognition to Moscow's Lublin puppets and decertify the anti-Reds of London. Thus, not with a bang and scarcely with a whimper, did the West surrender Poland to Stalin and his agents.

15.

THE MORGENTHAU PLANNERS

The conferences at Teheran and Yalta were the most important of the war, with the leaders of all three major powers on hand to make decisions that would shape the peacetime future. But there were along the way numerous other, bilateral meetings between Roosevelt and Churchill that were significant in their own right.

At these two-power summits, questions of strategy were thrashed out and plans made for the endgame of the fighting that would transform the postwar landscape. One such was the FDR-Churchill meeting at Casablanca in January 1943, when the President unveiled the "unconditional surrender" slogan that would become a source of fierce contention within the government and in the press corps. Another was the Quebec II conference of September 1944, where the two leaders signed off on the "Morgenthau Plan" for Europe, named for Treasury Secretary Henry Morgenthau Jr., proposing that Germany be demolished as an industrial nation and reduced to strictly agrarian status.

As with "unconditional surrender," when the Morgenthau Plan came to public notice, it caused grave concern among U.S. military leaders, who feared that such draconian notions would stir the Germans to desperate last-ditch fighting. (Army Chief of Staff General George C. Marshall, for one, deplored the plan in comments made to Morgenthau directly.) Nazi propagandists thought the same, seizing on both "unconditional surrender" and the Morgenthau scheme to rouse German troops and populations, apparently facing complete extinction, to greater frenzies of resistance.[1]

Military and press observers including General J. F. C. Fuller and

Hanson Baldwin of the *New York Times* would agree that these episodes prolonged the fighting in the West, where the Nazis had been inclined to surrender to the United States and Britain rather than to the Communists advancing from the East. In this sense, the Morgenthau Plan helped redraw the postwar map in Moscow's favor, as continued German opposition to the Anglo-Americans afforded time for deeper Red incursions into Europe.[2] However, the even more important aspects of the plan lay in its long-term implications. By converting a once thriving industrial state into an agrarian country, it would have reduced a population of 70 million to bare subsistence, if that, and ensured that there would be no nation on the continent that could hinder the growth of Soviet power.

The linkage of the Treasury plan to the interests and concerns of Moscow was stressed often by Morgenthau himself and the staffers who worked with him on the project. The Treasury spokesmen frequently complained that U.S. officials who opposed their scheme were simply afraid of Russia, and secretly wanted to build Germany up again as a barrier against the Soviets in the postwar era. Such accusations were in particular aimed at War Secretary Henry Stimson, who would emerge as the most vocal and effective critic of the program.

Morgenthau would vehemently address the Russian angle in his quarrel with Stimson. As the Treasury secretary remarked to Harry Hopkins (as seen, a supporter of the Morgenthau effort): "Of course what he [Stimson] wants is a strong Germany as a buffer state [against the USSR] and he didn't have the guts to say it. . . . I think if we would probe a little further we would find that he's like some of those other fellows that are afraid of Russia."[3] (A reference to anti-Soviet elements in the State Department.)

The point was likewise made by Treasury staffer Josiah Dubois, who took a leading role in drafting the plan and pushing for its adoption. At in-house Treasury meetings, Dubois attacked Stimson for envisioning Germany as a "bulwark of strength" against the Soviets, and said that trying to fortify the country "as a citadel against Russia" was an irrational concept. (A later Treasury state-ment went still further, saying that "any program which has as its purpose the building up of Germany as a bulwark against Russia would inevitably lead to a third world war.")[4]

Of course, the ideas thus branded as warmongering and irratio-nal would by 1948 become strategic notions embraced by Presi-dent Truman, the U.S. Congress, and Western European leaders trying to guard against the threat of Red aggression. The period 1944–45, however, was the height of the honeymoon with Mos-cow, and nowhere more so than at the Treasury, where "anti-Soviet" was used as a self-evident term of condemnation. (A Morgenthau memo in the run-up to Yalta said of State Department official Leo Pasvolsky, "his writings have not been sympathetic with the Soviet Union."[5] Pasvolsky conspicuously wasn't at Yalta, though his Soviet agent subordinate Alger Hiss conspicuously was.)

As with just about everything else at the Treasury of this era, the central figure in these backstage doings was Harry Dexter White. The proximate cause of the Morgenthau project was White's dis-covery in the summer of 1944 that plans were afoot elsewhere in the government to impose a moderate peace in Europe, insisting on de-Nazification of Germany but envisioning its eventual reentry into the family of nations. Embodying this idea was a State De-partment memo calling for "rapid reconstruction and rehabilitation of war-torn areas" of the defeated country. The Treasury planners further discovered the draft of an Army handbook meant to guide U.S. occupation forces and a draft military directive that suggested relatively humane treatment of the German population.

Such notions were anathema to White and Morgenthau, who responded with a Carthaginian scheme to crush Germany as a mod-ern nation and derail the plans of State and War for a more mod-erate occupation. Treasury discussions to this effect would occur during the summer of 1944, stepping up in tempo as the date neared for the September Anglo-American summit at Quebec, where the planners believed the issue of a soft versus hard peace would be settled. White and company were intent on developing a blueprint Morgenthau could sell to Roosevelt before this meeting, in the hope that Churchill could then be induced to support the project also.

At these Treasury sessions, the range of topics considered was extremely broad, and quite amazing. The main subjects of discussion were naturally of economic nature, as German deindustrialization was to be the major focus. But White and his colleagues went far beyond economic and financial issues to discuss a vast array of other measures, indicating that there were few items of postwar concern in Europe that the planners thought beyond their purview.*

One subject they discussed was the idea of shooting large numbers of Germans when they surrendered, and who should be treated in this summary fashion. Morgenthau, White, and other Treasury staffers weighed the feasibility of compiling lists of people to be killed, but weren't sure how such lists might be assembled. Morgenthau in these exchanges showed he was familiar with Stalin's Teheran remarks saying fifty thousand Germans should be shot at the earliest possible moment. The secretary (jokingly?) said that maybe Stalin's list could be used to identify appropriate targets. From these comments there emerged a proposal, meant for adoption at Quebec, saying German archcriminals, identities yet to be determined, "shall be put to death forthwith by firing squads."[6]

These discussions of mass executions were punctuated by Treasury worries that more moderate counsels might prevail in postwar planning. When White discussed the need for compiling lists of people to be killed, his departmental colleague John Pehle said this was a good idea, but that "it has to be done right away, or nothing will be done." Pehle recalled that after World War I, there had likewise been talk of

---

* These attitudes surfaced on other occasions and were an irritant to Secretary of State Cordell Hull, who often protested Treasury meddling in State Department business.

shooting Germans, but after a long delay there had been no shootings. He warned that such lack of follow-through could occur again.[7]

Apart from the substantive merits of these proposals, it wasn't quite clear what shooting people, either on sight or before firing squads, had to do with the Treasury and its economic mission. This thought at length occurred to Morgenthau, whereupon White, ever alert to Morgenthau's moods, had the item struck from the agenda. There remained, however, other topics that were also far afield from the Treasury's official functions, which would in fact make it to Quebec and thereafter be approved at Yalta.

Noteworthy among these were variations on the theme of slavery—the idea of using German prisoners as "reparations" in the form of conscripted labor to be sent to Russia, and a policy of capturing and handing over to the Soviets anti-Communist Russian refugees who had fled the embrace of Stalin. Forced labor and this update of the fugitive slave law would both be part of the Morgenthau package taken to Quebec, carried thence to Yalta, and adopted there as part of the settlement with Moscow. (See chapter 16.)

Other issues of interest to Treasury staffers were the redrawing of national borders and the shifting about of populations—projects that chiefly affected Germany and Poland, though Rumainia, Hungary, and others would be affected also. A premise of this planning, as earlier noted, was that half of Poland would be consigned to Russia, and that Poland would in turn be given territory that once was German. The planners also busied themselves with schemes to dismember Germany into three, five, or some other number of segments. (As one observer put it: "Those fellows are having a lot of fun cutting up Germany down there in the Treasury department.")*[8]

---

* A guiding premise of this activity was the need to separate Germany as a nation from its industrial heartland in the Ruhr valley, which connected up to the deindustrialization thesis. On the other hand, it's hard to see what the Molotov-Ribbentrop line bisecting Poland, or the total dismemberment of the German nation, had to do with the Treasury's mission.

Further on the noneconomic side of things, of intense concern to Morgenthau, was the education and upbringing of German children. As he put it in an exchange with Stimson: "Don't you think the thing to do is to take a leaf from Hitler's book and completely remove these children from their parents and make them wards of the state, and have ex–U.S. Army officers, English Army officers and Russian Army officers run these schools and have these children learn the true spirit of democracy?"*9

As the Quebec summit neared, Morgenthau met with a group of his advisers to finalize the program. At this session, various of the above-noted ideas were debated and fine-tuned. As the meeting ended, the secretary was effusive in praise of his hardworking staffers. They had done, he said, "a perfectly amazing good job, and I want to congratulate all of you." He added that the plan they had devised would "be very useful to the President at Quebec," and he hoped that out of it "will come a directive" on policy toward the Germans—which was in fact what happened.†10

---

* While Morgenthau and his staffers thought fear of Russia was at the root of opposition to their program, the arguments expressed by Stimson (and to some extent by Cordell Hull) were generally of a different nature. The critics stressed that immiseration would result from reducing Germany to pastoral status and that it would be impossible to sustain the lives of a population who in large numbers depended on industry for survival. Morgenthau was unmoved by such arguments, saying he couldn't care less what happened to the German population, and that leveling its economy to the ground was worth doing whatever the cost in human suffering. The secretary's comments to this effect, as reflected in his diaries, were many: "I don't care what happens to the population. I would take every mine, mill and factory and wreck it." And again: "Why the hell should I worry about what happens to their people?"

† As to the merits of his staff, he would later add that "we have a good team. They just can't break the team. . . ." Also covered in the Treasury sessions was the need to control expressions of opinion via publications and radio broadcasts, all of which in the Morgenthau scenario were to be under the thumb of Allied censors. Such ideas were, of course, inherent in the concept of a military occupation, but again would seem to have been in the jurisdiction of the War or State department, rather than Treasury's financial planners.

These Morgenthau comments about the excellence of his staffers take on added meaning when we note who some of the staffers were, and what was later learned about them. Of the people conferring with him on this occasion, no fewer than six would be named in sworn testimony, *Venona* decrypts, or other official security records as ideological Communists or Soviet agents. (The six so identified were Harry D. White, Solomon Adler, Josiah Dubois, Sonia Gold, Harold Glasser, and William H. Taylor.)

These were, to reiterate, people who happened to be present at this one meeting. There were other staffers of kindred nature who weren't on hand for this particular session but who worked on the program also. One such was V. Frank Coe, an oft-identified Soviet agent, who like Sol Adler would later abscond to Communist China. Another was Irving Kaplan, the subject of several such identifications.* (A number of those so named—Glasser, Dubois, Kaplan—not only helped draft the Treasury program but went on in varying ways to staff it.)

As these identifications suggest, the Treasury comrades practiced defense in depth, and in substantial numbers. They in effect had Morgenthau surrounded—not only in a metaphorical sense, but in a literal sense as well. This was a level of penetration that, as J. Peters bragged to Chambers, far surpassed the Communists of Weimar. It was indeed a formidable team Morgenthau had put together, but distinguished in a way he could scarcely have imagined.

The planning done by Morgenthau's staffers would pay off when

---

* White would be identified as a Soviet agent by Chambers, Bentley, and the *Venona* decrypts. The same identifications would occur with Adler, Glasser, and Coe. Kaplan would be named by Chambers and Bentley. Sonia Gold would be named by Bentley, then turn up in *Venona*. Dubois wasn't named by Chambers-Bentley but would appear in *Venona* as an "intimate friend" of Glasser, described by Glasser as a "fellow countryman" (meaning an ideological Communist) though not formally a member of the party (March 28, 1945). Of this group of eight, the only one not named by Chambers or in *Venona* was Taylor, as the sole identification we have for him is that of Bentley. Taylor would deny the allegation

FDR met with Churchill in Canada a few days later. Here would be demonstrated again the importance of access, which Morgenthau, second only to Harry Hopkins, enjoyed to an extent untrue of others. When the summit convened, though numerous military and diplomatic issues would be discussed, the top two cabinet officers of the U.S. government dealing with such matters—Stimson and Cordell Hull—would not be present. That both were in varying degree opposed to Morgenthau's scheme made their absence all the more important. Morgenthau and the Soviet agent of influence White would, however, both be very much on hand to advance the Treasury program.

In the event, Quebec was all that Morgenthau could have hoped for. By the end of the conference, both FDR and Churchill had signed off on the Treasury project, agreeing that German industry was to be abolished, with the goal of "converting Germany into a country primarily agricultural and pastoral in its character." The memo to this effect bore the initials of both leaders, the Roosevelt version saying "ok—FDR." Morgenthau was understandably exultant. It was, he said, the "high spot" of his career, a complete triumph over the views of Hull and Stimson.[11]

To all this those two veteran cabinet members would have predictably adverse reactions, both as to what was done and to the way it was accomplished. Stimson was especially irate, going directly to Roosevelt to voice his protest. The response he got was as revealing as the plan itself. As Stimson would disclose in his memoirs, when he read the Quebec memo aloud to Roosevelt, the President *"was frankly staggered by this and said he had no idea how he could have initialed this; that he had evidently done it without much thought."*[12] (Emphasis added.)

That such a matter could be decided on such a basis, and explained in such a fashion, suggests a lot about the maneuvering used to get FDR to sign off on the project and, by extension, a number of other projects. This was five months before Yalta, where many other postwar matters would be decided, of equal or even more important nature, and where as discussed Roosevelt's powers of comprehension would be even more seriously in question.

Churchill's acquiescence in the plan was different, since he well knew what he was signing. Here again, however, the Treasury role would be decisive. The prime minister at first opposed the scheme as "unnecessary, unnatural and unchristian" but was brought around by a Treasury promise of a $6.5 billion postwar loan to a financially stricken Britain. This was an offer he said he couldn't refuse, explaining to Anthony Eden that if he had to decide between the German people and those of England he would naturally choose the English.*

Confronted by the protests of Stimson, Hull, and others who deplored the Treasury plan as a counterproductive scheme that would prolong the fighting, Roosevelt seemingly backed off, saying that Morgenthau had blundered. The plan was thus nominally repudiated and, we're told in several histories, abandoned. There is ample reason, however, to conclude that this renunciation was merely pro forma and for the record, as beneath the surface of events the main components of the program kept grinding forward.

Experienced bureaucrats that they were, White and Morgenthau weren't deterred by Roosevelt's disavowals, which they put down to political pressure that would dissipate when the fall election was over. Their strategy was to plug away on specifics, dropping the stress on vengeance per se and repackaging their proposals to make them seem less drastic—for instance, describing the dismantling of German industrial plants as "reparations" rather than as destruction for its own sake.

This approach was the more feasible as the program initialed at Quebec was simply a statement of general purpose. Details would

---

* As later confirmed by both Harry White and Morgenthau, the go-between in bringing about Churchill's conversion was his confidant Lord Cherwell (Frederick Lindemann), who accompanied the prime minister to Quebec. After Churchill had voiced his opposition to the Treasury plan, Morgenthau broached the loan idea to Cherwell, who then sold it to Churchill.

be provided piecemeal in intramural dealings, where Morgenthau's high-level access continued to be a potent factor. As noted, more moderate occupation plans had been embodied in drafts from the State and War departments, including a handbook for the guidance of the Army and a draft directive called JCS 1067, a behavioral blueprint for U.S. occupation forces. In the Treasury campaign to derail these proposals, the first target was the Army handbook.

With Morgenthau's approval, White drafted a harshly worded memo that denounced the handbook as intolerably soft and completely unacceptable. When Morgenthau took this to the Oval Office, the result was a stinging White House rebuke to Stimson. In a letter signed by FDR, the war secretary was told in no uncertain terms that the moderate-seeming handbook must be altered. "The German people as a whole," this said, "must have it driven home to them that the whole nation has been engaged in a lawless conspiracy against the decencies of modern civilization."[13]

This letter has sometimes been cited as showing that Roosevelt personally subscribed to theories of racial guilt and collective vengeance, and it's possible that he did so. However, this particular language wasn't written by him, but was instead ghosted by the Soviet asset White. We know this because Morgenthau would reveal it in later comment informing White that once more they had the President in their corner. As the secretary told his aide, "the President has written a letter to Stimson *based entirely on the [White] memorandum which I gave him on the handbook,* telling them that they cannot put the handbook in force and have to rewrite the whole thing. . . . There is an introductory paragraph, *and then came your memorandum, verbatim,* the President said. . . ."[14] (Emphasis added.)

This episode had an obvious resemblance to what had happened at Quebec and raised similar questions about how things were being done behind the presidential arras. If FDR was unaware of what he agreed to at Quebec, as he said to Stimson (and explained in like fashion to Hull), was he any more aware of what he signed in this letter drafted by the pro-Moscow apparatchik White? Again, we have no way of telling. Suffice it to note that in both cases the President gave his imprimatur to proposals secretly concocted for him by Soviet henchmen.

White and his Treasury colleagues would undertake a similar critique of the proposed directive, JCS 1067. Over a span of months there would be backstage battles about this decree involving the Treasury, State, and War departments, in which the Treasury planners again invoked the prestige of FDR to get their views adopted. The net result was an edict imbued with the vengeful Morgenthau spirit. Suggesting the extent to which the Treasury view prevailed was White's approving remark at the end of the process that the new draft of JCS 1067 was "an excellent job and we are quite pleased with it."

The reasons for this approval may be found in what White called the "vital" paragraphs, wherein the Army was told to control the German economy to halt war production and divert resources toward reparations. To this there was added the proviso: "Except for the purposes specified above, *you will take no steps looking toward the rehabilitation of Germany nor designed to maintain or strengthen the German economy.*" (Emphasis added.)[15]

Other clauses reflected a similar outlook. One concerning the prevention of inflation (which was not in fact prevented) said this would not be grounds for importing goods or limiting "the removal, destruction or curtailment of productive facilities" from the German economic system. Throughout, the directive was of this punitive nature. As noted in the Senate compilation of Morgenthau's diaries, the end product was "an official but diluted version of the Morgenthau plan."*[16] It would remain on the books until the summer of 1947, with effects that lingered long thereafter.

---

* The "dilution" seems to have been mostly of cosmetic nature, as the substantive clauses quoted above were lifted almost verbatim from the original program.

16.

OPERATION KEELHAUL

For obvious reasons, analyses of the Big Three's wartime meetings focus mostly on geopolitical issues—changing boundaries, transfers of power, the balance of forces in struggles to follow. While this wide-angle view doesn't preclude attention to the human costs of what was being agreed to, the fate of countless people in Eastern and Central Europe and large parts of Asia tends to get glossed over in such treatment. Only by looking at specific cases from ground level can we get some sense of the human toll exacted by the summits.

As seen, the White-Morgenthau planners at the era of Quebec waged a strenuous backstage campaign to impose draconian measures on the German nation. These were to be inflicted on a country where cities had been bombed to rubble, disease and famine were rampant, shelter, clothing, and fuel ranged from scarce to nonexistent. But according to Treasury notions of collective guilt, this was as it should be. The Nazis had wrought tremendous suffering in Europe, killing Jews, Russians, Yugoslavs, Poles, and others. Since the German people, in the Treasury view, were guilty of these atrocities as a nation, they too were now to suffer at the hands of the avenging Allies.

However, even if such race-guilt theories were accepted, they couldn't explain the misery that was meanwhile inflicted on people who had no part to play in Hitler's depredations. Prominent instances have been noted in our discussion of Yugoslavia and Poland. The betrayal of Mihailovich and abandonment of the

London Poles were pivotal episodes in the looming East-West conflict, but were also huge personal tragedies involving deception, treachery, and murder, as trusting U.S. allies were sold out to Moscow and whole populations submitted to Soviet terror. The Yugoslavs and Poles thus left to perish were people who had resisted Hitler when Stalin was his chief accomplice, but were now scourged by Moscow without effective answer from the West as traitors to the Allies.

Making matters still more horrific were other European policy matters concealed or played down at the time that even today aren't widely noted. In these cases, the groundwork for what was done was laid by White and company in the run-up to Quebec, with pro-Soviet outcomes that were endorsed at Yalta. As a result of these maneuvers, the United States and Britain would consent to traffic in human beings for the benefit of Stalin, including the use of slave labor as "reparations" for Russia's wartime losses and a proviso consigning two million anti-Soviet refugees to the control of Moscow. In both instances, the best the victims might expect was enslavement in the Gulag, the worst, death sentences like those inflicted at Katyn.

Of course, neither slave labor nor dragging people to death chambers was a novelty for Stalin. By the time of World War II, millions of his subjects had been sent to forced labor in the Arctic, and millions more had died in Moscow's man-made famines and ruthless purges. All of this was standard operating procedure for the Soviet system. It was not, however, considered SOP for the United States and Britain, sponsors of the ringing phrases of the Atlantic Charter and allegedly waging a global war for freedom. All too obviously, their wartime concessions to Stalin would make a mockery of their high-sounding pledges, though they did their best to ignore or talk around this.

On the issues of slave labor and the handover of captives, the

United States and Britain in fact went beyond what they would do for Moscow in other cases. In these two episodes, the Western powers agreed not only to avert their gaze from Soviet crimes but to become complicit in them. This wasn't merely a matter of failing to speak out or mount some kind of resistance, bad as that was, but of expressly sanctioning slave labor and the handover of desperate people to the Soviet army. In these instances, the Western allies acted not simply as mute spectators but as Stalin's active partners.

In both cases, there was an explicit link between the 1944 conference at Quebec and what would later occur at Yalta. In the Treasury's Quebec proposals, the subject of slave labor as "reparations" had appeared in several guises. One draft specified, as a form of reparations, "forced German labor outside Germany." A modified draft three days later repeated this formulation, which would appear in other Treasury papers in slightly different language. The concept would then resurface at Yalta, expressed as the "use of German labour."[1] And while such postwar labor would be used to some extent by others among the Allies, there was no doubt in anyone's mind that the main intended beneficiaries were the Russians.

The truth of this emerged shortly after Yalta, when the issue was angrily joined behind closed doors inside the Washington administration. This intramural dispute indicated not only that the forced labor agreed to at the summit was a boon for Moscow, but that it was defended precisely on those grounds by the Treasury planners who espoused it. Their main antagonist was Supreme Court justice Robert Jackson, who would later become the American lead prosecutor at the Nuremberg war crime trials. Encountering the issue of slave labor in the Treasury proposals, Jackson thought he spotted a postwar war crime in the making, and pulled no punches in voicing his disapproval.

In denouncing the Treasury labor proviso, Jackson stated: "The plan is to impress great numbers of laborers into foreign service, which means herding them into concentration camps." Pursuing such a course, he charged, "will largely destroy the position of the United States in this war. . . . What the world needs is not to turn one crowd out of concentration camps and put another crowd in, but to end the concentration camp idea." He couldn't support a project, he said, the purpose of which was "to get labor for Russia."[2]

Jackson's talk of "concentration camps" and the "herding" of conscript labor was assailed in Treasury circles, where the goal was, precisely, to put a new crowd of victims into such confinement. Especially vocal on the point was Morgenthau aide Josiah Dubois, who deplored the justice's statements as "an effort by Jackson to block forced labor altogether." If such ideas were to prevail, complained Dubois, "it's going to look to the Russians as though we're trying to sabotage the whole labor program."[3] The evident meaning of which was that slave labor for Russia had to be sanctioned by the United States to keep from offending Moscow.

Equally startling, though from a different angle, were statements on labor-as-reparations by Secretary of State Stettinius, on whose watch at Yalta the slave labor proviso was agreed to. It's remarkable to note that Stettinius, the top U.S. diplomat at the conference, seemingly didn't know that this language had been approved as part of the Yalta summit. The point emerged from his interviews with historian Walter Johnson, discussed in chapter 3, when the two collaborated on the Stettinius memoir, *Roosevelt and the Russians*.

In these exchanges, the historian quizzed Stettinius about things done at Yalta and how matters there had been decided. When the question of forced labor came up, Stettinius was emphatic in denying that any such proviso was arrived at, saying, "Nothing was agreed to at all." And again: "The whole question was referred to the Reparations Committee, to investigate and recommend. No decision was reached on it." And yet again: "FDR was definite that we didn't want to approve German labor for reparations."[4]

All these assertions were mistaken—as Johnson knew but didn't say to Stettinius directly. At one point, as the former secretary was insisting that no such stipulation had been agreed to, Johnson interjected, "That's not clear," but went no further. Stettinius then declared again that forced-labor-as-reparations had not been approved at Yalta. (Johnson's note on this contains the handwritten comment "ERS is wrong.") Stettinius did say, however, as he would on other matters, "See Alger, and we'll discuss this again."[5]

These Stettinius comments were the more astounding as the Yalta protocols are clear on the subject, defining "reparations in kind" as material goods of one sort or another, plus levies on future German output, and listing, as a separate item, "use of German labor."[6] Documents reflecting this would turn up in Stettinius's own papers (as in the graphic on page 192), where Johnson probably got his information, and would later be published in the official State Department record. So there isn't any doubt that forced-labor-as-reparations was approved at Yalta.

Among the several mysteries that swirl around the Yalta agreements, this ranks among the strangest. Is it conceivable that slave labor for the benefit of Moscow was approved by the United States, but that the American secretary of state knew nothing of it? This seems incredible on its face, yet based on Stettinius's statements to Johnson appears to be what happened. Likewise, is it possible that such an immense concession to Moscow would have been made by the United States, despite Stettinius's statement that Roosevelt opposed it? And if Stettinius and FDR weren't aware of what was done, who was aware, and who approved it?

Stettinius Misstates Key Yalta Provision

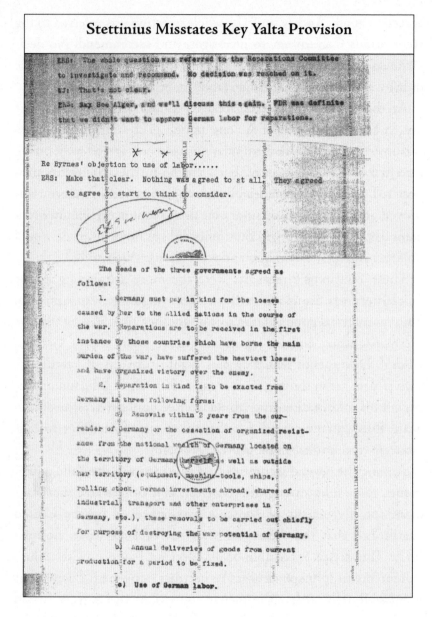

ERS: The whole question was referred to the Reparations Committee to investigate and recommend. No decision was reached on it.

WJ: That's not clear.

ERS: Jay See Alger, and we'll discuss this again. FDR was definite that we didn't want to approve German labor for reparations.

✳ ✳ ✳

Re Byrnes' objection to use of labor......

ERS: Make that clear. Nothing was agreed to at all. They agreed to agree to start to think to consider.

The heads of the three governments agreed as follows:

1. Germany must pay in kind for the losses caused by her to the Allied nations in the course of the war. Reparations are to be received in the first instance by those countries which have borne the main burden of the war, have suffered the heaviest losses and have organized victory over the enemy.

2. Reparation in kind is to be exacted from Germany in three following forms:

a) Removals within 2 years from the surrender of Germany or the cessation of organized resistance from the national wealth of Germany located on the territory of Germany herself as well as outside her territory (equipment, machine-tools, ships, rolling stock, German investments abroad, shares of industrial, transport and other enterprises in Germany, etc.), these removals to be carried out chiefly for purposes of destroying the war potential of Germany,

b) Annual deliveries of goods from current production for a period to be fixed.

c) Use of German labor.

The mistaken comments of Secretary of State Edward R. Stettinius Jr. that conscripted German labor as "reparations" to Moscow was not approved at Yalta. The handwritten comment in the notes of historian Walter Johnson—"ERS is wrong"—was confirmed by the Yalta protocol explicitly approving such conscripted labor. (*Source: Stettinius/Yalta records, University of Virginia*)

This background is further relevant in connection with the second Yalta protocol involving traffic in human beings—the treatment of anti-Soviet refugees who fled from Stalin seeking asylum in the West, only to be turned back over to their Soviet masters. How and by whom this policy was approved would be even bigger mysteries than the issue of forced labor.

In this case, again, there was a link between Treasury planning for Quebec and what occurred at Yalta. In the set of Treasury proposals that included the idea of shooting prisoners en masse when the war concluded, there was a further item concerning punishment of the conquered peoples. This was a draft "political directive" to be issued to U.S. commanders, targeting persons to be "arrested and held," pending further instructions. Specifically to be locked up, this said, was *"any national of any of the United Nations who is believed to have committed offenses against his national law in support of the German war effort."*[7] (Emphasis added.)

Once more the intended beneficiaries—and victims—were apparent from the wording. While there may have been a handful of U.S., British, or French nationals who fit this description, this draft decree, like the labor proviso, was obviously tailor-made for Moscow. The Soviet Union was the only Allied power that had any substantial number of its nationals fighting for the Germans, which among other issues raised the question of why this should be and what it said about the Soviet system. Potential embarrassment on that front would have been one motive among many for Stalin to corral such dissidents and ship them back to Russia.

This Treasury proposal would be folded into the final version of JCS 1067, repeated in Yalta working papers drafted in preparation for the summit, then endorsed in a secret protocol adopted on the last day of the conference. Interestingly, this agreement was signed by neither Roosevelt nor Stettinius, nor by any other U.S. political or diplomatic figure, but instead was handled purely as a military matter, and this not at the highest levels. The signatories were U.S.

Major General John R. Deane and Soviet Lieutenant General A. A. Gryzlov, to all appearances simply agreeing to a swap of military prisoners, seemingly not of interest from a diplomatic standpoint. In this accord, the United States consented to "hand over" prisoners of asserted Soviet nationality to the Russians. Along with a similar deal agreed to by the British, this became the legal basis for consigning millions of anti-Soviet refugees to the mercies of Soviet justice.*

As would be expected amid the chaos of war, the people to be treated thus were a mixed assortment. A sizable number were Russians who had been imprisoned by the Nazis and pressed into service as troops or work battalions. Others were anti-Communists who had joined with the Germans in the naïve and futile hope that they would be preferable to the Communists and could topple the hated Stalin. Expatriates in either category were obvious targets of Moscow vengeance and could expect no mercy when returned to Russia.

However, there were others in the diaspora who didn't fit these profiles. A substantial number had left the USSR before the war began, and had long since forsworn allegiance to the Kremlin. Others had been residents of states or provinces that in 1939 weren't part of the Soviet empire. Still others included the elderly, the infirm, and women or children caught up in the vast migrations of the war. All would be targeted for repatriation, and turned over by the West, if the Soviets so demanded.

That these fugitives faced not only imprisonment but in some cases certain death was known to the Western allies. British foreign minister Anthony Eden said it was British policy "to send all the Russians home, whether they want to go or not and by force if necessary." (He further said that "we shall be sending some of them to their death.") His successor Ernest Bevin agreed that "it

---

* In fact, such handovers had previously occurred, but without the legal sanction that was supplied at Yalta.

is important to get rid of these people as soon as possible . . . using as much force as may be necessary." Similar statements would be made by U.S. officials, as in the revised Army handbook reflecting the Morgenthau-White pro-Moscow mind-set, saying the captives would be "released expeditiously to the control of the USSR *without regard to their individual wishes.*"[8] (Emphasis added.)

Further suggestive of how the matter was viewed in U.S. circles was the code name given the project—"Operation Keelhaul." The allusion was to a barbaric form of punishment at sea, whereby captives were dragged beneath the keel of a ship, suffering agonizing death by torture. The name indicated little doubt as to the fate of the prisoners once in the clutches of the Russians. All this becomes the more appalling when we note that many captives had been induced to surrender to the West in the belief—and sometimes the promise—that they would be humanely treated.[9]

The captives now knew what they were in for and fought desperately to avoid going back to Russia. These struggles were brutally put down by U.S. and British forces (one British order said that "any attempt whatever at resistance will be met firmly by shooting to kill").[10] A number of fugitives would commit suicide, some first killing their children, rather than return to Soviet jurisdiction. Horrendous scenes ensued as British and American soldiers bludgeoned helpless prisoners, herding them into boxcars and forcing them onto ships that would take them to their fate in Russia.

Though this scheme was promoted by Treasury planners in the run-up to Quebec and signed by General Deane at Yalta, there were grave concerns expressed about it at high levels of the State Department. These were voiced by Undersecretary Joseph Grew, who remained at home while Stettinius and company were at the summit. As seen, Grew had earlier crossed swords with such as White, Currie, and Lattimore when he was trying to avert a U.S.-Japanese war and they were working to foment one. He would be in conflict with this group again in the *Amerasia* scandal (see chapter 18), and on the question of a hard versus soft peace to conclude the Pacific fighting. Now he would in effect go up against White and the Treasury staffers concerning the handover of refugees to the Russians.

On February 1, as Roosevelt, Stettinius, and the rest of the U.S. delegation were on their way to Yalta, the Soviets approached the State Department in Washington to obtain approval for turning over Soviet-nationality fugitives held by the United States, but got from Grew a flat refusal. A handover of unwilling captives, he said, would violate the rules of warfare concerning treatment of POWs as set forth in the Geneva Convention and be contrary to the long-standing U.S. custom of granting asylum to fugitives targeted for compulsory repatriation.[11]

Soon thereafter, Grew would be surprised to learn that the Red request he had turned down was being accepted by U.S. officials at Yalta, agreeing with the British-Soviet accord on the delivery of such captives. Whereupon he sent a cable to Stettinius noting that the British-Soviet deal ignored the Geneva Convention and American diplomatic practice, and that he had so informed the Russians. To this there was an instantaneous answer in the form of a Stettinius cable, curtly dismissing the issues raised by Grew and saying the U.S. delegation would definitely agree to turn the fugitives over, no two ways about it.

This cable was of unusual nature. Though peremptory in tone and categorical in conclusion, it was phrased in elliptical language that talked around the substance of the issue. As for the Geneva Convention, it said, there was a "consensus" at Yalta to ignore its provisions with respect to German prisoners in U.S. custody. Why this was so was not explained, nor was it clear who had reached this "consensus," nor were other points raised by Grew dealt with on their merits. His concerns thus weren't so much addressed as overridden. On that basis, the U.S. and Soviet generals on the last day at Yalta signed the secret protocol whereby some two million fugitives would be returned to Russia.[12]

Grew vs. Operation Keelhaul

TOP SECRET
AFHQ MESSAGE CENTER
INCOMING MESSAGE

U R G E N T

From: War

To : ARGONAUT

No. : 27   DTG 080218Z   8 Feb 45

Special message to the Secretary of State from the Acting Secretary. TOPSEC.

War Department has just made available message dated February 7 from Marshall which indicates that JCS on February 7 approved with certain changes British preliminary text on agreement with Soviet Union for exchange of prisoners of war and apparently also for liberated persons. While it is not definitely clear what preliminary British text is referred to, if it is the preliminary text included in JCS 1266, the agreement would not appear to cover the following specific points which were incorporated in the United States counterproposals forwarded to JCS Staff with you:

1. Protection of Geneva Convention which we have informed Soviet Government we will accord to Soviet citizens captured in German uniform who demand such protection.

2. Soviet citizens in the United States not prisoners of war whose cases the Attorney General feels should be dealt with on basis of traditional American policy of asylum.

3. Persons liberated by United States forces no longer in their custody.

4. Question of the liberation and repatriation of other United Nations citizens.

5. Persons claimed as citizens by the Soviet authorities who were not Soviet citizens prior to outbreak of war and do not now claim Soviet citizenship.

(continued)

ARGONAUT-IN-142

The cable sent to Yalta by acting secretary of state Joseph Grew, objecting to the Operation Keelhaul pact that consigned two million anti-Soviet refugees to their doom in Russia. Grew's protest that the agreement violated the Geneva Convention and American diplomatic practice was overridden by U.S. officials at Yalta to give the Soviets what they wanted. (*Source: Stettinius/Yalta records, University of Virginia*)

This episode was remarkable at several levels—not only for what was done and the secretive way it was handled, but also in that to all appearance it pitted the neophyte secretary of state at Yalta against the experienced acting secretary in Washington. As noted, Stettinius at this time had held his post for just two months and indicated in many ways that he was swimming in uncharted waters. Grew, conversely, was the most experienced diplomat in the State Department, having served there for forty years, and was well familiar with international law, American custom, and diplomatic practice. Yet the Stettinius cable from Yalta showed not the slightest hesitation in overruling and rebuking Grew to give the Russians what they wanted.

This sequence becomes more puzzling yet if we compare it with the above-quoted Stettinius statements on forced labor, and his peculiar lack of knowledge on that subject. Though this earlier proviso was expressly entered in the State Department's records as something agreed to at Yalta, Stettinius by his comments to historian Johnson made it clear that he knew nothing of it. Yet on the more esoteric matter of turning anti-Soviet fugitives over to Russia—a supposed military measure with no State Department involvement—his cable to Grew seemed knowledgeable and decisive. It's curious that Stettinius could be so clueless on one such matter but so thoroughly up to speed about the other.

But then, as Stettinius said to historian Johnson, the person to be consulted on such issues was Alger Hiss, who, as Hiss himself would comment, was also the person at Yalta "in charge of receiving and dispatching reports from and to the State Department." Perhaps if he had been questioned on Operation Keelhaul, Hiss could have explained who exactly received Joe Grew's protesting cable, who drafted the peremptory answer, and how a policy sought by Moscow was thus secretly approved at Yalta—sending two million captives to their doom in Russia.

17.

STALIN'S COUP IN ASIA

B ased on a now considerable mass of data, it's evident that the real victors of World War II weren't the United States and Britain, France or China, but the Soviet Union and its worldwide web of vassals, satellites, and agents.

Much of Moscow's advantage at war's end stemmed from the situation on the ground, but a good deal of it derived from the ability of Stalin and his subalterns to shape events in favor of the Soviet interest. In comparison, the Western allies seemed remarkably unskilled, and U.S. officials in particular behaved as if there were nothing going on in which skill was needed. These trends were on display at Teheran and Yalta as Stalin and his agents outmaneuvered the Western powers on a host of European issues. They would be even more successful with affairs of Asia.

Throughout the conflict in the Pacific, the Communists positioned themselves to run few risks to speak of, but to gain maximum benefit from the fighting. As earlier recounted, pro-Soviet operatives in the United States and Asia worked in the months before Pearl Harbor to ensure that there wouldn't be an attack on Russia, and that Japanese power would be unleashed instead against American, Dutch, or British outposts. All this in turn was a beginning—not only of Japanese-American conflict, but of further maneuvering in the far Pacific that would serve the ends of Moscow.

In the spring of 1941, as KGB agent Pavlov was counseling Harry White on how to prevent a Washington-Tokyo rapprochement, the Soviets signed a neutrality treaty with Japan, which they would observe for four full years of combat. Thus, while clamoring for a "second front" in Europe, they avoided opening a "second front" in Asia as American power destroyed their nemesis in the region—a nice kind of geopolitical parlay if one could get it. (A strategy vividly summarized by Soviet deputy foreign commissar Ivan Maisky. The Soviets, he said, should "by clever maneuvers" avoid "open involvement in the war with Japan," since it would be far more advantageous to let the British and Americans defeat the Japanese. By such tactics, he said, "the USSR could obtain [its] goals without firing a shot in the Far East.")[1]

However, when it became clear in the latter months of 1943 that Japan was definitely going to be defeated, the nature of Stalin's policy would be somewhat different. With Allied victory in prospect, he would begin reversing course in Asia to claim the spoils of war in the Pacific. This turnabout began at Teheran and would culminate at Yalta, where the Red dictator signed a secret pact with FDR, ratified by President Truman the following summer at Potsdam. By these agreements, the Communists would gain the lion's share of benefits from the Far East conflict, while scarcely lifting a finger to deserve them.

At Teheran and Yalta, Stalin told Roosevelt that Russia, despite its treaty with Japan, would enter the Pacific war "two or three months" after the Nazis surrendered (which occurred on May 8, 1945)—a deadline that would be met, if barely, in the early days of August. In return, FDR agreed to a vast array of benefits for Moscow: sanctioning Soviet control of Outer Mongolia, ceding to Russia the southern part of Sakhalin Island north of Japan and the Kurile chain that stretches between Japan and Russia, plus de facto control of seaports and railways in Manchuria, the main industrial zone and richest part of China.

Of these provisos, those concerning Sakhalin and the Kuriles were justified on the grounds that the islands had been seized wrongly by Japan and were being "returned" to Russia. But the agreements concerning Outer Mongolia and Manchuria were at the expense of China, whose territorial integrity was the pretext for our involvement in the fighting. This was done though China's leaders weren't at Yalta, weren't consulted, and would learn to their dismay about the concessions only later. The pact gave the Soviets commanding power over Manchuria, along with a sizable store of munitions the Japanese would leave behind them. A substantial portion of these would be turned over to the Red Chinese, who flocked to Manchuria once the Soviets were in control there.

To obtain this cornucopia of riches, the Soviets would take part in the Pacific fighting for a grand total of five days before Japan's announced surrender (August 9 through August 14, 1945), with some brief skirmishing to follow when they drove into Manchuria and the northern islands to secure the booty. It was an amazing coup that put not only China but other nations of Asia at risk of Communist domination—among the most stunning diplomatic triumphs ever recorded by one major power against another.

In the European case, U.S. and British concessions to Moscow were rationalized on the grounds that the Soviets had done the hard slogging on the ground, were already in possession, had "killed more Germans" than anyone else, and so earned dominion over half of Europe. Whatever the merits of all this regarding Europe, none of it applied to Asia. Here the Soviets at the time of Yalta had done no fighting, weren't killing any Japanese (had in fact per OSS provided them assistance), and had otherwise done nothing to aid the Western allies. Accordingly, the reasons for concessions to Stalin in Asia would be drastically different from those alleged for Europe—not what the Soviets *had* done for the common effort, but what they *would* do for it at some point in the future.

As argued by Secretary of State Stettinius, the U.S. Joint Chiefs of Staff, and defenders of Yalta, victory in the Pacific would have required an invasion of Japan's home islands against fanatical resistance, in which apocalyptic battle the help of the Soviets would be needed.

The record, however, does little to support this thesis. For one thing, the United States at the time of Yalta knew from multiple sources that Tokyo was desperate to end the fighting—the main hang-up in this respect being the "unconditional surrender" doctrine, which as with Germany spurred bitter-end resistance.* Given that information, it was far from a consensus of the U.S. military that ground invasion or Soviet assistance would be required to bring about Japan's surrender. It's noteworthy indeed how many American military leaders opposed the Asia strategy approved at Yalta.

On the Navy side, the dissenters included Admirals William Leahy, Ernest King, and Chester Nimitz, to name only the most famous. The views of Leahy are of particular interest since he was chief of staff to FDR, a post he would also hold with Truman. Though a loyal defender of Roosevelt and Yalta, Leahy was emphatic in saying the Russians shouldn't have been brought into the Asian conflict. "I was of the firm opinion," he wrote, "that our war against Japan had progressed to the point where her defeat was only a matter of time and attrition. Therefore we did not need Stalin's help to defeat our enemy in the Pacific."[2]

Naval officers might of course be expected to deprecate the need for a ground invasion, believing seagoing victories and blockades—along with aerial bombardment—were sufficient keys to winning. Similar views as to the role of Moscow were, however, voiced by General Douglas MacArthur, Army supreme commander in the region, who was prepared to do a ground invasion of Japan if so ordered but who knew and reported to Washington in the run-up to Yalta that the Japanese were ready to parley for surrender. His views were doubly significant, both because he spoke for the Army and because he would later be cited by defenders of Yalta as someone who thought the Soviets should be brought into the Pacific conflict.

---

* The main problem, from Japan's perspective, was what it implied about the fate of Emperor Hirohito.

Omitted from this scenario was that MacArthur by his own account *had* favored Soviet help (and any other that he could get) at the outset of the war, when he and his men were waging a lonely battle against Japan. But by the time of Yalta, many U.S. victories later, his thoughts would be quite different. As he would comment, "had my views been requested I would most emphatically have recommended against bringing the Soviets into the Pacific war at that late date. To have made vital concessions for such a purpose would have seemed to me fantastic. . . . I had urged Russian intervention in 1941 to draw the Japanese from their Southward march and to keep them pinned down in Siberia. By 1945 such intervention had become superfluous."[3]

Despite these MacArthur statements, the Yalta deal on Asia is often attributed to "the military" or sometimes "the Army."* On examination, this meant Army Chief of Staff General Marshall and his staffers in the Pentagon. Subsequently defenders of Yalta would explain this stance by referring to "intelligence" data that indicated the need for a ground invasion against massive Japanese resistance, hence the need for the pact with Russia.

But this reliance on "intelligence," it turns out, is also open to serious challenge. As we now know, there were other intelligence estimates at the time that gave a totally different picture of the fighting and the state of Japanese defenses. Moreover, there were briefing papers prepared by State Department experts that warned against giving the Soviets control of southern Sakhalin and the Kuriles. But none of these analyses would make their way to U.S. policy makers at Yalta. As explained by Admiral Ellis Zacharias, a Navy intelligence specialist dealing with affairs of Asia:

---

* Stettinius in his memoir would stress this argument in numerous places to justify the Asia pact at Yalta.

*[The] decision to bring the USSR into the Pacific war was based on
a crucial document drafted in the fall of 1944. . . . Its pessimism, its
exaggeration of Japanese potentialities, made Russian participation in
the war seem imperative. . . . Later we found that the War Department had prepared two estimates instead of one, but somehow the
more accurate and from our point of view optimistic assessment of
Japanese potentialities was pigeonholed by a special intelligence outfit
in the assistant secretary's office, which allowed only the pessimistic
report to go up to the Joint Chiefs and through them to Roosevelt.*[4]

A similar fate would befall other intelligence reports that said Soviet entry into the Pacific war would not be needed. As Zacharias
would note of intelligence data assembled for the Navy: "An estimate—prepared for [Navy] Secretary [James] Forrestal . . . explicitly advising against Soviet participation in the Pacific war on the
grounds that it was not required by our own military necessities . . .
ended up in the same Pentagon pigeonhole."[5] Thus the only intelligence on the Asian fighting provided to policy makers at Yalta was
that pointing to the need for Soviet involvement.

Also, while it wasn't an "intelligence" report as such, the information received from MacArthur was of similar import. As would
later be revealed, the general in the run-up to Yalta had communi-
cated to FDR that the Japanese were ready to sue for peace—on
terms remarkably similar to those agreed to the following August.
This MacArthur communiqué, however, was reportedly dismissed
out of hand at the White House, would play no part in the Yalta
negotiations, and would be concealed from public view for months
thereafter.[6]

The pattern of disappearing intelligence data would continue
after Yalta. A further instance would be recorded by Senator Styles
Bridges (R-NH), when he obtained a copy of an intelligence summary saying Soviet entry into the Asian war not only wasn't needed
but would be a strategic disaster. Among the authors of this report

were Army intelligence specialists Colonel Truman Smith and the earlier noted Colonel Ivan Yeaton. The date of their estimate was April 12, 1945, two months after Yalta but well before the Potsdam meeting in July, where Truman would confirm the Asia pact with Stalin. This discussed the endgame of the war as follows:

> *It may be expected that Soviet Russia will enter the Asiatic war, but at her own good time and probably only when the hard fighting stage is over. . . . Strong enough to crush Japan by ourselves, the United States should make no political or economic concession to Soviet Russia to bring about or prevent an action which she is fully determined to make anyway.*[7]

Further, and even more prophetic: "The entry of Soviet Russia into the Asiatic war would destroy America's position in Asia quite as effectively as our position is now destroyed in Europe East of the Elbe and beyond the Adriatic. . . . If Russia enters the Asiatic war, China will certainly lose her position to become the Poland of Asia. . . . Under no circumstances should we pay the Soviet Union to destroy China. . . . [T]he United States Army is by no means united in believing it wise to encourage the Soviet Union into the Pacific fighting."[8]

This was uncannily accurate as to what would occur in Asia, and obviously would have been helpful reading for Truman when he and Secretary of State James Byrnes set sail for Potsdam. There is no record, however, that this prescient memo ever made its way to Truman, Byrnes, or other top officials. When Senator Richard Russell (D-GA) of the Armed Services Committee asked the Pentagon what happened to it, he was told the Army didn't know, but that "since no action was taken on its recommendations it was probably destroyed."[9]

Beyond the "intelligence" rationale, Stettinius and some historians of Yalta would argue that nothing was given to the Russians there that they couldn't have taken anyway. Again, whatever the applicability of this to Europe, its relevance to the Pacific is doubtful. As recent scholarship has shown, the Soviets were hypercautious in affairs of Asia until they knew what the U.S. stance would be, and at pains to cover their actions with provisos we agreed to or policies we announced. One reason for this was that our Far East position was immensely strong while theirs was by comparison weak—designedly so, since their treaty with Japan had protected them in the region.[10]

Stalin himself would stress the point in saying he couldn't enter the Pacific war unless we gave him the means to do so. This was a routine sort of request for Moscow, which had received billions of Lend-Lease aid in Europe and now wanted to do the same in Asia. As was routine for the United States as well, we made haste to comply, launching a major buildup of Soviet strength in the Pacific. As described by General Deane (who as has been seen was a significant figure at Yalta) our additions to the Soviet forces were many:

> We were given a list of the needs of the Soviet Union for a two months' supply of food, fuel, transport equipment and other supplies, calculated on a force of 1,500,000 men, 3,000 tanks, 75,000 motor vehicles and 5,000 airplanes. The total tonnage involved was 860,410 tons of dry cargo and 206,000 tons of liquid cargo. . . . [T]he end result was that the Soviets got their supplies and the United States got nothing except a belated and last minute Russian attack against the Japanese.[11]

Thus America generously paid the Soviets to do what it was in their interest to do in any event (and which Stalin at Teheran had promised to do unbidden, with no quid pro quo suggested).* Nor

---

* Stalin had previously said the same thing to Cordell Hull at a 1943 conference in Moscow. The Soviet leader made his unsolicited offer at Teheran on November 28, in the context of "second front" discussions. It was Roosevelt who two days later raised the issue of concessions to Moscow in Asia.

were the items named by Deane the full extent of the aid provided. The United States would also agree to supply to the Soviets an armada of small combat vessels in the Pacific and train Russian personnel to man them. When the war concluded, the Soviets were in possession of more than seven hundred ships provided in this manner. The materiel thus furnished would have been more useful to the Reds in postwar Asia than in their mopping-up skirmishes with Japan.[12]

All of this, like most of what occurred at Yalta, was mantled in concealment. The Asia protocols were agreed to on the last day of the conference by FDR and Stalin, Churchill not being present (he signed in pro forma manner later). No official notice was given of what was done, and Roosevelt would later say no Far East arrangements were even discussed at Yalta, much less agreed to. The document was meanwhile spirited back to Washington and locked up in a White House safe, where it would stay for months thereafter. It wasn't until February 1946 that Byrnes found the pact and made it public—a year to the day after it was signed at Yalta.[13]

This curtain of secrecy seems more significant yet when we note that the Asia protocol was written verbatim by the Russians. The go-between in this was Averell Harriman, who carried the document from the Soviets to FDR and back again, while suggesting some marginal changes of his own. This backdoor method made things still more clandestine, as it steered around State Department channels where a bit of checking could have shown that various Soviet claims in Asia were bogus. The justification for this hush-hush approach was that the accord was a "military" matter— the rationale likewise used for the Operation Keelhaul pact agreed to that same day, also in secret.

That the Asia protocols were written by the Soviets doesn't seem surprising, given the blatantly pro-Moscow nature of the provisions. Also significant, as Harriman would note, the most glaringly pro-Soviet clauses—regarding the "pre-eminent interests of the Soviet Union" and guaranteeing that Moscow's claims "shall unquestionably be fulfilled"—were last-minute additions by the Russians. Harriman said he objected to this, but that Roosevelt "was not disposed to haggle over words"—or indeed over much of anything the Soviets wanted.[14]

As some histories treat all this as no big deal, something Roosevelt had to do, and so on, it's noteworthy that such FDR supporters as former undersecretary of state Sumner Welles and Hopkins biographer Robert Sherwood would judge the Far East agreements harshly. Welles would say the Manchuria concessions were "tantamount to full control of that ancient province," the "more objectionable in view of China's absence from the conference table." Sherwood condemned the pledge that Moscow's claims on China "shall unquestionably be fulfilled," noting that this committed the United States and Britain to coercing Chiang Kai-shek into compliance.

Why FDR would have agreed to these one-sided provisos remains a puzzle. Sherwood opined that Roosevelt wouldn't have assented to the Soviet-drafted language except that "he was tired" and thought he could straighten things out with China later. Harriman's version was that the President had other goals in view (chiefly, getting the Soviets into the U.N.) and that "he may have been trying to save his strength" in agreeing to such concessions. All of which sounds like a polite way of saying FDR weakly gave away the freedom of China because of his impaired condition.[15]

At all events, the Asian protocol was an even more flagrant version of what had happened at Quebec, when Roosevelt signed off on postwar plans crafted for him by Harry White and other Soviet secret agents. The Yalta Far East accord went this one better, since it was drafted by the Russians themselves and came, via Harriman, direct from Stalin and his foreign commissar, V. M. Molotov. As Roosevelt would say he didn't recall what he initialed at Quebec, and at Yalta was even more enfeebled, it's a fair question whether he understood or remembered what was in the Far East concessions he agreed to.*

A further mystery was the nature of the "intelligence" relied on to justify the Asia provisos. As noted, there were other estimates concerning the endgame of the Pacific war, plus State Department papers warning against aspects of the Far East agreements, that didn't rise to policy-making levels, while a single estimate favorable to the goals of Moscow did so. In the case of the State Department memos, it's not mysterious that these didn't get through, since the person in charge of managing such papers was Hiss. That he would have passed along information adverse to the Stalinist cause may well be doubted.

It's also useful to recall the disinformation being sent back at the time of Yalta by the Soviet agent Adler (and his roommate Service) and being circulated in Washington by pro-Soviet operatives such as White. These bogus reports were all part of the "intelligence" mix on China, believed and acted on by U.S. officials. Relevant too were the findings of the Madden committee on Katyn, discussed in chapter 14, which found that pro-Soviet elements in intelligence ranks had deep-sixed information adverse to Moscow. The cover-up of Katyn, important as it was, would be far exceeded in strategic impact by what occurred at Yalta.

A final item worth noting is the interaction between happenings overseas and what was occurring on the home front. From Stalin's standpoint, it was essential that Japan's surrender be delayed to give him time to get into the Pacific fighting, move his armies east, and otherwise conduct a military buildup to back his postwar claims in Asia. In this respect, the Japanese played into his hands, believing—or hoping—that as their treaty partner he would negotiate some kind of settlement with the United States short of

* Recall also the statement of Hopkins that Roosevelt arguably didn't hear half of what was said at Yalta.

their complete destruction. Since Stalin's motives were the reverse of this, he instead strung them along until he was ready to attack them.

Aiding the process of delay were elements in the United States demanding a "hard" peace in Asia, which meant no give on "unconditional surrender" and—most important—no guarantees about the safety of the emperor. Absent these factors, as indicated in the pre-Yalta report provided by MacArthur, the Japanese arguably would have surrendered months before they did so. Thus demands by domestic radicals and pro-Soviet spokesmen for a "hard" peace in the Pacific dovetailed nicely with the needs of Moscow. Opposing them, as ever, was the State Department's Grew, who for his trouble would be branded an appeaser. Thus did the same cast of players, abroad and on the home front, appear repeatedly in the struggle for control of Asia.

18.

THE *AMERASIA* SCANDAL

Though not usually recognized as such, April 12, 1945, would be a fateful day in American Cold War history, and thus the history of the world in general.

On that day, two months after the Yalta summit ended, President Roosevelt's tenuous lease on life expired, as he suffered a massive stroke early in the afternoon and died two hours later. He would be succeeded in the Oval Office by a disconcerted Harry Truman, who had been vice president for less than ninety days and knew almost nothing of Roosevelt's dealings with Moscow or other foreign powers. In particular, Truman hadn't been privy to the decisions made at Yalta or Teheran (the latter occurring when he was still in the Senate) and of course knew even less about the penetration of the government by Alger Hiss and other Soviet agents—matters that would be sources of contention and strife for Truman throughout his tenure in the White House.

Also on April 12, a second important but far less conspicuous event occurred, one that would lead the FBI to discover a lot about the Communist penetration problem and the manner in which pro-Soviet forces were working to shape American policy toward Asia. On that day as well, diplomat John Stewart Service would arrive in Washington from China, ending his tempestuous tour of duty in that country. In the months preceding he had run afoul of the new U.S. ambassador to Chungking, Patrick Hurley, who had been perusing some of the dispatches Service and other Foreign Service officers sent back from China and didn't like what he was reading.

Pat Hurley was a Republican of some note (secretary of war under Herbert Hoover) but also a confidant of FDR, who liked movers and shakers of all descriptions who could get things done and was partial to Hurley on this basis. The ambassador had been sent to China in late 1944 to strengthen the war effort there, and contra General Stilwell understood this to mean supporting the regime of Chiang Kai-shek, while uniting different elements of the country in common cause against Japan (as he and others would discover, an impossible task). Though no student of Communist methods, Hurley knew blatant propaganda when he saw it, was shocked by the pro-Red material that Service and others like him were producing, and demanded their recall from China. Hence Service's arrival in Washington on April 12, rebuked and chastened but by no means ready to call off his anti-Chiang vendetta. On the contrary, as events would show, he was now prepared to pursue the project with equal fervor on the home front.

Soon after his arrival in Washington, Service would connect up with Andrew Roth, a lieutenant in the Office of Naval Intelligence (ONI) whose official bailiwick was Asia. The two had met the preceding fall when Service on a brief visit to the U.S. capital addressed a meeting of the IPR, where Roth and others mentioned in our discussion (notably Professor Owen Lattimore) were in attendance. At this meeting, Service and Roth had obviously hit it off, since within a week of Service's return in April they were once more in contact. Through Roth, Service would be introduced to a group of Asia-policy activists and writers who shared his anti-Chiang opinions, were avid supporters of the Communists at Yenan, and were anxious to tap into his firsthand knowledge.

The foremost member of this shadowy group was journalist/activist Philip Jaffe, publisher of a pro-Communist magazine called *Amerasia*, which as the name suggests was concerned with U.S. policy in the far Pacific. Jaffe was a Russian-born naturalized American citizen who combined entrepreneurial skills as a small businessman (manufacturer of greeting cards) with zeal for Marxist doctrine. *Amerasia* was but one of several sidelines he pursued in trying to serve pro-Communist causes. The journal was linked in multiple ways to the IPR, featuring among its editors and staffers such prominent IPR figures as Lattimore, the millionaire Communist Frederick Field, and the Communist operative Chi Chao-ting, who as noted had been a Service housemate in China. Jaffe was so ardent a fan of the rebels at Yenan that he had gone there in 1937 with Lattimore and Soviet intelligence asset T. A. Bisson to meet with Mao and Chou En-lai to show his solidarity with the Communist revolution.

In connecting up with Roth and the *Amerasia* crowd, John Service had unwittingly stepped into the middle of a wide-ranging FBI investigation that had been in progress for several weeks before then. This was a major inquest into suspected pro-Red spying linked to *Amerasia* involving Bureau wiretaps, microphone surveillance, and physical monitoring of the journal's staffers. Now the circle of suspects would be expanded to include the much more imposing figure of John Service. His recent important post in China, and his many official contacts, would escalate the FBI's inquiry up to the highest levels and lead to one of the most significant espionage cases of the Cold War.

This Bureau investigation was triggered by the discovery that the contents of a secret OSS memo had appeared, in some respects verbatim, in the pages of *Amerasia*—the obvious implication being that someone had been leaking official data to the journal. This led agents from OSS, and then the FBI, to conduct an in-depth probe of the magazine and its personnel, including dragnet coverage of the suspects and their contacts, plus entry into *Amerasia*'s New York offices to photograph papers being held there. In the course of this inquiry, the Bureau noted Jaffe's multifarious dealings with Service, Roth, State Department official Emmanuel Larsen, and journalist Mark Gayn. Interspersed with these, Jaffe was also surveilled meeting with U.S. Communist Party chief Earl Browder, visiting Chinese Communist bigwig Tung Pi-wu, officials at the Soviet consulate in New

York, and self-described Soviet espionage courier Joseph Bernstein.*

Given the emphasis of this probe on the hemorrhaging of official data, the FBI would predictably take notice when Service, in his contacts with Roth and Jaffe, immediately started sharing confidential information. This was both oral (including a statement about a military matter Service said was "very secret") and written (including a sheaf of documents Jaffe would take back with him to New York). The number and nature of these papers would later be disputed by Service and his defenders; suffice it here to note that the FBI would retrieve some fifty documents from the premises of *Amerasia* that, based on their official markings, were traceable to Service.[1]

Having observed a fair amount of this activity, including Jaffe's tête-à-têtes with Service, his meetings with high-ranking Communists and Soviet agents, and the frequent handing back and forth of papers, the FBI was authorized by the Department of Justice to proceed with arrests, preparatory to indictments and prosecution. Accordingly, on June 6, 1945, the Bureau rounded up three main suspects in New York City—Jaffe, *Amerasia* coeditor Kate Mitchell, and the journalist Gayn—and three more in Washington—Service, Roth, and Larsen. In the course of the arrests, the Bureau impounded copies of more than one thousand government documents found at *Amerasia*'s offices and in possession of the suspects. It was a substantial haul of people and a mother lode of data—constituting, in the view of FBI Director Hoover, an "airtight case," primed and ready for prosecution.[2]

And so at first it seemed. In a matter of weeks, however, the airtight case would be deflated, and the prosecution would collapse in mysterious fashion. In the end, nobody would be charged with espionage or any other major offense. Instead minor charges would be filed against

---

* In conversations with Jaffe monitored by the FBI, Bernstein revealed that he had been in contact with Soviet espionage operatives and was seeking to obtain information on their behalf.

Jaffe and Larsen, which were handled in perfunctory manner, while charges against Andrew Roth would later be dropped entirely. Service, Kate Mitchell, and Mark Gayn would in the meantime walk scot-free, no-billed by a U.S. grand jury (that is, with no indictments handed down against them). With this result, so far as the Truman Justice Department was concerned, the *Amerasia* case was over. Thereafter, Service and his defenders would portray him as a vindicated martyr— cleared of any wrongdoing by the grand jury and thus a Cold War victim, harassed because of his unfashionable views on China.

So the matter would be treated at the time and was still being treated decades later in State Department publications and purported Cold War histories. All of it, however, would turn out to be not only a whitewash of Service and his codefendants but something considerably worse—a felonious conspiracy to break the law, dupe the public, and cover up a case of pro-Red spying. As we now know, the suppression of the case was the result of a plot among U.S. officials to rig the grand jury process and falsify the legal and historical record. It was an elaborate scheme involving a host of people then holding federal office, much of it recorded by the FBI, preserved in Bureau records made public decades later.[3]

As it happened, when the *Amerasia* probe was winding down, the FBI hadn't ceased its wiretapping efforts but had simply turned them in a new direction. This further eavesdropping was ordered by President Truman in a case that at the outset had no connection to *Amerasia*, involving Washington wheeler-dealer Thomas ("Tommy the Cork") Corcoran, mentioned previously in our discussion, whom Truman suspected of malfeasance. In conducting this new series of wiretaps, the Bureau would discover Corcoran knee-deep in the *Amerasia* quagmire, trying to get the Service prosecution fixed, covering up the facts about the case, and making substantial progress in the effort.

At the center of this plot, along with Corcoran, was Roosevelt White House assistant Lauchlin Currie, pro-Soviet agent of influence and friend of Service, whose behind-the-scenes activities have been noted often in these pages. Likewise involved, though remaining in the background, was Corcoran's law partner Benjamin Cohen, then also a White House staffer, who would soon transfer to the State Department. As the Bureau records show, Currie, Corcoran, and a high-ranking group at the Justice Department in the summer of 1945 were conspiring to manipulate the grand jury and get Service off the hook—the other suspects being of minor interest but benefiting from their ties to Service.

In conversations tapped by the FBI, Corcoran discussed with Currie, Service, and others the steps being taken to fix the case and have Service no-billed or skip the grand jury altogether, thus officially "cleared" of all wrongdoing. Corcoran's contacts at Justice went to the very top, including lead prosecutor Robert Hitchcock, Assistant Attorney General James McInerney, and recently named attorney general Tom Clark. All these, so far as available records show, concurred in the goal of fixing the case and getting Service off, the only disagreement being on how to do this. The following exchanges suggest the flavor:

> SERVICE: Munter [Service's attorney] talked to Hitchcock yesterday to say I hadn't made up my mind [about appearing before the grand jury] and Hitchcock said, "Well, I hope you realize by this time that we want to have Service cleared by a legal body. . . ."

> CORCORAN: . . . Only thing is when I have a flat deal like that you are going to be cleared. . . . I don't like anyone to have to talk before a grand jury.

> SERVICE: Well, the statement by Hitchcock yesterday was the most encouraging. . . .

> CORCORAN: [after the decision was reached to go ahead to the grand jury] Don't worry when you go in. This is double riveted from top to bottom.[4]

These assurances turned out to be on target. Service would indeed be no-billed, by a grand jury vote of 20 to 0 (no great surprise when the prosecutor said this was the outcome that he wanted), and returned to the good graces of the State Department. There his next assignment would be a posting to Japan, where he would assist General MacArthur in his peacetime occupation efforts. (Also departing at this juncture for State Department duty in Japan were Service-Currie associates Lattimore and T. A. Bisson, and IPR figures Miriam Farley and Philip Keeney, along with others from the *Amerasia*-IPR contingent, including Cambridge alumnus Herbert Norman.)

It is thus apparent that, far from proving the innocence of Service, the grand jury proceedings and FBI records show the reverse—that he was the beneficiary of an illegal fix, grand jury rigging, and obstruction of justice by a wide-ranging conspiracy at high levels. He would later perjure himself about the matter in testimony to Congress. Perjury about the case would likewise be committed in congressional hearings by members of the Justice Department who did the fixing. Thus Service and others involved not only should have lost their federal jobs because of *Amerasia*, but arguably were candidates for serious jail time for the felonies that were committed.

All of this would be an eye-opening experience for the FBI, not only as to the machinations of pro-Red agents in the United States but also the willingness of some in official places to conceal the facts about such matters from the public. There had been cases before in which significant data on subversion were ignored—most notably, the strange indifference to the revelations of Whittaker Chambers. (There had been a further such instance in the early 1940s in which Justice buried a report from the House Committee on Un-American Activities concerning more than a thousand security suspects on official payrolls.) But *Amerasia* went well beyond those cases, since in this instance officials not only ignored the security intelligence but engaged in felonious actions to conceal it.

Compounding the problem, when the case later came partially

to public view through congressional hearings, the Justice Department would try to explain the failure of the prosecution by scapegoating the FBI for allegedly mishandling the *Amerasia* papers. Since Hoover and his agents knew what they had done in gathering evidence, and further knew via their wiretaps that Justice itself was complicit in the fix, these allegations were doubly galling to the Bureau. Disagreement about such topics would lead to tense exchanges between the FBI and Truman Justice as to what should be said to Senate investigators who probed the scandal.

The angriest of such exchanges—though far from the only one—concerned a newspaper account saying that Hoover had indeed viewed the *Amerasia* affair as an "airtight case" and said so to a reporter. This was directly contrary to the administration line that the case was no big deal, consisting simply of Service's efforts to provide "background" to a member of the press corps. Accordingly, Justice officials made haste to disavow the Hoover quote, drafting a proposed public statement declaring that he never said it. This further enraged the director, who told Assistant Attorney General Peyton Ford: "... I have carefully reviewed this [statement] and cannot approve it.... [I]n the event I had been asked about the case at the time the arrests were made whether I thought we had an airtight case, I would have stated that I thought we had. Further, if I were asked today I would have to so state." (Justice would issue the disavowal anyway.)[5]

Similar conflicts between the FBI and Truman officials would occur in the months succeeding, as further information about the penetration problem came to light. Most significant in this respect was the earlier noted testimony of defecting Soviet courier Elizabeth Bentley. Bentley went to the FBI with her story in November 1945, just as the *Amerasia* case was nearing a conclusion. In a series of debriefings, she gave the Bureau an overview of Soviet U.S. operations of the war years, naming more than two dozen alleged agents, Communist Party members, and fellow travelers then still in federal office. Coming in the immediate aftermath of *Amerasia*, this was a further wake-up call for Hoover and the Bureau.

Bentley's disclosures triggered the investigation noted in chapter 6, as the FBI shadowed her suspects and their contacts, conducted wiretaps, engaged in "bag jobs," and otherwise kept the Bentley people under tight surveillance. It also went back and looked at other security records, including its interviews with Chambers, and found numerous overlaps between his suspects and those named by Bentley. From this endeavor the Bureau put together a huge compendium of files and reports, running to tens of thousands of pages, concerning such Cold War figures as Hiss, White, Currie, Silvermaster, and scores of others. These reports were provided in copious fashion to the agencies where the suspects were or had been working, to the attorney general, and to the White House.

However, in keeping with earlier disregard for the data supplied by Chambers and the cover-up of *Amerasia*, the Bureau reports on Bentley's cases were received mostly with indifference, if not outright resentment. In some cases, departmental security forces did move against the suspects, pressuring them quietly to resign from their positions. A good deal of activity along these lines occurred in the State Department, at the direction of security officer J. Anthony Panuch, who tried to deal with the problem behind the scenes by forcing through such resignations. But in early 1947 Panuch and his security team would themselves be ousted from their jobs, to be succeeded by officials who took a markedly more lenient view of security issues.[6]

The security efforts of Panuch and his colleagues were occasionally matched in other venues, but for the most part FBI reports concerning suspects on official payrolls were buried, ignored, or "lost"—a source of further annoyance to Hoover. In some instances official higher-ups not only disputed the security intelligence but worked to discredit the people who supplied it. Thereafter, when data pertaining to such matters began leaking to members of Congress, the

The FBI Chart on Hiss

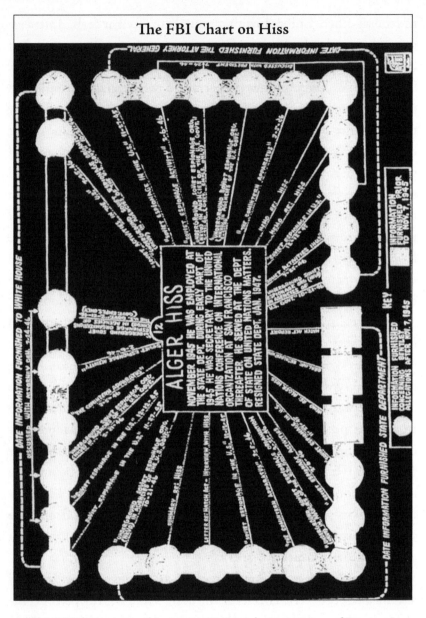

This FBI chart, prepared in August 1948 on the instructions of Director J. Edgar Hoover, indicates the large number of Bureau reports about Soviet agent Alger Hiss provided to the State Department and other federal agencies, beginning in November 1945—almost three full years before the case became a public scandal. (Diagonal lines refer to specific reports, circles to receiving agencies.) (*Source: FBI Silvermaster file*)

administration handed down a stringent order that forbade disclosure of security information by executive agencies under any and all conditions—a secrecy edict that would stand for decades.

All this would be followed by a series of congressional hearings in 1948 in which Hill investigators developed information that tracked closely with the Bureau's inquest. The most famous of these were the Hiss-Chambers hearings held by the House Committee on Un-American Activities in the summer of 1948. In these sessions information concerning Hiss, White, Currie, Silvermaster, and others was to some degree made public. Records held in secret archives and some equally secret grand jury sessions were now no longer entirely secret. For members of Congress and the media who had no previous inkling of the wartime penetration, the data thus supplied were shocking.

As occurred with *Amerasia*, executive officials in the wake of these hearings tried to pin responsibility for inaction on the FBI. Rumors were floated that the Bureau had been asleep at the wheel, failed to inform officials of the danger, and withheld information from President Truman. (Similar tales of supposed FBI ineptitude and inaction would be heard in the 1990s when the *Venona* decrypts were published.) All of this, again, would anger Hoover, who knew what the FBI had done about the cases and how inert the response had been at higher levels.

Accordingly, in August 1948, Hoover had his staffers draw up a series of summaries and charts showing the vast number of FBI reports about the suspects that had been supplied to top officials. The master chart concerning these indicated that no fewer than 380 oral and written reports had been provided, the vast majority going to the White House and Truman Justice.[7] Individual charts on major suspects showed the vast number of reports that had been filed in specific cases. That the Bureau had done its job in tracking and reporting the penetration was thus evident at a glance; responsibility for the failure to do much of anything about it obviously lay elsewhere.

19.

STATE AND REVOLUTION

One obvious effect of the *Amerasia* fix was that numerous suspects who might have been exposed by any halfway competent inquest were allowed to walk when John Service was acquitted.

High on this list of suspects was Roosevelt White House assistant Currie, who as noted was a top-ranking pro-Soviet asset, and not so coincidentally one of the major fixers. Also concealed from view were Service's Chungking housemates Chi and Adler, both of whom were Soviet agents and had multiple other contacts of like nature. Of note in this respect were Adler's Treasury colleagues Harry White and V. Frank Coe, two more high-level Soviet agents of influence who were thus protected.

Add to these a group of Service colleagues who worked foreign policy issues and shared his pro-Maoist views on China. These included Far Eastern expert John Carter Vincent, State Department officials Haldore Hanson and O. Edmund Clubb, former OWI staffers Lattimore and Barnes, and a sizable crew of others. On the edges of this circle were activists of the IPR with links not only to Jaffe and his journal, but to such pro-Red apparatchiks as T. A. Bisson, espionage courier Joseph Bernstein, Sorge spy alumni Guenther Stein and Chen Han Seng, and members of the Cambridge connection, including Michael Greenberg and Herbert Norman. This network or a considerable portion of it could have been uncovered by an adequate follow-up of the *Amerasia* scandal but was screened from view by the grand jury fixers.[1]

This failure to bring pro-Soviet operatives to light was not, however, the total story. Arguably as important was the manner in which the cover-up became the pretext for increasing the already formidable leverage that Service and his allies exerted on U.S. policy toward China. This was, if not the most significant aspect of the case, certainly the most ironic. An episode that should have resulted in unearthing the swarm of clandestine forces working to promote the Reds of Asia instead resulted in strengthening those forces and in the ouster from official posts of people who opposed them.

In this respect, the *Amerasia* case was the culmination of a process that had been going on at State for almost a decade, affecting not only personnel and policy toward China, but Soviet-Communist interests in general. Behind the serene façade of the department there had been waged since the latter 1930s a series of bitter struggles between conservatives in the diplomatic corps and staffers amenable to the concerns of Moscow. In some phases of this contest, the conservatives would win the day, but in the last decisive battles would be defeated.

Contrary to its later image, and despite the presence of Hiss, Duggan, and other pro-Red infiltrators, the State Department in the 1930s and early '40s was known mostly as a conservative place, with prominent anti-Communists in key positions. Foremost among these was Undersecretary Joseph Grew, a longtime mainstay of the department, respected diplomat, and no great fan of Moscow.* Others who shared his outlook included Robert Kelley of the Russia desk, Soviet expert Loy Henderson, Far Eastern specialist Stanley Hornbeck, and security analyst Raymond Murphy. All were knowledgeable students of the Communist problem and

---

* Grew was a forty-year veteran of the department, a founder of the Foreign Service, had served as ambassador to Japan, and was twice appointed to the high position at State of undersecretary/acting secretary.

skeptical of Stalin and his agents, and all would in due course be targeted for dismissal from their positions.

This purge had begun in the 1930s as FDR and various of his advisers sought closer ties with Russia, building on their recognition of the Red regime there. By 1937, Roosevelt's first appointee to the Moscow embassy, William Bullitt, had soured on the Red experiment and said so in dispatches. FDR's more accommodationist stance would be signaled by Bullitt's departure from the USSR and the advent of the pro-Soviet Joseph Davies, whose views as to the virtues of Stalin and the Communist system have been noted.

This switch coincided with backstage efforts to muzzle anti-Red department staffers on the home front. The first to feel the effects of this crackdown was the Russian division, headed by Robert Kelley, a unit considered to be a bastion of anti-Soviet expertise and counsel. Kelley was a scholarly sort who had followed the Soviet revolution from the outset, maintained an extensive library and filing system on its doings, and knew a lot about the Reds and their objectives. In June 1937, concurrent with the rise of Davies, Kelley was informed that his division was to be abolished and he himself shipped off to a job in Turkey.

A retrospective of this coup would be provided by State Department officials Charles E. Bohlen and George F. Kennan, who in the 1930s were up-and-coming young diplomats serving at the embassy in Moscow. Given their eventual fame as Cold War experts—both would later serve as U.S. ambassador to Russia—their comments on the origins of the diplomatic purge are of interest.

As Bohlen would describe it, what happened in the 1930s was a battle between "State Department old line officers and powerful figures in the White House" concerning Russia. As to who the powerful figures were, Bohlen said he was uncertain but that departmental sources thought Mrs. Roosevelt and Harry Hopkins were the leaders of the White House faction. He further stated that, in the background, "the Russians themselves, I believe, took part in the campaign against Kelley."[2]

Concomitant with Kelley's ouster was an effort to disperse the library and files on Communism he had assembled, a move Bohlen took measures to forestall by concealing and protecting records targeted for such treatment. As his colleague Kennan would remember:

> *The entire shop was to be liquidated, and its functions transferred to the division of East European affairs. . . . The beautiful library was to be turned over to the Library of Congress, to be distributed there by file number among its other vast holdings and thus cease to exist as a library. The special files were to be destroyed. . . . Here, if ever, was a point at which there was indeed the smell of Soviet influence, or strongly pro-Soviet influence, somewhere in the higher reaches of the government.*[3]

As might be guessed from earlier comment, pressures against anti-Soviet officials would intensify in the pro-Moscow climate of the war years. A noteworthy instance occurred in the winter of 1943, when Admiral William Standley, our then ambassador to the USSR, made remarks to members of the press corps about Soviet conduct relating to Lend-Lease supplies shipped to Russia. The extent of this assistance, said Standley, wasn't being disclosed to the Russian people by Red officials. His statements stirred up a furor in the United States, since any criticism of our Soviet ally, however truthful, was verboten. Demands were made for Standley's ouster, and he would in a matter of months be gone from his post in Moscow.

Running parallel with the Standley case was that of Loy Henderson, a top-ranking expert on Soviet affairs who served in Eastern Europe at the time of the Bolshevik Revolution and then at the embassy in Moscow (where he mentored both George

Kennan and Chip Bohlen). Henderson was an intramural ally of Kelley and shared his view of Red intentions. Henderson's ideas to this effect were well-known to Soviet diplomats and agents, pitting him against Soviet ambassador Maxim Litvinov, whom Henderson neither liked nor trusted and with whom the hostility was mutual.

In the dustup over Standley, a member of Congress had named Henderson as the likely source of the admiral's negative view of Moscow. Publicity to this effect escalated pro-Soviet pressures against Henderson, with decisive impact at the State Department and the White House. In a remarkable episode, the Soviets via Litvinov presented to Undersecretary of State Sumner Welles a list of U.S. personnel they deemed unfriendly, on which list Henderson was predictably included. Thereafter, Litvinov would explicitly urge that Henderson be ousted from his job dealing with East-West issues—a startling instance of a foreign power presuming to dictate the makeup of America's diplomatic service.

According to Henderson's memoir of these events, this Soviet demand would be complied with—though Secretary of State Cordell Hull tried to resist it and initially thought that he could do so. In the end, Henderson was called in by Hull and told he was to be dismissed from his position. "The people over there," said Hull, gesturing toward the White House, "want a change." And what "the people over there" wanted, they got. Soviet/East European expert Henderson, sharing in the Mideast exile of Kelley, was transferred to Iraq.[4]

The purge of Henderson would be followed by a campaign against security specialist Raymond Murphy. Murphy was another important player in the drama, since he kept track of Communist machinations in domestic matters as well as in the global context, and like Kelley maintained extensive records on such topics. In 1944 he too was told his assignment would be altered and his files disposed of. As related by diplomatic historian Martin Weil,

Murphy at this juncture said to Loy Henderson: "Current Communist tactics [are] to force from government service any public official who will not go along with what they conceive to be the best interests of the Soviet Union and the Communist Party of the United States."*5

Rather than abating, these State Department battles would become more intense as the war neared a conclusion, with sharp disagreements as to what peacetime course to follow toward the Kremlin. One group argued that harmony with Moscow could be attained by still more accommodation, the view that would prevail at Yalta. Another group took a tougher line, saying we needed to be firm in dealings with the Russians. A participant in these disputes was Assistant Secretary of State Adolf Berle, who in 1939 had received security data from Whittaker Chambers. As Berle later said in congressional hearings relating to Alger Hiss:

> *As I think many people know, in the fall of 1944 there was a difference of opinion in the State Department. I felt that the Russians were not going to be sympathetic and cooperative. . . . I was pressing for a pretty clean-cut showdown when our position was the strongest. The opposite group in the State Department was largely the men—Mr. [Dean] Acheson's group, of course, with Mr. Hiss as his principal assistant in the matter. . . . I got trimmed in that fight, and as a result was sent to Brazil, and that ended my diplomatic career.*[6]

---

* The Henderson case was unusual in that the Soviet intervention was so overt, which wasn't the normal method. More typically, such pressures were exerted either from within the government, by outside groups such as the IPR, or by members of the press corps. As noted by Weil, key players in this respect were White House staffer David Niles, Treasury Secretary Morgenthau, and Vice President Henry Wallace. In the press corps, leading critics of the anti-Soviets at State included the columnist Drew Pearson, Joe Barnes of the *New York Herald Tribune* (and OWI), and press gadfly I. F. Stone. All would keep up a steady drumbeat of criticism against conservatives in the department.

Thus Berle would join Kelley and the others in diplomatic exile. In this context the Acheson reference may come as a surprise to readers accustomed to recent histories depicting him as a Cold War hawk and foe of Stalin, which he would one day become, at least on matters involving Western Europe. How this change occurred is the topic for another essay. For now, enough to note that Acheson at the period referred to had a profile sharply different from his later image, as he was then considered the State Department's foremost "progressive" on issues involving Russia.

All the episodes thus cited, though important, were merely prelude to the seismic changes that would rock the department in the wake of *Amerasia*. These would be even more significant than the treatment of Kelley, Henderson, et al., as they reached up to the highest levels. In this instance, the target was the respected Joseph Grew, a senior diplomatic figure and doyen of the Foreign Service. He was also a man of generally conservative views, which made him a thorn in the side of the "progressives" on many issues.

As discussed, Grew had been on the opposite side from Currie, White, Lattimore, and other leftward spokesmen in the run-up to Pearl Harbor. He then clashed with pro-Red elements at the time of Yalta over Operation Keelhaul, which consigned two million helpless victims to their doom in Russia. As the end of the war approached, he would be accused by Soviet apologist Lattimore and others of favoring a "soft" peace in the Pacific. All of this would align the "progressives" against Grew in angry phalanx. However, the episode that triggered the most violent opposition to the undersecretary was the wrangle over *Amerasia*.

When the scandal surfaced in June 1945, it fell to Grew as acting secretary (Stettinius at that time attending the San Francisco founding conference of the United Nations) to give a State Department green light for arrests and prosecution. In a press statement, Grew said there had been a noise "in the chicken coop," security officials had responded, and measures were being taken to head off such problems in the future. These comments ignited a firestorm in the radical press, chiefly in the *Daily Worker*, where it was charged that Grew was waging a vendetta against federal staffers (such as arrestee Andrew Roth) who opposed "soft peace" notions for Japan.[7]

The *Worker* and others now demanded that Grew and like-minded colleagues be ousted, thus upping the ante from the attacks on Kelley-Henderson-Murphy. Remarkably, within two months of the arrests, Grew would in fact resign, to be replaced by Acheson in the powerful post of undersecretary. Making the transition even more important, it coincided with the arrival on the scene of a new secretary of state, former senator and Supreme Court justice James F. Byrnes. An experienced politician but foreign policy tyro, Byrnes was unschooled in the inner workings of the department, and would remain so. During his year and a half as secretary, he would spend a vast amount of time overseas, attending conferences on postwar issues. While he was away, whoever was undersecretary would be acting secretary, wielding day-to-day control of the department. The switch from Grew to Acheson meant this vital role would be performed not by a seasoned diplomat skeptical of Moscow, but by a relative newcomer to the department* and point man for the "progressives."

Most important in *Amerasia* context, Acheson was in close alignment with the China policy faction represented by John Service. This meant first and foremost John Carter Vincent, like Service a China specialist hostile to Chiang Kai-shek and well disposed toward the rebels at Yenan. One of Acheson's first acts when he assumed de facto control at State was to name Vincent head of the Far East division, shunting aside such Asia experts as Stanley Hornbeck and Grew deputy Eugene Dooman. With those changes the course of China policy was foreordained, since Vincent was

---

* Acheson had been at State only since 1941, one-tenth as long as Grew.

thick not only with Service but with the Soviet agent of influence Currie, the pro-Soviet Lattimore, and others of the IPR contingent.

With a new president who knew nothing of the matter, a new secretary of state whose interests were elsewhere, and knowledgeable anti-Communists ousted, Acheson, Vincent, Service, and company would have a free hand conducting policy toward Asia, driving the final nails into the coffin of China. Their methods included a complete cutoff of military aid to Chiang, matching the Treasury cutoff of economic aid engineered by Soviet agents White and Adler. (The denial of military aid, ordered by George Marshall on his China mission, would be explicit from July 1946 to May 1947, after which Acheson would obstruct deliveries by backdoor tactics like those used by White and Adler to block the gold loan.)[8] It was on Acheson's watch also that other blows were struck against Chiang, including the several plots to overthrow him on Formosa.

Among those sidetracked in these various purges was Stanley Hornbeck, a veteran diplomat well versed in Far Eastern matters.* Now, following the path marked out by Kelley, Henderson, and Berle, he too would be assigned to extraneous duties—becoming U.S. ambassador to Holland. As he would later comment, "it was . . . in the year 1945 . . . that the government of the United States . . . embarked upon what became a course of intervention in the civil conflict [in China] exerting pressures upon the National government . . . not against the Communists but in their behalf. . . ."[9]

Beyond these high-level changes were further shifts in State Department personnel that are worth mention. Wartime agencies such as OSS, OWI, and BEW were as has been discussed heavily penetrated by Communists, fellow travelers, and Soviet agents. In the fall of 1945, when these units were abolished, thousands of

---

* Though not so well versed in matters of Red infiltration, as he was one of the State Department bosses of Alger Hiss who didn't view him with suspicion.

their staffers would be transferred to the State Department. The security problems hatched in the war would thus come to roost at State. The merger would replicate, on a broader scale, previous "trapdoor" operations such as the National Research Project of the 1930s and the Short Wave/OWI connection of the early 1940s.

Though less momentous than some other changes at State, the new staff brought in by the merger would tilt things still further in pro-Red directions. Among the new inductees were such Elizabeth Bentley suspects as Robert Miller and Bernard Redmont, *Venona* alumni Maurice Halperin and Donald Wheeler, OSS employees Franz Neumann and Stanley Graze, and many others of like nature. All would eventually be targets of investigation by the FBI, State Department security screeners, and committees of Congress. Equally important, many would be subjects of an inquest by a U.S. grand jury, whose curious doings, like the *Amerasia* case, revealed a lot about security standards of the era.

This mysterious merger was engineered by the Bureau of the Budget, and is thus treated in some histories as a boring technical business, simply blending several bureaucracies into one as an economy measure. An examination of the record, however, suggests more substantive reasons for the merger. The head of the Bureau at this time was a civil servant named Harold Smith, who as his diaries and other records show was a frequent adviser to the Truman White House. In the spring of 1945, after the death of Roosevelt, Truman was trying to find out what was going on in the bureaucracy and often relied on Smith for briefings. Smith used this access to promote the merger of OSS and OWI into State as a measure favored by FDR. Truman, knowing nothing different, told Smith to proceed according to the plan that Roosevelt had sanctioned.[10]

The record further shows that Smith was more than a technician. State Department security chief Panuch would identify him as a close ally of Alger Hiss, a description Panuch likewise applied to Smith aides Paul Appleby and George Schwarzwalder. Smith's daybooks show him in frequent contact with this duo, as well as with former budget official Wayne Coy and former vice president Henry Wallace. Appleby and Coy, as earlier noted, were attendees at the wartime soirees put together by Harry White. Schwarzwalder would be identified to the FBI by security expert Ben Mandel as one of the budget officials who visited federal agencies urging that security archives be abolished.[11]

As the record shows as well, Smith was also the official who came up with the executive order merging parts of OSS into State, where Acheson as acting secretary would welcome the new arrivals and set out to organize them as a brand-new intelligence unit. This resulted in yet another internal struggle, as the security forces under Panuch, who knew something about the problems at OSS, fought against the planned new service as a dangerous incursion. In the end, Acheson would lose this battle—one of the few in which he was ever defeated. These developments would lead in turn to a final showdown between the Acheson contingent and the Panuch security forces.

Having battled Panuch about the recruits from OSS and other security issues, Acheson was now determined to oust the security chief from his position. This he was able to do early in 1947 when George Marshall became secretary of state and gave the already influential undersecretary virtual carte blanche over State's internal workings. By the end of the first day of the Marshall-Acheson era at State, Panuch was out of office. The rout of the more conservative forces was now all but complete and State's huge security problem further concealed from press and public. Thereby would the stage be set for the historic congressional hearings of 1948, plus some grand jury sessions that have received far less attention but are equally worthy of our notice.

20.

A NOT SO GRAND GRAND JURY

A mong many unsolved mysteries left over from our domestic Cold War is the strange tale of the U.S. grand jury that convened in 1947 to hear Elizabeth Bentley's charges of subversion. This specially summoned, potentially crucial, and to this day inscrutable panel met in New York City off and on for eighteen months, from June 1947 to December 1948. During its extended life span, it heard from approximately one hundred witnesses, some forty of whom were Bentley suspects, weighing her account of Red conniving in high places.

Throughout, these grand jury sessions tracked the FBI investigation of Bentley's statements, covering much of the same ground and featuring the same cast of players. The witnesses weren't then famous, but would be known to history later. They included Alger Hiss, Harry White, Lauchlin Currie, N. G. Silvermaster, William Remington, V. Frank Coe, Harold Glasser, Maurice Halperin, Robert Miller, Solomon Adler, and dozens more of like persuasion. (The complete list of grand jury witnesses heard from June 1947 to April 1948 appears on page 234.)

Gauged by what we know today, this was a spectacular lineup—an all-star team of Soviet agents, Communists, and close-in fellow travelers, all familiar to the FBI though not yet to the public. Among them were two suspects eventually sent to prison for lying about their Red connections (Hiss and Remington), two more who would defect to Communist China (Coe and Adler), and numerous others named in *Venona* and other official security records as assets of the Kremlin (Currie, Miller, Halperin, White, Silvermaster, Glasser).

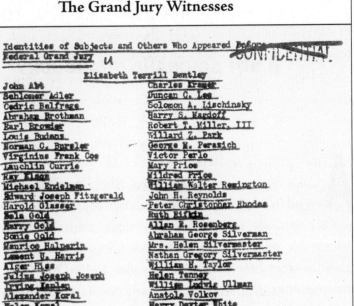

The FBI list of witnesses before the mysterious federal grand jury of 1947–48, which considered ex-Communist Elizabeth Bentley's charges of subversion. The list featured a galaxy of Soviet agents, Communists, and fellow travelers, including Alger Hiss, Lauchlin Currie, Harry Dexter White, Nathan G. Silvermaster, Solomon Adler, and many others allowed to walk free by the grand jury and Truman Justice. Noteworthy also are potential witnesses not on the list, most conspicuously Whittaker Chambers, who could have confirmed Bentley's story. (*Source: FBI Silvermaster file*)

All these, plus a considerable number of their friends and allies, had been working not long before this for the U.S. government, or the global organizations, often in fairly high positions. By the time the grand jury met, many had been eased out by pressures from the FBI, backstage congressional protests, and the actions of security forces. Even so, some veteran apparatchiks (Coe, Remington, Glasser, Adler) were still on official payrolls, as were a sizable group of other suspects not on the Bentley roster.

In short, about as important a case as a grand jury could consider, featuring life-and-death security issues and an array of suspects that reads today like a who's who of Communist moles and Soviet agents. It would be hard to imagine a more significant proceeding, or one more fraught with potential drama.

Yet after this grand jury had met for over a year and questioned two-score Bentley suspects, nothing whatever resulted from its labors. In the summer of 1948, when the jurors finished the Bentley phase of their inquiry (they would reconvene for other purposes later), they handed down not a single indictment of her cases. Nor did they file a presentment, as grand juries sometimes do, calling attention to the issues they'd considered. So not only did the suspects walk but, as important, the graphic picture of pro-Red subversion sketched by Bentley would be kept completely secret.

With that, so far as the Justice Department was concerned, the Bentley case was closed. To replace it, on July 20, Justice launched a surprise maneuver, switching official notice to a different matter—indictment of the leaders of the open Communist Party for alleged violations of the Smith Act. As the witness list through April 1948 makes clear (none of the party leaders of that day was on it),* this wasn't the reason the jury was empaneled, and wasn't

---

* Earl Browder was on the list, but three years before this he had been ousted from his party leadership position.

the issue it was weighing. But in the summer of 1948 it would be the major headline emerging from its inquest.

Various theories have been advanced as to why all the Bentley suspects, including such egregious cases as Hiss and White, were given a pass by this grand jury. The reason cited in the usual histories is that the prosecutors had only Bentley's word to go on, with no other witness to support her story. Nor, per the standard treatments, did she have proof of spying in the form of purloined official papers connected to her suspects.

Perjury indictments were another option—but again the Bentley-only thesis blocked the way to action. With no second witness or supporting data, any perjury charge would have been a she-said, he-said affair, all but impossible to prove in court. As FBI official Edward Morgan put it, the case was "nothing more than the word of Bentley against the word of the conspirators." [1]

This study in futility ground to a halt in midsummer 1948, to be closely followed by events that took things in a totally new direction. The jury's failure to indict was prelude, not only to the surprise move against the Communist Party bosses, but to an explosive series of congressional hearings that ran from late July through the end of August. These were separate but parallel sessions of a Senate Expenditures subcommittee* and the House Committee on Un-American Activities, in both of which Bentley would be the leadoff witness and the people she named were called to answer her assertions.

These hearings, especially those of the House committee, would

---

* The Expenditures Committee would later be renamed the Committee on Government Operations. The subcommittee's hearings, chaired by Senator Homer Ferguson (R-MI), would be focused on the case of William Remington.

be of historic nature—would be, indeed, among the most famous such hearings ever, and among the most important, with results completely different from those reached by the New York grand jury. Nevertheless, the Bentley-only version of why that jury acted as it did—or, more precisely, failed to act—has long been the accepted theory of the case, much repeated in Cold War studies.

Today, however, we have information that wasn't available in previous decades, including some of the jury minutes and archives of the FBI pertaining to the cases. These tell a story starkly different from the accepted version. By far the most significant thing they tell us is that, contra the statements of Edward Morgan, the Justice Department, and the usual histories, federal prosecutors from the outset *did* have a confirming witness to back up Bentley and thus pave the way for indictments, but as of the summer of 1948 had simply failed to call him.

That uncalled witness, cooling his heels for over a year while the grand jury was in progress, was Whittaker Chambers. Chambers didn't know all the people on Bentley's list, but did know, or know of, a considerable number, so there was a substantial overlap between her suspects and those who could have been named by Chambers. Chief among these were Hiss and White, two hugely important suspects, both appearing before the jury and both well-known to Chambers. Indeed, Chambers knew far more about this duo than did Bentley, since he had worked with them directly, as she hadn't.* So he unquestionably could have backstopped her on these cases, giving the prosecutors the confirming witness they allegedly were in search of. Yet though the FBI was well aware of Chambers and what he could have told the jury, prosecutors for

---

* Running third to Hiss and White as a significant Cold War figure was former White House assistant Lauchlin Currie, a close friend of White, named as a pro-Soviet mole by Bentley—another identification that matched with data known to Chambers.

over a year refused to call him. Hence no second witness in the cases—hence no indictments.*

Though glossed over in the usual write-ups, the fact that Chambers up through the summer of 1948 hadn't been called by the grand jury is alluded to in several places in Bureau records. These make it clear why he wasn't called and provide a suggestive picture of attitudes at the Justice Department that guided the grand jury process.

Thus one FBI entry from March 1948 raised the question of whether Chambers should be called in the Bentley sessions and concluded that he would not be. According to this update, federal prosecutor Thomas Donegan was *of the opinion that Chambers testimony would not be helpful and has decided against any attempt to have the latter appear before the grand jury.*[†2] (Emphasis here and elsewhere in this chapter added.) This thumbs-down on Chambers occurred toward the tag end of the jury sessions in the spring of 1948 dealing with the Bentley cases.

The question of a Chambers appearance would come up again in the wake of the congressional hearings four months later that put his charges on the record, and in the headlines. Once more, however, he would not be summoned by Truman Justice. A Bureau memo dated September 20, 1948—almost a month after

---

* Only after Chambers appeared before the August sessions of the House committee was he brought before a reconvened and reenergized grand jury—this occurring in mid-October 1948.

† The issue of whether he had been called would arise in August, during the House committee hearings, when the Chambers testimony against Alger Hiss would rock the nation. On August 3, the first day of Chambers's appearance before the House committee, FBI officials did a double check as to whether he had been called before the grand jury. The memo on this informs us: "Whittaker Chambers did not testify before GJ NYC and no indication ever received from Messrs. [Vincent] Quinn [the assistant attorney general assigned to the case] or Donegan that he prepared any statement whatever for the GJ."

Chambers and Hiss had their sensational clash before the House committee—says Donegan and the grand jury had "discussed the desirability of having Whittaker Chambers and General William J. Donovan [former head of the Office of Strategic Services]" appear before them, but ". . . *no decision was reached on either Chambers or Donovan.*"[3]

So Chambers still wasn't called, though his House testimony had by this time sparked a deadly feud with Hiss, touched off a national furor, and caused ideological armies to line up for an apocalyptic struggle that hasn't yet abated. The case of the century was mushrooming to huge proportions, with vast legal and historical issues riding on the outcome. But federal prosecutors still hadn't called the former Soviet courier who would later be the most famous witness of the Cold War.

Almost as peculiar as the fact that Chambers hadn't come before the jury was the reason cited for his absence. According to the Bureau archives, he had been asked if he would give evidence in a separate matter: an executive loyalty hearing in the case of Solomon Adler, an earlier noted Treasury staffer, Bentley suspect, and China roommate of John Service. Though Chambers hadn't dealt with Adler directly, he did know something of Adler's doings and so informed the FBI. For unstated reasons, prosecutors would tie Chambers's possible grand jury testimony on all of the other Bentley cases to what he might say about this separate hearing. In which connection, the above-quoted Donegan memo says that "*in view of the negative info supplied by Chambers re Adler,*" grand jury testimony from Chambers would not be helpful.[4]

Considering what the FBI knew of Chambers, this Donegan comment rings hollow. As the records show, the Chambers take on Adler wasn't "negative info," except that he didn't claim to have dealt with Adler directly. Rather, according to Chambers, Soviet spy chief J. Peters had said he was receiving reports from Adler, which led Chambers to conclude that Adler was a Communist Party member. If testimony about this would be of use, said Chambers, he would so testify. This was hearsay of a type not uncommon in conspiracy cases, but scarcely rated as "negative info." To describe it thus without explanation was grossly misleading—conveying the notion that Chambers had nothing to say concerning Adler, or else refused to say it, neither of which was true.

And even if Chambers had come up totally empty on Adler, what of it? That wasn't a valid reason for not asking him about *other* Bentley cases concerning whom he knew plenty—a fact of which the FBI was already conscious. When the grand jurors convened in 1947, the Bureau in fact had an excellent grasp of the things Chambers could tell them—since he had previously told much of his story to Hoover's agents.

The FBI first interviewed Chambers on May 14, 1942, and a year later obtained Adolf Berle's notes concerning his revelations of 1939. The Bureau interviewed Chambers again in 1945 and 1946, months before the grand jury assembled. His information was featured in one of the earliest FBI reports about the infiltration problem—"Soviet Espionage in the United States," dated November 27, 1945. This was based on the Bentley revelations, data concerning *Amerasia*, and other developing cases. It also contained a summary of the Hiss case, based on the Chambers disclosures. Thus the FBI, thanks to Chambers, had a bead on Hiss almost three full years before the case became a public scandal.*[5]

---

* Further disclosures concerning Hiss would appear in subsequent FBI reports, including "Underground Soviet Espionage Organization (NKVD) in Agencies of the United States Government," February 1, 1946, and "The Comintern Apparatus (COMRAP)," March 5, 1946. The latter included Chambers's statements concerning Alger and Donald Hiss, Henry Collins, Lee Pressman, and Sol Adler. Thereafter, a lengthy Bureau memo of March 26, 1946, directed to J. Edgar Hoover, summarized Chambers's statements on Hiss and his brother Donald, as well as Collins, Pressman, Nathan Witt, John Abt, and Harold Ware.

Asked by the FBI in March 1946 if he would testify about Hiss, Chambers said that "if he were called to testify he did not see how he could refuse to do so," though he hoped this might be in executive session. He further stated that he wanted "to do everything in his power to expose Communism in this country." The interviewing Bureau agents concluded that *"Chambers was receptive, cordial and cooperative and it is felt that if the Bureau decided to conduct an investigation of Hiss' Communist activities that Chambers will agree to anything within reason."*[6] Such was the positive FBI appraisal of Chambers twenty-four months before Justice officials casually dismissed him as a source of "negative info" not worth calling as a witness.*

If "negative info" didn't explain the Chambers absence, other items in the record make the matter clearer. A recurring theme in the FBI reports is the notion, adopted by Justice from the outset, that the grand jury wouldn't hand down indictments in the Bentley cases, but would, as with *Amerasia*, "no bill" the suspects, letting them walk free from legal sanctions.

Thus an FBI memo from early 1947 says Justice wanted the Bureau to interview various Bentley people, but with a proviso: "... that subsequently consideration might be given to *presenting the*

---

* If Justice and the FBI had forgotten all this by the time of the grand jury sessions, their memories would be refreshed while those sessions were in progress. In October 1947, the Bureau received two copies of memoranda summarizing data Chambers could provide, recorded by State Department official Raymond Murphy in 1945–46 interviews at the Chambers farm near Westminster, Maryland. These memos, reproduced in the Bureau records, recite once more the story of Hiss, Ware, Pressman, and others named in previous Chambers statements. In these memos also, Chambers was reported as having named Harry White, Laurence Duggan, Noel Field, V. Frank Coe, and various others as parts of the apparatus—some as Communist Party members, others as close-in fellow travelers. Again, the overlap with the Elizabeth Bentley cases was extensive. As FBI official Lou Nichols would comment, "if this individual in Westminster will talk this might very well be a connecting link in this Gregory [Bentley] case." And so it might—except that Chambers wasn't called by the grand jury for more than a year after Nichols made this statement.

evidence to a grand jury with the idea of letting them no bill the case.
Further that in the event Congressman [J. Parnell] Thomas [R-NJ]
of the Un-American Committee should ever raise a question, it
would be possible to answer by *saying that the grand jury had considered the evidence and it had not deemed it sufficient to justify criminal
action.*"[7]

These thoughts about grand jury inaction, expressed before the
jury was even empaneled, would be repeated when filing a presentment was considered. The Bureau entry on this says Attorney General Tom Clark was "opposed to returning any presentment. The
AG indicated that *in the event of subsequent news inquiry, that he, the
Attorney General, can always say that the matter was referred to the
Grand Jury, which took no action.*"[8]

In similar vein were FBI comments concerning the last-minute
switch from the myriad secret Reds who had been sheltering on
the federal payroll to known leaders of the open Communist Party.
A March 1948 Bureau entry on this said a brief against the open
party leaders was already in existence (though the switch wouldn't
be public until July) and added: "It is apparently the thought of
the Department that if they can get favorable action on the case of
the Communist Party . . . *they will overcome any bad publicity which
might result from the Grand Jury returning in effect a no bill report on
the Gregory [Bentley] case.*"[9]

The net meaning of these memos doesn't need much comment.
The guiding premise from the outset was that there would be
no Bentley-case indictments, and such would be the conclusion
reached when the Bentley sessions ended. The failure to indict or
file a presentment would then be imputed to the grand jury, not to
Truman Justice. The last-minute switch to the Communist leaders
would meanwhile divert attention from the fact that no Bentley
indictments were arrived at. Justice would thus be off the hook for
inaction on the Bentley cases.

Against that backdrop, it's hardly surprising that Chambers wasn't called by the jury until the fall of 1948, after his public testimony to the House committee, when there was no way to avoid him. Far from seeking another witness to back up Bentley, the strategy spelled out in these memos made it necessary *not* to have one. With his knowledge of Hiss, White, Currie, Glasser, and other Soviet agents of influence, Chambers would have been the Banquo's ghost at the proceedings. His testimony would have made it virtually impossible to avoid indictments of various Bentley suspects—for perjury, if nothing else, during their statements to the inquest.

That Chambers was an unwelcome guest is plain from other items in the record. In the wake of his congressional testimony in August 1948, the Truman White House and Justice Department launched a campaign to indict him—not Hiss—for perjury. An August 16 White House memo, capsuling a meeting with Attorney General Clark and other officials, contained a to-do list concerning the House committee hearings, saying, *"Justice should make every effort to ascertain if Whittaker Chambers is guilty of perjury."*[10] There was no entry concerning a perjury rap for Hiss.

Even when Chambers came up with documentary evidence that Hiss was lying, Justice didn't relent in its pursuit of Chambers. Following a November 1948 Chambers deposition conducted by Hiss's lawyers (see below), Assistant Attorney General Alexander Campbell told the FBI: *"It is desired that an immediate investigation be conducted so that it can be ascertained whether Chambers committed perjury."*[11] Again, no similar entry targeting Hiss.

Similar memos from Campbell to FBI Director Hoover continued into December 1948, as the grand jury was nearing its expiration. A Campbell memo of December 2 reemphasized that Justice wanted "an immediate investigation by the Bureau to determine whether Chambers committed perjury." Hoover's handwritten comment on this was "I can't understand why such effort is being made to indict Chambers to the exclusion of Hiss."[12]

In the light of now available data, the answer to this puzzle is apparent. If Chambers had been indicted, the single most important witness who could confirm the Bentley revelations and expose the massive Communist infiltration of the government would have been badly damaged—if not sent to prison. Hiss and his fellow suspects would again have been shielded from exposure, and, perhaps even more to the point, the officials who allowed the penetration to happen then covered up the facts about it would have been shielded also.

And so it might have ended, if not for the House committee and the "pumpkin papers" brought forth by Chambers at the last minute. These papers would be the pivot on which domestic Cold War history turned from that time forward.

When Chambers was asked by Hiss's lawyers if he could supply documentary proof of the relationship between the two in the 1930s, he to their consternation did just that. At the November deposition, he presented sixty-five typed copies of official papers he said he received from Hiss during the latter's tenure on the federal payroll. When the initial shock wore off, the attorneys agreed that the documents be turned over to the Department of Justice as evidence of possible espionage or perjury by one or the other of the parties.

This could have been the undoing of Chambers, as Justice proceeded to impound the papers and planned to use them as proof of his lying. This charge as far as it went was true, since he had previously denied that Communist espionage occurred but now said it had happened. At this stage, however, he had purged himself of his earlier testimony, while Hiss persisted in his denials. Despite which, Truman Justice remained focused strictly on the crimes of Chambers.

Meanwhile, Representative Richard Nixon (R-CA) and House committee chief investigator Robert Stripling asked Chambers if there were other relevant documents that he hadn't given to Justice. His answer was that such documents existed—in the form of microfilmed data he had stashed away, which would now be famously, if briefly, concealed in a pumpkin patch at his mid-Maryland farm.* This material, obtained by House investigators during the first week of December, was definitive proof that Chambers was telling the truth and Hiss was lying. Equally important, it was proof that Justice couldn't deny, and couldn't sequester.

It was this evidence in the hands of the House committee that broke the case and led to the indictment of Hiss. These outcomes were made possible by the pumpkin papers and the unwillingness of Nixon and Stripling to turn them over without proper measures for safekeeping. Small wonder the left never forgave Nixon, despite later efforts at placation, for his role in the Hiss-Chambers struggle.

Though the details were different, there were numerous parallels between the Bentley inquest and the grand jury probe that buried the *Amerasia* scandal three years before.

In the *Amerasia* case, there had been a crude and explicit fix, wiretapped by the FBI, featuring perjury by high officials, obstruction of justice, and grand jury rigging, to cite only the most obvious offenses. In the Bentley case, there was no such wiretap evidence we know of, though the FBI records indicate an unswerving purpose throughout to quash indictments. In both cases, the course favored by Justice was followed, the suspects walked, and the fact that they went free was imputed to a grand jury.

---

* Chambers later explained this melodramatic touch by saying there had been not only numerous reporters but also anonymous prowlers spotted on his property and he felt that special measures for concealment of the microfilm were needed.

In these instances, the grand jury functioned essentially as a shield for Truman Justice as it deep-sixed cases of Communist infiltration; a procedure supposedly geared to enforcing the law was thus used as a device for thwarting its enforcement. As Service and Andrew Roth had walked in the *Amerasia* case, so would Hiss, White, Currie, and numerous others walk from the Bentley sessions—until the House committee at last turned the tables in the matter of Hiss and Chambers.

21.

RECOVERING THE COLD WAR RECORD

A joke that made the rounds in Moscow during the Communist heyday there ran more or less as follows: "I'm confident of the future, and reasonably sure about the present, but the past seems to be constantly changing."

The point of this sardonic gibe was that "history" in the USSR and elsewhere in the Communist world was typically the most convenient fiction, made to turn this way or that to serve the interests of the ruling powers. As those interests changed, the history would change as well, to justify in retrospect whatever stance the regime adopted. Such was, for instance, the origin of the "memory hole" made famous by George Orwell, down which uncongenial data from the past would be disposed of.

Among the most obvious Soviet cases to this effect were the purge trials of the 1930s, whereby Stalin wiped out a whole generation of Bolshevik leaders who in one way or another threatened his claim to power. In this pursuit, the history of the Soviet revolution was rewritten, as formerly lauded heroes of the cause would be reviled as double-dealing scoundrels. Foremost among these supposed miscreants was Trotsky, who had much to answer for on other grounds, but whose only real crime in the eyes of Stalin was that he had been and still considered himself to be a competitor for the leadership mantle of Lenin.* As an aspect of

---

* Stalin accordingly waged a nonstop vendetta against Trotsky and his forces, pursuing them from place to place and finally tracking the main offender to Mexico, where he would be murdered by one of Stalin's henchmen.

this deadly feud, history would be revamped to turn Trotsky from hero into villain.

In this grim episode, the Soviet approach to history was a subset of the commitment to deception that marked the Communist outlook from the beginning, in which any ruse was justified if it advanced a Moscow purpose. Soviet claims to scientific prowess, fantastic growth rates and other economic wonders, the alleged elimination of crime and mental illness, the supposed service of the USSR in bringing "democracy" to conquered nations, were all absurdly bogus, but nonetheless served the Kremlin's interests and thus were incessantly repeated.

As has been seen, these deceptions also had historiographic implications, though that presumably wasn't their initial object. Pro-Moscow falsehoods were recited so widely and so often, from such a seemingly diverse array of sources, as to become embedded in the historical record, often going unchallenged by Western journalists and authors. A classic instance was the man-made famine of the 1930s that Stalin imposed on Russia's suffering peasants. As later shown by Eugene Lyons, Robert Conquest, and some others, the toll of death and misery thus inflicted was horrific, but was effectively covered up by Western newsmen, with Duranty of the *New York Times* providing the premier example.

Other instances along these lines might be cited almost ad infinitum. To this day, documentable facts about the Communist subversion of Poland, Rumania, Yugoslavia, China, and other targeted nations aren't widely known to the public. More remarkable still, pro-Red disinformation about such matters may be found even now in Cold War histories and biographies of recent vintage. Perhaps the most obvious case is China, where many modern studies repeat as gospel the Maoist propaganda that undercut the anti-Communist Chiang Kai-shek and helped bring the despotic Red regime to power.

All this obviously makes it difficult for researchers to track down facts of record, as Cold War falsehoods are passed on by writers who apparently don't know that they're recycling disinformation. Nor is that the only difficulty encountered by scholars trying to unearth the Cold War story. Other, related problems stem from our own official and academic practice, making the truth about such matters hard to come by. One such problem, mentioned often in this study, is the continuing censorship, withholding, or disappearance of relevant data from official records. This is a difficulty that should improve with the passage of time, and in some cases has done so, but in others seems to be getting worse instead of better.

Thus, six or seven decades after they were first assembled, FBI files about Communist penetration of the U.S. government are still heavily "redacted," with page after page of information blacked out by official censors. This despite the strictures of the Freedom of Information Act and the fact that data from that far-off time can't plausibly pose security problems for the modern era. More remarkable still, the amount of FBI information available to the public in some cases seems to be decreasing, when logic would dictate that more data instead of less should be forthcoming. Likewise, the authors have found that security records of fifty years ago pertaining to the Cold War were being officially *withdrawn* from the National Archives up through the 1990s (the most recent instance we know of occurring in 2000).*

These problems have been pyramided on top of others created when the Cold War was in progress and investigations of the infiltration issue were triggering fierce debates and angry headlines. In some instances, reports and related data about such matters were picked clean from official records: the U.S. Army memo showing Soviet complicity in the massacre at Katyn, a State Department

---

* A document withdrawn in 2000 concerned the case of Soviet agent Gustavo Duran, dating to the 1940s. When we called attention to this problem, the document was restored to the file.

summary discussing the level of Soviet and pro-Communist penetration of that agency, rosters of security suspects submitted to Hill
committees, intelligence estimates that differed from the policy line
pursued at Yalta. These and similar significant data have vanished
from official records (though in some fortunate instances found in
other places).

In certain cases of this nature, it's evident that there has been a
deliberate cover-up of crucial information reflecting the extent of
the pro-Red penetration and the policy effects that followed. The
classic instance was the *Amerasia* scandal, where there was not only
a fix and cover-up, but the felonious rigging of a grand jury to make
the plot successful. We now have transcripts of the wiretaps that
show the jury-rigging in progress and the significant role therein of
Soviet agent of influence Lauchlin Currie. The manipulations that
surrounded the later grand jury of 1947–48 were arguably even
more important, since many more pro-Reds and Soviet agents were
thereby allowed to escape exposure.

In such episodes there was back then—and remains to some
extent today—a layer cake of motives for concealment, which
among them have served to deep-six, deny, or disguise important
aspects of the record. At the first and most obvious level, when
these matters were going forward in the late 1940s and early 1950s,
the people who most urgently wanted to cover up the facts were of
course the Communists and Soviet assets themselves. Hiss, White,
Currie, Lee, Adler, Glasser, and the rest had an urgent personal interest in not having the truth about their perfidy established.

However, there were others involved in these disputes who
weren't Communists or Soviet agents, but who nevertheless had
compelling reasons to deny or cover up the record. These were
the officials who by their complicity or indifference had let the
penetration happen. Compounding their offense, many ignored
the alarming data they were later given about such matters, beginning with the Whittaker Chambers revelations to Adolf Berle. The

responsible officials of the Roosevelt and Truman administrations would have had a heavy price to pay if the full truth about their performance had been made known to the public. They thus had powerful motives to conceal the facts and often were in positions where they could do so.

A further reason to ignore or obscure the record is vested ideological interest. For decades there has been an established narrative about our domestic Cold War and related security matters, the main theme of which is that the internal Communist problem was vastly overstated, if not entirely nonexistent, and that the people accused as infiltrators were innocent victims. A whole library of books has been written to advance such notions, downplaying the security problem, defending the accused, and denouncing the accusers. This mind-set has yielded inch by inch to the ever-mounting body of data that show the reverse of these conceptions, yet there is an obvious lingering yen to cling to the established story.

In pursuing this project, some authors use what might be called, for want of a better term, "minimization" procedures, a phrase taken from federal law pertaining to counterintelligence efforts. It refers to measures designed to limit the amount of information security officials can obtain about a suspected group or individual. The government thus by a kind of self-denying ordinance has blocked its own access to data relating to terrorism or subversion, data that might conceivably have prevented the deadly attacks of 9/11, though that is the topic for another sermon.

Similar tactics have long affected historical writing on the Cold War. An exclusive focus on espionage, as noted frequently in these pages, has been a significant factor in this process. As has been seen, there were many instances in which Communists and Soviet agents were able to influence American policy overseas to the benefit of Moscow. But a fixation on cases in which suspects were caught *passing documents* to Soviet handlers excludes numerous agents, contacts, and episodes with impact on policy matters. As espionage convictions were relatively few and far between, this self-denying method drastically understates the extent of the Cold War security problem.*

A variation of this approach might be called "what we now know is all we need to know, so we don't need to push any further." In the earliest going, this translated to the mind-set that, since we didn't know very much, there wasn't very much to know. This idea stemmed to a large extent from the unprecedented nature of the penetration, its huge scope, and the levels to which it reached, which made it seem incredible to many who were ignorant of the Communist project and Soviet methods of deception.†

A further such example has been treatment of the *Venona* decrypts. In some cases it's said or implied that, if a given suspect doesn't show up in *Venona*, he wasn't a Communist or Soviet agent. But this is on the face of it untrue. The *Venona* decrypts that we have number less than three thousand out of hundreds

---

* The Communists and their defenders have understood the point quite well, contending that unless someone was *convicted of espionage*, then he (or she) wasn't a security danger. A salient instance was the secret Communist Lee Pressman, identified early on by Chambers, who boldly challenged congressional investigators to say whether anyone had charged him with committing espionage. Since the answer to that was no, the inference sought by Pressman was that he thus wasn't a threat to security interests. This ignored the fact that, as a high-ranking official of the CIO linked to comrades at the National Labor Relations Board, he had been in position to promote the objectives of the Communists and their Soviet bosses. Such "minimization" made sense from the standpoint of Pressman and other Communists; it makes a good deal less from the perspective of historical studies trying to determine what actually happened in the Cold War.

† An added example of this outlook is the oft-stated view that the internal Communist problem had in essence been eliminated by 1948, when the Truman administration was conducting an alleged crackdown on Red agents via the President's loyalty program and indictment of the leaders of the Communist Party. But as seen in preceding chapters, this portrayal is far off the mark. The *Amerasia* cover-up, the manipulation of the subsequent grand jury that let the Elizabeth Bentley suspects walk, the routine dismissal of FBI reports about such matters, and the administration's effort to go after Chambers all tell a different story.

of thousands of such missives—and the decrypts in many cases are only partial. And with a few exceptions, cable traffic for Soviet military intelligence wasn't read at all. Since some of the most important Soviet agents, most notably Alger Hiss, worked with the GRU, this is another sizable gap in the Cold War record.

These comments aren't meant to disparage *Venona*, but rather to place it in context. It was a critical part of the mosaic of evidence on the Communist penetration problem, but it was indeed a part, not the total picture. In many cases, its value was that it confirmed the revelations provided by such witnesses as Chambers and Bentley and the investigations of the FBI. Countless suspects had already been named by Bentley, Chambers, and others before the Bureau had access to *Venona*.

A final variation on these themes is a tendency toward slack-cutting, which reflects again the lingering effects of the established story. In some cases a considerable effort has been made to save appearances for favored suspects once acclaimed as martyrs. A foremost instance is the oft-referenced John Service, who collaborated with the hard-core Soviet agent Solomon Adler in supplying pro-Red disinformation to U.S. officials, passed confidential data to the pro-Maoist Philip Jaffe, and was the prime beneficiary of a cover-up and grand jury fix in part orchestrated by a Soviet agent of influence who had been serving in the White House. All this is demonstrable from the record, yet few Cold War histories spell it out clearly for the reader, while many don't refer to it at all.

Another and even more prominent beneficiary of such treatment has been famed physicist J. Robert Oppenheimer, the World War II scientific leader of the atom project and a leading figure in nuclear matters for almost a full decade of the Cold War. It's clear beyond all peradventure that Oppenheimer was considered by Communist leaders to be a secret member of the party when he went into the atom program—a point made explicit in the records of the FBI—and that this was known to U.S. officials years before his security clearance was suspended. Even so, Oppenheimer is routinely depicted in our histories as a martyr, the evidence of his Communist Party membership and false testimony about it being glossed over or denied in discussions of the matter.*

From all these considerations, it should be apparent that there is still much to do in developing a full and accurate Cold War record. A great deal of digging needs to be done, both in the cases that we already have and in others waiting to be discovered. Yet, despite such knowledge issues, we do have sufficient data in hand to draw certain firm conclusions, many stated or implied in our discussion, but worth reemphasis here by way of wrap-up.

First and foremost, there can no longer be any serious question, at least among serious people, that Communist and pro-Soviet penetration at the American government was extensive, involving many hundreds of suspects, and that by the era of World War II and early stages of the Cold War reached up to significant levels. The now available documentation to this effect is massive.

Second, the infiltrators in numerous instances were able to wield important leverage on U.S. policy overseas in the war years and the early Cold War era. This was achieved by pro-Soviet operatives who variously controlled the flow of official information, propagandized their superiors in favor of pro-Red causes, or in some cases actually made or guided key decisions. By such leverage the likes of Lauchlin Currie, Harry White, and Solomon Adler (or in Great Britain, the Communist James Klugmann) were able to steer the policies of the West in favor of pro-Communist interests.

Third, pro-Red penetration and the resulting policy damage

---

* In such cases also, some historians have shown a remarkable willingness to accept exculpatory statements by the suspects, in preference to independent data. This is of course contrary to the rules of evidence, and common sense, which say one doesn't give preference to self-serving statements rather than to credible independent sources. Again, what we have in these cases is the use of "minimization" tactics to save something, or someone, from the ruins of the established story.

occurred because Soviet agents preyed on the credulity of officials who were ignorant of Communist methods and apparently had no interest in learning. A striking pattern in the record is the extent to which sophisticated Soviet agents attached themselves to naïve U.S. officials who were highly susceptible to disinformation. The classic cases were White with Henry Morgenthau at the Treasury and Alger Hiss with Stettinius at State, but there were many similar match-ups elsewhere during the course of the Cold War struggle.

The net effect of these converging factors was a series of free-world retreats, as pro-Communist forces triumphed in a host of European countries during the earliest stages of the Cold War, followed by the fall of China to Communism a few years later. These events would be a prelude to Marxist conquests elsewhere, in places as disparate as Indochina; the Latin American states of Cuba and Nicaragua; African nations, including Zimbabwe and Angola; and numerous other cases of like nature.

It's significant that these pro-Red victories were in the usual instance achieved not by conventional armies marching past national borders, but by the actions of subversive elements inside the target nations, prompted and aided by outside Communist powers and with frequent assistance from forces in the United States or other Western nations. Only when conventional warfare occurred or threatened, as in Korea or Western Europe, did the free world effectively mobilize resistance. As with the case of spying versus policy influence, we seemed incapable of gauging the threat we faced unless it was presented in the most explicit and glaring fashion.

In the preceding pages we have sought, despite the historical blackout that still exists in too many places, to pull together some of the available data on such matters and tell part of the Cold War story. However, we stress again that the information set forward here is fragmentary and episodic. There is much more out there still to be tracked down by researchers of the future.

NOTES

Introduction: The Greatest Story Never Told

1. For background on *Venona*, see *Venona: Soviet Espionage and the American Response, 1939–1957*, Robert Louis Benson and Michael Warner, eds. (Washington, DC: National Security Agency and Central Intelligence Agency, 1996); Herbert Romerstein and Eric Breindel, *The Venona Secrets* (Washington, DC: Regnery, 2000); and John Earl Haynes and Harvey Klehr, *Venona: Decoding Soviet Espionage in America* (New Haven, CT: Yale University Press, 1999).
2. Whittaker Chambers, *Witness* (Chicago: Regnery Gateway, 1988), p. 427.
3. Ibid.

Chapter 1: Even If My Ally Is a Fool

1. Winston Churchill, *Closing the Ring* (New York: Bantam Books, 1962), p. 297.
2. Various drafts of the charter, including the final text, are given in Winston Churchill, *The Grand Alliance* (New York: Bantam Books, 1962), pp. 366–70.
3. Winston Churchill, *The Gathering Storm* (New York: Bantam Books, 1962), p. viii.
4. Robert E. Sherwood, *Roosevelt and Hopkins* (New York: Harper & Brothers, 1948), p. 749.
5. Quoted in Robert Nisbet, *Roosevelt and Stalin* (Chicago: Regnery Gateway, 1989), p. 6.
6. Ibid., p. 26.
7. Joseph E. Davies, *Mission to Moscow* (Garden City, NY: Garden City, 1943), p. 217.
8. George Racey Jordan, *From Major Jordan's Diaries* (New York: Harcourt Brace, 1952), p. 19.
9. Quoted in Nisbet, *Roosevelt and Stalin*, p. 15.
10. George F. Kennan, *Russia and the West* (New York: Mentor Books, 1962), p. 333.

11. Winston Churchill, *Triumph and Tragedy* (New York: Bantam Books, 1962), p. 311.

Chapter 2: The Ghost Ship at Yalta

1. Charles E. Bohlen, *Witness to History* (New York: Norton, 1973), p. 143.
2. Turner Catledge, *My Life and the Times* (New York: Harper & Row, 1971), p. 144.
3. James A. Farley, *Jim Farley's Story* (New York: Whittlesey House, 1948), pp. 363–65.
4. Charles A. Willoughby and John Chamberlain, *MacArthur* (New York: McGraw-Hill, 1954), p. 235.
5. Steven Lomazow and Eric Fettmann, *FDR's Deadly Secret* (New York: PublicAffairs, 2009), p. 143; Henry L. Stimson and McGeorge Bundy, *On Active Service in Peace and War* (New York: Harper & Brothers, 1948), p. 575.
6. Lomazow and Fettmann, *FDR's Deadly Secret*, p. 153.
7. Bohlen, *Witness to History*, p. 172.
8. George McJimsey, *Harry Hopkins* (Cambridge, MA: Harvard University Press, 1987), p. 374.
9. Churchill, *Triumph and Tragedy*, p. 341.
10. Lomazow and Fettmann, *FDR's Deadly Secret*, pp. 166–69.
11. Elliott Roosevelt, *As He Saw It* (New York: Duell, Sloan & Pearce, 1946), p. 189.
12. Papers of Edward R. Stettinius Jr., University of Virginia, The Conference in Crimea, Box 279.
13. *Foreign Relations of the United States: The Conferences at Malta and Yalta* (Washington, DC: U.S. Department of State, 1955), p. 849 (hereafter cited as Yalta Papers).
14. Sherwood, *Roosevelt and Hopkins*, pp. 833–34.
15. Churchill, *Triumph and Tragedy*, p. 361.
16. Robert Ferrell, *The Dying President* (Columbia: University of Missouri Press, 1998), p. 83.
17. Ibid., p. 106.

Chapter 3: See Alger Hiss About This

1. Yalta Papers, p. 439.
2. "Hiss Says His Job at Yalta Was U.N.," *New York Times*, March 18, 1955.

3. Bryton Barron, *Inside the State Department* (New York: Bookmailer, 1961), pp. 22–23.

4. Hearings of House Committee on Un-American Activities, August 5, 1948, pp. 656–57.

5. Stettinius Papers, Box 278. This version of the exchange would also appear, two decades after the State Department compilation, in a condensed edition of the Stettinius papers, *The Diaries of Edward R. Stettinius, Jr.,* Thomas M. Campbell and George C. Herring, eds. (New York: Viewpoints, 1975), p. 229.

6. Yalta Papers, p. 502.

7. Stettinius Papers, Box 277.

8. Ibid., Box 278.

9. Edward R. Stettinius Jr., *Roosevelt and the Russians* (Garden City, NY: Doubleday, 1949), pp. 31, 270.

10. Allen Weinstein, *Perjury: The Hiss-Chambers Case* (New York: Knopf, 1978), pp. 353–54.

11. Yalta Papers, p. 42.

12. John Earl Haynes, Harvey Klehr, and Alexander Vassiliev, *Spies* (New Haven, CT: Yale University Press, 2008), p. 13.

Chapter 4: Moscow's Bodyguard of Lies

1. "Soviet Active Measures," hearings of House Intelligence Committee, June 1982, p. 50.

2. "Political Intelligence from the Territory of the USSR," Andropov Institute of the KGB, Moscow, 1989.

3. The Trust is described by Herbert Romerstein and Stanislav Levchenko in *The KGB Against the Main Enemy* (Lexington, MA: Lexington Books, 1989), pp. 29–32, and by Edward J. Epstein in *Deception* (New York: Simon & Schuster, 1989), pp. 22ff.

4. *Operation Caesar,* publication of the Communist Party of Poland, 1954.

5. Claud Cockburn, *Cockburn Sums Up: An Autobiography* (New York: Quartet Books, 1981).

6. Jung Chang and Jon Halliday, *Mao* (New York: Knopf, 2005), p. 204.

7. Donald Downes, *The Scarlet Thread* (London: Derek Verschoyle, 1953), p. 78.

8. "Political Intelligence," Andropov Institute.

Notes

9. Vassiliev Papers, Black Notebook, quoted by Christina Shelton, *Alger Hiss: Why He Chose Treason* (New York: Threshold Editions, 2012), pp. 264–65.

Chapter 5: Three Who Saved a Revolution

1. Robins's activities in Russia are described by George F. Kennan, *Russia Leaves the War* and *The Decision to Intervene* (both New York: Atheneum, 1967), and Neil V. Salzman, *Reform and Revolution* (Kent, OH: Kent State University Press, 1991), passim.
2. The most concise discussion of Gumberg and his relationship with Robins may be found in Kent Clizbe, *Willing Accomplices* (Ashburn, VA: Andemca Publishers, 2011). A highly sympathetic biography is James K. Libbey, *Alexander Gumberg and Soviet-American Relations* (Lexington: University Press of Kentucky, 1977). The Robins-Gumberg relationship is addressed at many places by Kennan and Salzman.
3. Edgar Sisson, *100 Red Days* (New Haven, CT: Yale University Press, 1931). Sisson describes his break with Robins beginning at p. 213.
4. Kennan's summing up on Robins appears in *The Decision to Intervene*, chapter 10.
5. Documents in possession of the authors.
6. Edward J. Epstein, *Dossier: The Secret History of Armand Hammer* (New York: Random House, 1996), pp. 40ff.
7. Ibid., p. 81.
8. The photograph of Reagan and Hammer, with their wives, appears in Epstein, *Dossier*, p. 304.
9. FBI/CIA report, re "Dr. Armand Hammer and Family," August 1, 1972. Document in possession of the authors.
10. Ibid.
11. Quoted in Eugene Lyons, *Assignment in Utopia* (New York: Harcourt Brace, 1937), p. 573. See also S. J. Taylor, *Stalin's Apologist* (New York: Oxford University Press, 1990), pp. 210 ff.

Chapter 6: The First Red Decade

1. The Berle memo recording the names provided by Chambers is reprinted in the hearings of the Senate Internal Security Subcommittee, May 6, 1953, p. 329.
2. Hearings of the House Committee on Un-American Activities, August 24, 1948, p. 1293.

3. Chambers, *Witness*, pp. 342ff.

4. The most complete survey of the Bentley case, with supporting data from the Bureau investigation, may be found in the FBI Silvermaster file, vol. 145.

5. Chambers, *Witness*, p. 338.

6. McJimsey, *Harry Hopkins*, p. 74.

7. Testimony of Lee Pressman, House Committee on Un-American Activities, August 28, 1950, p. 2849.

8. The correspondence from Gardner Jackson concerning Gibarti and State Department comments date from January 1939. Documents in possession of the authors.

9. The Paul Appleby memorandum defending Jackson was written on August 4, 1942. Document in possession of the authors.

10. "The Harry Dexter White Papers," hearings of the Senate Internal Security Subcommittee, August 30, 1955, p. lix.

11. Quoted in Haynes and Klehr, *Venona*, p. 133.

12. *Institute of Pacific Relations*, report of the Senate Internal Security Subcommittee, 1952, p. 97 (hereafter cited as IPR Report).

Chapter 7: Remember Pearl Harbor

1. The most complete, albeit sympathetic, biography of Sorge is Robert Whymant, *Stalin's Spy* (New York: St. Martin's Press, 1996).

2. "A Partial Documentation of the Sorge Espionage Case," prepared for the House Committee on Un-American Activities, U.S. Military Intelligence, Far East Command, 1952.

3. "Hearings on American Aspects of the Richard Sorge Spy Case," House Committee on Un-American Activities, August 23, 1951, pp. 1202–3.

4. Forrest Davis and Ernest K. Lindley, *How War Came* (New York: Simon & Schuster, 1942), p. 258.

5. Joseph C. Grew, *Turbulent Era* (Boston: Houghton Mifflin, 1952), pp. 1351ff.

6. IPR Report, p. 180.

7. Quoted in Anthony Kubek, *How the Far East Was Lost* (Chicago: Regnery, 1963), p. 17.

8. IPR Report, p. 180.

9. Institute of Pacific Relations, hearings of the Senate Internal Security Subcommittee, August 9, 1951, pp. 381–82.

10. George Morgenstern, *Pearl Harbor* (New York: Devin-Adair, 1948), pp. 154, 156.
11. Vitaliy Pavlov, *Operation Snow* (Moscow: Gaya, 1996), p. 44.
12. Morgenstern, *Pearl Harbor*, pp. 160, 288.
13. Pavlov, *Operation Snow*, p. 41.

Chapter 8: The Enemy Within

1. FBI, Silvermaster file, vol. 37.
2. The names of federal employees as listed in the Gorsky memo are taken from the Vassiliev papers. See John Earl Haynes, "Alexander Vassiliev's Notes on Anatoly Gorsky's December 1948 Memo," <http://johnearl haynes.org>, October 2005.
3. This unredacted version of the New York to Moscow KGB cable of September 22, 1944, is taken from OSS files at the National Archives. (Copy in possession of the authors.)
4. These and other OWI cases are discussed in M. Stanton Evans, *Blacklisted by History* (New York: Crown Forum, 2007), pp. 88–92.
5. Ibid.
6. Ibid.
7. Ibid.
8. FBI, Silvermaster file, vol. 3.
9. Ibid.
10. IPR Report, p. 147.

Chapter 9: Friends in High Places

1. McJimsey, *Harry Hopkins*, pp. 10–52.
2. Jordan, *From Major Jordan's Diaries*, pp. 78–84. Major Jordan testified on these matters to the House Committee on Un-American Activities on December 4, 1949, and March 3, 1950.
3. McJimsey, *Harry Hopkins*, p. 293.
4. Memo of Gen. F. L. Anderson, September 7, 1944, Carl Spaatz Papers, Library of Congress, Box 18.
5. McJimsey, *Harry Hopkins*, p. 344.
6. Ibid., p. 305.
7. The McJimsey book is replete with statements to this effect, especially chapter 22, "Dawn of a New Day."
8. Sherwood, *Roosevelt and Hopkins*, p. 860.
9. Ibid., p. 890.
10. Romerstein and Breindel, *The Venona Secrets*, p. 214.

11. Christopher Andrew and Oleg Gordievsky, *KGB: The Inside Story* (New York: HarperCollins, 1990), p. 287.
12. Romerstein and Breindel, *The Venona Secrets*, p. 180.

Chapter 10: The War Within the War

1. Hearings of the Senate Internal Security Subcommittee, March 2, 1954, p. 1320.
2. Extension of the Remarks of Senator Styles Bridges of New Hampshire, *Congressional Record*, January 2, 1951, pp. 8002ff.
3. Hearings of Senate Internal Security Subcommittee, March 2, 1954, p. 1329.
4. Testimony of Lieutenant Colonel John Lansdale, In the Matter of J. Robert Oppenheimer, proceedings of the Atomic Energy Commission, April 1954. Lansdale gave this testimony in the context of defending Oppenheimer from charges of being a security risk.
5. Hearings of the House Committee on Un-American Activities, August 4, 1948, p. 626.
6. Evans, *Blacklisted by History*, p. 79.
7. FBI, Silvermaster file, vol. 42.
8. Hearings of the Select Committee on the Katyn Massacre, U.S. House of Representatives, November 1952, pp. 1852, 1883, 1932.
9. Memoirs of Colonel Ivan Yeaton, Hoover Institution, Box 4, pp. 37–38. Copyright Stanford University, Stanford, California.
10. Romerstein and Breindel, *The Venona Secrets*, pp. 218–19; Yeaton, Memoirs, p. 40.
11. This FBI report may be found among the Yeaton Papers at the Hoover Institution.
12. Yeaton, Memoirs, p. 58.
13. Ibid., p. 62.
14. Ibid., p. 60.
15. Ibid., p. 81.
16. Ibid., p. 64.
17. Ibid.

Chapter 11: The Media Megaphone

1. Romerstein and Breindel, *The Venona Secrets*, pp. 435–36.
2. Haynes, Klehr, and Vassiliev, *Spies*, p. 150.
3. Straight's account of these events appears in his memoir, *After Long Silence* (New York: Norton, 1983).

4. Rushmore's testimony to the Senate Committee on Immigration and Naturalization was read into the *Congressional Record* by Senator Joseph R. McCarthy on December 19, 1950.

5. Romerstein and Breindel, *The Venona Secrets*, pp. 138–39.

6. Hearings of the Senate Permanent Subcommittee on Investigations, February 23, 1954, p. 351; Jack Anderson, *Confessions of a Muckraker* (New York: Random House, 1979), p. 6.

7. IPR Report, pp. 147–48.

8. Harvey Klehr, John Haynes, and Kyrill Anderson, *The Soviet World of American Communism* (New Haven, CT: Yale University Press, 1998), p. 336; IPR Report, pp. 115–16.

9. Haynes and Klehr, *Venona*, p. 237.

Chapter 12: The Plot to Murder Chiang Kai-shek

1. The Rogov article, originally published in a Russian journal, was reprinted in the *Daily Worker*, August 14, 1943; Bisson's article appeared in the *Far Eastern Survey*, July 14, 1943. Both reprinted in IPR hearings, loc. cit., pp. 531–34.

2. The White cable to Adler of October 11, 1943, is reprinted in *Morgenthau Diary: China*, published by the Senate Internal Security Subcommittee in 1967, pp. 911–12.

3. Donald M. Dozer, "The State Department Won't Tell You," unpublished monograph, copy provided by Charles Dozer.

4. *Morgenthau Diary: China*, pp. 1468, 1134.

5. Ibid., p. 1052.

6. In these discussions and related memos, White and Adler cited Chi Chao-ting and John S. Service to Morgenthau as sources of information on China, neglecting to tell the secretary that Adler, Chi, and Service were housemates in Chungking.

7. Currie was so named by both Elizabeth Bentley and Whittaker Chambers, identifications confirmed in *Venona* and the Gorsky memo.

8. See Evans, *Blacklisted by History*, pp. 104–5.

9. Quoted in Kubek, *How the Far East Was Lost*, p. 206.

10. Roosevelt, *As He Saw It*, pp. 163–64.

11. Frank Dorn, *Walkout: With Stilwell in Burma* (New York: Thomas Y. Crowell, 1970), pp. 76–82.

12. "Well-Kept Secret Gets Its Due," *Chicago Tribune*, December 20, 1985.

Chapter 13: Betrayal in the Balkans

1. Nazi troops invaded Yugoslavia on April 6, 1941. Tito did not declare war against the Axis until July, three months later, after the Germans invaded Russia.

2. At the end of 1941, Mihailovich had been proclaimed by *Time* magazine as "Man of the Year," and other press treatment was of like nature. See David Martin, *The Web of Disinformation* (New York: Harcourt Brace Jovanovich, 1990), pp. 29ff. One year later, press treatment of Mihailovich would be quite different.

3. See Michael Lees, *The Rape of Serbia* (New York: Harcourt Brace Jovanovich, 1990), p. 58.

4. Martin, *The Web of Disinformation*, p. 122.

5. Quoted in Slobodan Draskovich, *Tito: Moscow's Trojan Horse* (Chicago: Regnery, 1958), p. 90.

6. Lees, *The Rape of Serbia*, p. 360.

7. MI5 transcript and summary of Klugmann's talk with British Communist leader Robert Stewart, August 23, 1945. Documents in possession of the authors.

8. FRUS, *The Conferences at Cairo and Teheran* (Washington, DC: U.S. Department of State, 1961), p. 547. Hereafter cited as Teheran Papers.

9. Lees, *The Rape of Serbia*, pp. 360ff.

10. Wolff would plead the Fifth in hearings of the Senate Internal Security Subcommittee on June 14, 1953, pp. 767ff.

11. The story of the Farish memo is told in Martin, *The Web of Disinformation*, pp. 220–25, 363–77.

Chapter 14: The Rape of Poland

1. Teheran Papers, p. 594.

2. Ibid., pp. 594–95.

3. Report of the Select Committee of the House of Representatives, "The Katyn Forest Massacre," December 22, 1952.

4. Romerstein and Breindel, *The Venona Secrets*, pp. 399ff.

5. See Edward Rozek, *Allied Wartime Diplomacy* (New York: John Wiley, 1958), pp. 248ff.

6. Ibid.

7. Various of these identifications are made in FBI reports, including "The Comintern Apparatus" (December 1944) and a special survey of individuals involved in shaping U.S. policy toward Poland. (See below.)

8. Report from FBI Director J. Edgar Hoover to Commander James Vardaman, Naval Assistant to the President, August 17, 1945. Document in possession of the authors.

9. Ibid.

10. Katyn report, p. 8.

11. *Congressional Record*, June 17, 1943, p. 6000.

12. Select House Committee investigation, November 11, 1952, pp. 1984ff.

13. "Polish Views Here on Russia Sought," *New York Times*, August 20, 1943.

14. Martin Weil, *A Pretty Good Club* (New York: Norton, 1978), p. 166.

15. *The Amerasia Papers*, published by the Senate Internal Security Subcommittee, 1970; memo of January 25, 1944, p. 341.

16. Joseph Persico, *Roosevelt's Secret War* (New York: Random House, 2002), p. 262.

17. Correspondence between J. Edgar Hoover and Harry Hopkins, April 6, 1945; Niles response to Hopkins, April 20, 1945. Documents in possession of the authors.

Chapter 15: The Morgenthau Planners

1. *Morgenthau Diary: Germany*, published by the Senate Internal Security Subcommittee, 1967, p. 41.

2. J. F. C. Fuller, *The Second World War* (New York: Da Capo Press, 1993), p. 33; Hanson W. Baldwin, *Great Mistakes of the War* (New York: Harper & Brothers, 1950), pp. 14ff.

3. *Morgenthau Diary: Germany*, p. 31.

4. Ibid., pp. 49, 53, 175–76.

5. Ibid., p. 897.

6. Ibid., p. 507.

7. Ibid., p. 26.

8. Ibid., p. 23.

9. Ibid., p. 16.

10. Ibid., p. 595, 596.

11. Ibid., p. 36.

12. Stimson and Bundy, *On Active Service in Peace and War*, p. 581.

13. *Morgenthau Diary: Germany*, p. 18.

14. Ibid., p. 484.

15. William H. Chamberlin, *America's Second Crusade* (Chicago: Henry Regnery Company, 1950), p. 309.

16. *Morgenthau Diary: Germany*, p. 44.

Chapter 16: Operation Keelhaul

1. *Morgenthau Diary: Germany*, pp. 464, 505; Yalta Papers, p. 979.
2. *Morgenthau Diary: Germany*, pp. 1280, 1498.
3. Ibid., p. 1493.
4. Stettinius Papers, Box 278.
5. Ibid.
6. Yalta Papers, p. 979.
7. *Morgenthau Diary: Germany*, p. 511.
8. Nicholas Bethell, *The Last Secret* (New York: Basic Books, 1974), pp. 110, 182, 38.
9. Julius Epstein, *Operation Keelhaul* (New York: Devin-Adair, 1973), p. 28. This is the best-documented and most authoritative American book about the subject.
10. Bethell, *The Last Secret*, p. 112.
11. Stettinius Papers, Box 277.
12. Yalta Papers, p. 757.

Chapter 17: Stalin's Coup in Asia

1. Tsuyoshi Hasegawa, ed., *The End of the Pacific War* (Stanford, CA: Stanford University Press, 2007), p. 152.
2. William Leahy, *I Was There* (New York: Whittlesey House, 1950), p. 293.
3. Quoted in Kubek, *How the Far East Was Lost*, p. 120.
4. Admiral Ellis Zacharias, *Behind Closed Doors* (New York: Putnam's, 1950), p. 56.
5. Ibid., pp. 56–57.
6. Walter Trohan, "Bare Peace Bid U.S. Rebuffed 7 Months Ago," *Chicago Tribune*, August 19, 1945.
7. Hearings before the Committee on Armed Services and the Committee on Foreign Relations, United States Senate, June 21, 1951, p. 2916.
8. Ibid.
9. Ibid.
10. See, among other recent studies, Sergei N. Goncharov, John W. Lewis, and Xue Litai, *Uncertain Partners* (Stanford, CA: Stanford University Press, 1993), passim, and Katherine Weathersby, "Soviet Aims in Korea and the Origins of the Korean War," and "Korea, 1949–50: To Attack or Not to Attack," Cold War International History Project, Woodrow Wilson Center, November 1993 and spring 1995.

11. Major General John R. Deane, *The Strange Alliance* (New York: Viking, 1947), pp. 248–49.
12. Richard A. Russell, *Project HULA* (Washington, DC: Naval Historical Center, 1997), pp. 32–38.
13. James F. Byrnes, *All in One Lifetime* (New York: Harper & Brothers, 1958), p. 259.
14. W. Averell Harriman with Elie Abel, *Special Envoy* (New York: Random House, 1975), pp. 398–99.
15. Sumner Welles, *Seven Decisions That Shaped History* (New York: Harper & Brothers, 1951), p. 138; Sherwood, *Roosevelt and Hopkins*, p. 867.

Chapter 18: The *Amerasia* Scandal

1. Hoover to James Hatcher, May 25, 1950; FBI *Amerasia* File, Section 51.
2. Though this quote was at the time (and has been since) disputed, the proof of Hoover's views to this effect is clear in the *Amerasia* records. (See below.)
3. The data pertaining to the *Amerasia* case and official measures to conceal it are set forth in the Bureau's *Amerasia* File, some twelve thousand pages of which were made available to researchers under the Freedom of Information Act.
4. FBI *Amerasia* File, released in 1986, from D. M. Ladd to Director Hoover, June 30, 1952.
5. FBI *Amerasia* File, Section 54.
6. See Evans, *Blacklisted by History*, pp. 164ff.
7. Hearings of the House Committee on Un-American Activities, July 31, August 28, 1948.

Chapter 19: State and Revolution

1. Details about these and related cases are given in the IPR Report.
2. Bohlen, *Witness to History*, pp. 39–41.
3. George F. Kennan, *Memoirs* (New York: Bantam Books, 1965), p. 88.
4. Oral history interview with Loy W. Henderson, conducted by Richard D. McKinzie, June 14, 1973, July 5, 1973, Harry S. Truman Library, Independence, MO.
5. Weil, *A Pretty Good Club*, p. 139.
6. Berle testimony to House Committee on Un-American Activities, p. 1296.

7. *Daily Worker* attacks on Grew and like-minded colleagues were documented in the IPR hearings by former *Worker* managing editor Louis Budenz on August 23, 1951, pp. 609–19.
8. See Evans, *Blacklisted by History*, pp. 418–19.
9. IPR Report, pp. 202–3.
10. Harold Smith Papers, Roosevelt Library, Hyde Park, NY.
11. FBI Silvermaster file, vol. 42.

Chapter 20: A Not So Grand Grand Jury

1. Quoted in Kathryn S. Olmsted, *Red Spy Queen* (Chapel Hill: University of North Carolina Press, 2002), pp. 116ff.
2. FBI Silvermaster file, vol. 135.
3. Ibid., vol. 143.
4. Ibid., vol. 135.
5. The chronology of FBI contacts with Chambers appears in the FBI Hiss-Chambers file, vol. 13.
6. FBI Silvermaster file, vol. 31.
7. Ibid., vol. 96.
8. Ibid., vol. 137.
9. Ibid.
10. Memorandum of White House staffer George Elsey reproduced in CIA/NSA volume on the *Venona* papers, 1996.
11. FBI Hiss-Chambers file, vol. 12.
12. Ibid., vol. 1.

ACKNOWLEDGMENTS

The security documents and other data on which this study is based come from a wide array of sources that the authors wish gratefully to acknowledge.

Among official sources overseas, three in particular were most helpful in assisting our researches: the British National Archives in Kew, the archives of the Russian Intelligence Services in Moscow, and the archives of the Institute of National Remembrance at Warsaw. The cooperation of archivists at these institutions is much appreciated.

In the United States, we have relied on numerous official agencies and private research organizations for information and assistance. Most important in this respect have been the vast security archives of the Federal Bureau of Investigation, publications of the Central Intelligence Agency and National Security Agency, and the voluminous records of committees of the U.S. Congress that have dealt with security issues.

Extremely valuable also, on these matters as on others, are the extensive holdings of the U.S. National Archives and Records Administration and the Library of Congress, both of which we have consulted on countless occasions. We in particular acknowledge the help of the Franklin D. Roosevelt Library in Hyde Park, New York, which provided us with photographic and documentary records.

In tracking down significant data on the Yalta Conference and related Cold War topics, we were greatly aided by the Albert Small Special Collections division of the University of Virginia Library in Charlottesville, Virginia, and the research staff of the Hoover

Institution at Stanford University, Stanford, California. We also wish to thank the Associated Press for permission to reproduce the photograph appearing on page 33.

Among the many individuals who have assisted in the preparation of the book, we want to thank Mark LaRochelle and Ann Trevor, both of whom supplied large quantities of data referred to in our discussion. We are likewise indebted to John Earl Haynes, Charles Dozer, Stanley Sandler, Christina Shelton, Diana West, David Vuich, and Kent Clizbe, all of whom provided or directed us to materials essential to understanding the Cold War story.

Others who have aided in production of this volume include Allan Ryskind, who reviewed the manuscript with a discerning eye; Mary Jo Buckland, who managed a host of communications and research assignments; Kate Rowinsky, who provided much-needed technical assistance; and the invaluable Patricia Romerstein, who devoted so many hours to revising and correcting the manuscript that she qualifies as a virtual coauthor of the volume.

Finally, we extend our thanks to Mitchell Ivers, Natasha Simons, Kevin Smith, and Tom Pitoniak of Threshold Editions, who worked with us closely on preparation of the book, and to our agent Alex Hoyt, without whose diligent efforts this long-contemplated study would not have happened.

INDEX

Page numbers in *italics* refer to illustrations

Index